# Understanding British Party Politics

# Understanding British Party Politics

STEPHEN DRIVER

polity

First published in 2011 by Polity Press

Polity Press
65 Bridge Street
Cambridge CB2 1UR, UK

Polity Press
350 Main Street
Malden, MA 02148, USA

ISBN-13: 978-0-7456-4077-8
ISBN-13: 978-0-7456-4078-5(pb)

A catalogue record for this book is available from the British Library.

Typeset in 9.5 on 13 pt Swift Light
by Toppan Best-set Premedia Limited
Printed and bound in Great Britain by MPG Books Group Limited, Bodmin, Cornwall

The publisher has used its best endeavours to ensure that the URLs for external websites referred to in this book are correct and active at the time of going to press. However, the publisher has no responsibility for the websites and can make no guarantee that a site will remain live or that the content is or will remain appropriate.

Every effort has been made to trace all copyright holders, but if any have been inadvertently overlooked the publisher will be pleased to include any necessary credits in any subsequent reprint or edition.

For further information on Polity, visit our website: www.politybooks.com

# Contents

# Acknowledgements

I would like to thank Louise Knight, David Winters and Neil de Cort at Polity for their patience and encouragement – and Leigh Mueller for preparing the manuscript. Thanks also to two anonymous reviewers whose detailed comments were of enormous help in shaping the final version of the text. The mistakes are, of course, all mine. Ruth Gardiner and Alice and James make it all worthwhile.

Figure 1.2 is reproduced from Giovanni Sartori, *Parties and Party Systems: A Framework for Analysis* ([1976] Colchester: ECPR Press, 2005), with permission from the European Consortium for Political Research at the University of Essex.

# Introduction

The 2010 general election saw the façade of two-party politics crumble as the Liberal Democrats joined the Conservative Party in coalition government at Westminster. The new arrangements were quickly billed as a 'new politics' for Britain, breaking with one-party rule – and two-party bickering. Competition at the ballot box was giving way to something more collaborative in power. Reform of the voting system might make such politics a more permanent feature of British government, just as it is in many other parts of Europe.

Time will tell how new this politics is; and much depends on political parties adapting to the possibility of sharing power with each other. Certainly the chances of hung parliaments have increased as the traditional social alignments of two-party politics have shifted. Over the past thirty years or so, the slice of the electorate that has become less partisan in its politics has grown. Political parties have had to adapt to these less certain times. Having a core vote is important, but it is not enough. The 2010 general election was dominated by those who couldn't make up their minds who to support. Political parties have to make their pitch to these undecided voters.

In 2010, the Conservative Party did enough to end thirteen years in opposition. Since David Cameron became leader in 2005 (the fourth since the party's crushing loss to Labour in 1997), the Tories had reconnected to mainstream public opinion by moving back to the centre ground of British politics. The party had spent too long talking to itself and falling out with itself. Cameron's Conservatives talked about schools and hospitals – and much more besides – just as the electorate were. The shadow cast by radical Tory governments in the 1980s and 1990s ('Thatcherism') lifted, although memories of this period lie deep in the party and on parliamentary backbenches.

If the 2010 election marked the return of the Conservatives to government, the election also saw the Liberal Democrats move from being a party of protest at Westminster to becoming a party of power. (The paradox of the new politics was that both parties in the coalition had their roots in the 1830s and before.) While the Liberal Democrats had, on local authorities and in the devolved administrations in Scotland and Wales, already become an important partner in government, at the national level Liberals last shared in power in peacetime in the 1930s; and last won an election in 1910. In the future, the Liberal Democrats are likely to get the chance of government more often, but who they join in power, Labour or the Conservatives, goes to the heart of what kind of party they are.

The general election in 2010 also marked the end of Labour's great winning streak. The party had never before managed three election victories in a row. Back in the early 1990s, some analysts doubted whether Labour could ever win a general election again on its own. 'New Labour' not only proved to be a formidable vote-winning machine, but also reshaped centre left politics in Britain for a generation. By moving social democracy post-Thatcherism, Tony Blair and Gordon Brown brought Labour back in line with public opinion, even if only one of them proved capable of leading the country as prime minister.

The 2010 general election also saw the smaller parties in British party politics hold the ground they had won in recent years. Since the 1950s, the proportion of votes going to the two main parties, Labour and the Conservatives, has fallen from well over 90 per cent to around two-thirds. The Liberals, then the Liberal Democrats, have been the great beneficiaries of this electoral shift. But in the 2000s, the slice of votes going to 'other' parties has increased to around 10 per cent. In 2010, the first Green Party candidate was elected to Westminster (the party had already won seats in the Scottish parliament, the London Assembly, the European parliament and local council chambers). On the right, while the United Kingdom Independence Party (UKIP) and the British National Party (BNP) failed to win their target seats in 2010, both increased their share of the national vote. This followed the 2009 European elections in which UKIP came in second to the Tories, and the BNP won its first seats at Strasbourg. British politics has become more fragmented and ideologically stretched, and the smaller parties more focused on winning votes and gaining representation.

This shift to a more multi-party politics was given a boost by the devolution of government in 1998, although the revival of nationalist politics in Scotland and Wales dates back to the 1960s. Devolution created new political opportunities for the Scottish National Party (SNP) and Plaid Cymru, as well as exposing a territorial dimension to British politics long overshadowed by the class character of post-war two-party politics. At the time of the 2010 general election, both the SNP and Plaid were in power in the devolved administrations in Edinburgh and Cardiff. The SNP had sneaked past Labour in Scotland in elections in 2007 to form a minority government; Plaid joined Labour in another coalition running the principality. These elections confirmed the growing view in the study of politics that Britain had not one but multiple party systems: systems where different parties were in the running in different places. Party politics in Northern Ireland was often regarded as the exception to the class-based Conservative/Labour politics on the British mainland. Today, the political geography of the UK is far more complex.

The turnout in general elections has been a real cause for concern since it dipped below 60 per cent in 2001. Democracy, some thought, was in danger.

In this febrile political atmosphere, British party politics was fragmenting and polarizing. The electorate was not simply avoiding the polling station, but turning in greater numbers to smaller parties all too happy to attack the mainstream parties for being elitist and out of touch. At a time when trust in politics has hit an all-time low, political parties are facing a crisis in confidence. Membership of the big parties has melted away, while support for pressure groups campaigning on issues such as human rights abuses or climate change has grown (though whether levels of activism are any higher is a moot point). At the same time, political parties have come to rely on hired professionals to win support among the growing number of independently minded voters. Political parties certainly still need members, but not in the number or in the way they once did.

While understanding how political parties have become much more aggressive, professionally driven organizations, concerns have been raised about their capacity to engage and mobilize an increasingly critical and disenchanted electorate. The public, rightly or wrongly, perceive politicians and their parties as unrepresentative, self-serving, more interested in spin than substance, and funded by rich donors out to advance their own positions of power. But there is a real danger, as this book will argue, that, in acknowledging the faults of contemporary political parties (faults the leadership of parties, in all fairness, have tried to address), we miss why democracy needs political parties.

Love them or loathe them, democratic government and politics rely on political parties to recruit political activists and politicians, run election campaigns, organize the business of government and act as representatives of the plurality of interests and viewpoints across society. Without them, we'd have to invent some other institutional device to perform these roles – unless, that is, you believe that politicians should be untutored and their recruitment one of chance (the view of the classical 'direct democrats' in the Athenian *polis* in ancient Greece). Political parties provide government with a stable and ultimately accountable platform to run the country for four to five years before an election is held again. Parties matter because, at election time, voters can make a judgement about which group they want to run the country – and that group (or groups, in a coalition government) then have to do it knowing that somewhere down the line the electorate will hold them to account.

As parties have become professionalized, no one would doubt their capacity to mount political campaigns and organize the business of government and opposition. But as the more voluntary side to their organizations has declined, political parties have in other respects become weaker, more dependent on rich donors (or the state, in other countries) for funding, and less able to play their role in promoting and supporting political activity in wider society. These are all activities crucial to the democratic health of the country. If these are absent, it is argued, citizens are less likely to get involved in politics, the legitimacy of government is compromised, and democracy becomes prey to the power of special interest lobby groups.[1] In understanding how British political parties have changed, in part under the extraordinary pressure of social change that has reshaped political alignments, these issues remain for parties to address if confidence in British politics is to be restored.

The first two chapters of this book look at the background to the shifts in British party politics in recent decades. Chapter 1 examines the decline of two-party politics in the UK and the 'de-alignment' of politics and society that has driven the growth in multi-party politics. Chapter 2 assesses the implications of these changes in partisanship for how parties are organized and how they go about winning votes. The next three chapters focus on the three main parties in national politics. Chapter 3 looks at how the Conservative Party struggled with the legacy of Thatcherism in the 1990s and 2000s – and how David Cameron turned the Tories around to win the 2010 general election by a narrow margin. Chapter 4 considers how Labour tore itself apart in the 1980s, only to recover in the 1990s as 'New Labour' to win three elections in a row. Chapter 5 examines how the Liberal Democrats turned themselves from a party of protest into a party of power – and where this left them in the British party system. The rise of nationalist and far right politics is considered in chapter 6 – in particular, how UKIP and the BNP entered the mainstream of British party politics. Chapter 7 looks at why socialist parties on the far left of British politics have made such little impact, but the Green Party has become a more significant force at the ballot box. Chapter 8 examines the growth in nationalist politics in Scotland and Wales, not least as a result of devolution; and how political allegiances have been overturned on both sides of the community divide in Northern Ireland in recent years. The final chapter considers the dangers facing democratic politics and what political parties need to do to help to restore trust in British politics.

# CHAPTER ONE

# The British Party System

## Counting parties

Today, there are around 400 parties registered with the Electoral Commission, the body overseeing British politics.[1] This is an extraordinary number – and in most cases, there is very little to them. But how do we count which parties are important in British politics? And how can we measure the changes that are taking place in the British party system?

Any study of British political parties will start with the three national parties that contest seats across Britain (but not necessarily the UK): the Conservatives, Labour and the Liberal Democrats. Six regional parties stand candidates in constituencies exclusively in Scotland, Wales or Northern Ireland. There are also a number of other smaller green, socialist, nationalist, and far right parties that compete, with varying degrees of success, in national, European, devolved and local elections. In most cases, candidates for these parties get no further than the ballot paper. But this is changing. These 'minor parties' are making in-roads into political representation in local and devolved government, the European parliament and even at Westminster. In 2009, twenty out of sixty-nine seats in the European parliament (not counting Northern Ireland) were taken by smaller parties. The following year, the Green Party won a seat in the general election.

Inevitably, the study of politics and political parties is full of numbers. At the very least, democracy generates votes that have to be counted. There is one set of numbers that offers an insight into these changes taking place in Britain's party system. These numbers concern the proportion of voters across half a century that support one or other of the two main parties in British politics: the Conservative Party and the Labour Party. Figure 1.1 shows the results of the 1955 and 2005 general elections. In the 1950s, it is clear that well over 95 per cent of votes went to Labour or Conservative candidates in what were high-turnout elections. The number of votes for other parties was tiny by comparison. Most people, as is clear in figure 1.1, voted for one or other of these two parties.

Looking back at this period, Labour and the Conservatives dominated national elections and political representation in the Westminster parliament: the vast majority of MPs were members of one or other of these two

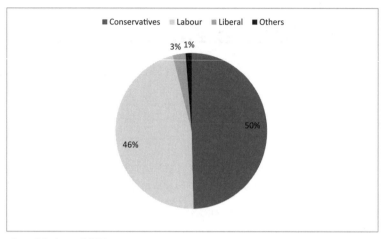

a General election result 1955

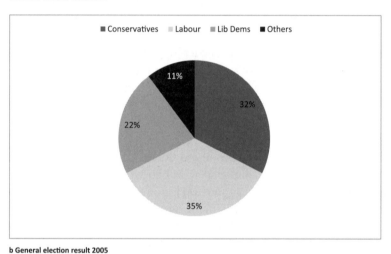

b General election result 2005

Figure 1.1 *British general election results, 1955, 2005*

parties. Support for these two parties was also relatively evenly balanced. This meant that Labour and the Conservatives took turns, if not equally, in government. Despite the strong record of the Conservatives in the 1950s, there was a reasonable expectation that each party had a chance of winning power: the opposition was a government in waiting. No one party, then, was 'predominant'. Between 1945 and 1970, Labour and the Conservatives alternated in government three times across seven elections. Despite the head-to-head nature of Westminster politics, however, Labour and the Conservatives were not separated by a wide ideological and policy divide. Both parties shared in a broad post-war consensus, even if they often disagreed on some of the details of policy. For the Labour and Conservative parties this made good electoral sense. Political competition drew both parties towards the ideological centre ground to maximize their share of the vote. All this cemented a view that Britain was a model of two-party politics, a party system distinguishable from that in other democratic countries where multiple parties competed for political power.

Now look at the result of the 2005 general election in figure 1.1. The number of voters supporting Labour or the Conservatives has fallen dramatically – down to 67.6 per cent. In 2010, this figure dropped further to around 65 per cent. While these two parties still account for a majority of votes cast, there are a significant number of votes going to other parties, in particular the Liberal Democrats whose 6.8 million votes in 2010 was just 1.8 million behind Labour.

So, what has happened? And what models can we use to understand these changing patterns of party politics in the UK?

## Party systems

A party system is a recurring pattern of relationships between political parties.[2] Instead of elections producing quite different results over time – say, most of the votes going to two parties at one election and spread more thinly across three or four parties at the next poll – voting patterns are reasonably stable. Moreover, these stable patterns tend to vary from country to country. The United Kingdom and the United States have traditionally been thought of as two-party systems: that is, ones where two parties dominate in both elections and government. By contrast, most countries across Europe are multi-party systems: that is, systems where at least three or four parties are in the political running and where election results produce multi-party parliaments and government by coalitions of parties.

So, what are the features of party systems that help to distinguish between different types? Giovanni Sartori, an Italian political scientist, identified in the 1970s two key dimensions of a party system:[3]

1. The number of parties in parliament (the 'relevant' parties)
2. The ideological differences between parties.

According to Sartori, the number of parties is an indicator of the degree of *fragmentation* in a party system: the more parties there are, the more fragmented the party system is. The ideological distance between parties on a left–right scale measures the *polarization* of a political system (see figure 1.2).

How does a party count as 'relevant'? According to Sartori, a relevant party must have participated in government or be a potential coalition partner or have 'blackmail' potential – by which he meant that it could influence government even if it wasn't part of it. In post-war Italy, for example, the Communist Party was a powerful player in national politics, but was regarded as

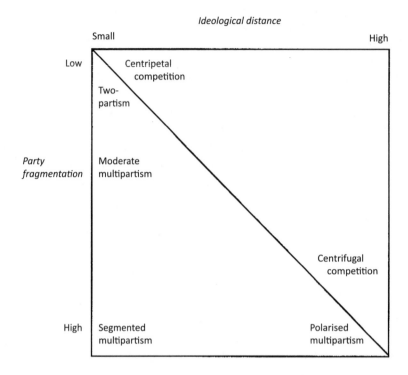

Source: Sartori, Parties and Party Systems, fig. 36, p.260.

Figure 1.2 *Sartori's simplified model of party systems*

beyond the ideological pale for any role in government dominated by the centre right Christian Democrats.

These two measures or indicators of a party system, the number of parties and the ideological difference between parties, form the basis for two basic types of party systems: the two-party system and the multi-party system.

In a two-party system, politics is dominated by two large parties competing for power – and this competition is regarded as 'centripetal'. This means that both parties are pulled to the centre of politics ideologically by the need to maximize the number of votes the party attracts: moving away from the centre alienates too many potential voters. By contrast, in multi-party political systems, there is a greater chance of 'centrifugal' competition. That is, parties are drawn to particular groups of voters and to aiming political campaigns at a relatively narrow segment of the political marketplace. The resulting polarization of politics can be extreme. In the past, Germany in the 1920s (the Weimar republic) and France in the 1950s (the Fourth Republic) were characterized by a high degree of ideological polarization and party fragmentation – and both became by-words for political instability. Sartori contrasts these examples of extreme or 'polarised pluralism' with cases of 'moderate pluralism' in which we see a combination of multi-party politics and limited ideological polarization. Contemporary examples include Germany and Spain. In countries such as France, Italy and the Netherlands, there is a greater degree of ideological polarizationand party fragmentation.

Some multi-party states have a dominant party. In such dominant or pre-dominant party systems, there is multi-party competition, but one party predominates in winning elections and forming governments over a number of decades. Sweden and Italy were examples of predominant party systems in the post-war period. In Japan, the Liberal Democratic Party ruled the country from 1955 to 2009 apart from a brief eleven-month period out of office in 1993–4. By contrast, other multi-party systems have no dominant party. France has in the past fallen into this category. However, the success in national elections of the main centre right party – the Union for a Popular Movement under Nicolas Sarkozy – in the 2000s, and the relative weakness of the main centre left party – the socialists – signalled that the French party system might be changing.

In between the two-party and multi-party systems is the two and a half party system, where a small 'half' party is a potential coalition party for both main parties. The Free Democrats have traditionally played this role in German, and before that West German, politics. Following the result of the 2010 general election, the Liberal Democrats look set to play this role more often in British politics, just as the old Liberal Party just about did in the 1970s and as the Lib Dems have done from time to time in the devolved administrations in Scotland and Wales since 1998.

A simple way of illustrating a party system is a bar chart showing the number of votes and seats won for each party in an election as a proportion of the total seats available. The charts in figure 1.3 give examples of each of the model party systems (the results are taken from elections around 1970 before substantial changes to party systems in Europe kicked in). The visual impression is striking. In predominant and two-party systems, most of the votes cast and seats won are taken by one or two parties. By contrast, in a more multi-party system, the distribution of votes and seats is more widely spread. In a two and a half party system, in this case West Germany *circa* 1969, we see a potential coalition partner in a smaller party, the Free Democrats. The other smaller party, the Christian Social Union, it should be noted, is the sister party of one of the two leading parties – the Christian Democratic Union (CDU) – in Bavaria, and so its votes and seats should be added to those of the CDU.

Political science has taken the analysis of party systems a step further using a mathematical formula known as the effective number of parties (ENP).[4] The formula can be applied to both the number of votes parties win in elections and the number of seats. The objective of the formula is to come up with a figure that corresponds to the number of political parties that are 'effectively' competing in a particular party system. Simply put, the effective number of

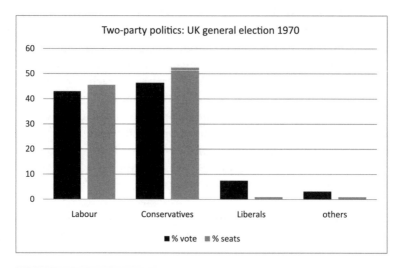

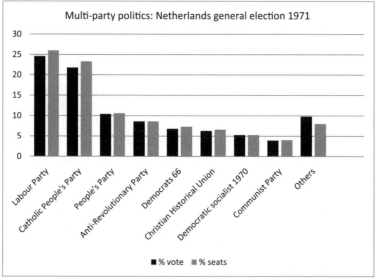

Figure 1.3  *Pary systems in four states*

parties is the fraction of votes or seats parties win in an election. The higher the value of the effective number of parties, the more multi-party a system is. For a two-party system, a score close to 2 would be expected. Where there are two parties running neck and neck plus another significant party in the mix – the two and half party system – the score will be around 2.5. Above this number, there are multi-party systems, some with predominant parties and others with no dominant party. ENP data for the UK, West Germany, the Netherlands and Sweden for the elections illustrated in the bar charts are summarized in figure 1.4.

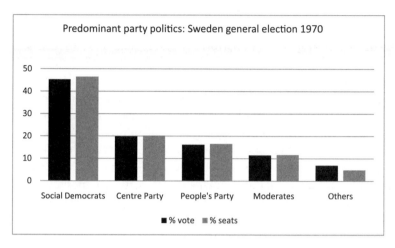

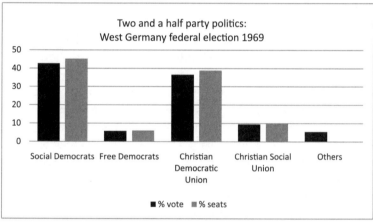

Figure 1.3    *(Continued)*

| | ENP votes | ENP seats |
|---|---|---|
| **United Kingdom (1970)** | 2.46 | 2.07 |
| **Netherlands (1971)** | 7.09 | 6.4 |
| **Sweden (1970)** | 3.48 | 3.32 |
| **West Germany (1969)** | 3.03 | 2.71 |

*Source: ENP scores online: www.tcd.ie/Political_Science/staff/michael_gallagher/ ElSystems/Docts/ElectionIndices.pdf; see also M. Gallagher and Paul Mitchell (eds.),* The Politics of Electoral Systems *(Oxford: Oxford University Press, 2008).*

Figure 1.4  *Effective number of parties in four states* circa *1970*

These conceptual models of party systems help political science to compare party competition in different states around the world. There are differences in methodological approaches. Sartori's is largely qualitative and considerable emphasis is placed on the ideology of parties and the degree of polarization of the party system on a left–right continuum. This continuum focuses on the role of the state in the economy and providing welfare: moving to the left, this role increases; to the right, the role decreases. Generally, it is assumed that the more parties there are in a party system, the greater the ideological polarization as parties try to stake out their own distinctive niche in the political marketplace. Research shows, however, that the number of parties and the degree of polarization can be 'relatively independent': party systems with the same number of parties can vary on the degree of ideological pluralism.[5]

The approach taken by the effective number of parties index is quantitative because the characteristic of a party system is reduced to a number based on election data on the votes and seats won by parties. Such a methodology makes cross-national comparative study easy but, critics argue, it doesn't address the question of political power directly enough. In particular, it underestimates the extent to which minor parties that have a small impact on the index, such as the Free Democrats in Germany, tip the balance of power. One way of addressing this is to extend the calculation of the effective number of parties in votes and seats to the effective number of parties with power over legislation and in government. Figure 1.5 is taken from research comparing the situations in Germany and the UK.[6] It highlights the significance of the Free Democrats in Germany in running the country, despite their relatively small size. The data also demonstrate that, whatever the shift in British politics since 1970 towards a more multi-party system in terms of votes (and to a lesser extent seats), two-party politics continued to hold sway in terms of the effective number of parties with real power in parliament and in the cabinet. The Conservative / Liberal Democrat coalition formed after the 2010 election changed all that.

| | ENP Votes | ENP Seats | ENP Parliament | ENP Cabinet |
|---|---|---|---|---|
| **UK** | | | | |
| **1945-2005** | 2.8 | 2.1 | 1.3 | 1.0 |
| **1974-2005** | 3.2 | 2.2 | 1.4 | 1.0 |
| **Germany** | | | | |
| **1949-2005** | 3.0 | 2.7 | 2.4 | 1.6 |

*Source: Blau, 'The effective number of parties at four scales', table 1.*

Figure 1.5 *Effective number of parties in UK and Germany*

But before we turn in more detail to the British party system today, why are some states two-party systems (with a correspondingly low effective number of parties) and others more multi-party (with a higher effective number of parties)? Explanations fall, broadly speaking, into two camps. One approach focuses on the underlying political sociology of a country, while another emphasizes institutional factors, in particular the relationship between electoral systems and party systems.

## Political sociology, social cleavages and party families

What shapes a party system? One way of answering this question is to think about the underlying political sociology of a country – in particular, how many significant social divisions there are in a society, for example by class, religion or geography. These divisions are known as social cleavages. There are three features of a social cleavage that are important for understanding political parties. First, the cleavage must divide people living in a society into groups. These social divisions should be sufficiently striking to give rise to tensions and conflicts over particular issues of interest or point of view between groups on either side of the cleavage. Second, these social divisions must sustain a sense of collective identity within the groups, forming the basis for a broad political ideology about how the world is and what it might be. Third, this collective identity should lead to the formation of political organizations, generally political parties, to advance the interests or point of view of the group and that help to mould the collective ideology of the group through their actions and campaigns.

Political cleavages are associated with particular 'party families'. This is a term used to describe a group of parties that share common ideological features and which draw support from particular groups in society. Like many other European countries, British politics in the twentieth century was dominated by a class social cleavage – and other social divides that did exist were marginalized. This class division between property owners and workers in industry arose in the nineteenth century and produced sharply different interests and points of view on issues such as the rights of workers, income distribution and the freedom of the individual. On the left, this class divide underpinned the formation of the socialist and social democratic family of parties, committed to greater equality of income, wealth and opportunity through the provision of welfare and the regulation of the capitalist system. On the right, the interests and points of view of middle-class property owners were represented by a mix of pro-business liberal and conservative parties.

In Britain, this class politics overlay earlier political divides between those whose interests and world views were bound up with land (largely farming) and those whose interests and ideologies were interwoven with business, manufacturing and urban society. Initially, the Conservative and Liberal parties stood either side of this social cleavage – with the added dimension that the Liberals generally represented non-conformist church groups against the authority of the established Church of England (reputedly the Conservative Party at prayer). But, over time, the Conservative Party successfully bridged this divide and became the dominant party representing the interests of all property owners, whether they lived in the countryside or not. The modern Conservative Party came to articulate both a conservative view on traditional social relations and the nation state, and a liberal perspective on the free market. In this way, it became a liberal conservative party.

On the continent, despite the importance of class cleavages, religion continued in the twentieth century to shape political divides through the influence of Christian democracy in countries such as Italy, Germany and the Netherlands. This social cleavage sprang from the resistance of churches, in particular the Catholic Church, to the rise of the modern secular state. Generally on the centre right of the political spectrum, the Christian democratic party family offered a conservative ideology of community, traditional morality and an interventionist welfare state. It introduced another dimension to some European party systems. Post-war German politics, for example, was (and still is) split not two ways but three: by secular left parties (notably the SPD); by a secular pro-business party (the Free Democrats); and by the pro-church centre right Christian Democrats. In the UK, the Social Democratic and Labour Party rooted in Catholic communities in Northern Ireland falls into this party family though on the centre left (see chapter 8). It has also been suggested that New Labour might be thought of in Christian democratic terms.[7]

Across Europe, the rise of the modern state also gave rise to social divisions between sub-national territories or regions. This 'centre–periphery' social cleavage saw political parties emerge committed to defending the interests of these sub-national regions and, very often, the ethno-nationalist groups within them, against what was seen as the power of the dominant region and/or ethno-nationalist group. In Belgium, such social divisions between distinct sub-national communities continue to shape political divides. The Belgium party system is today split on strict community lines: all the main parties are organized on a regional basis, representing either the Dutch-speaking community in Flanders or the French-speaking community in Walloon. In British politics, region-based parties were largely absent from the party system until the 1960s and 1970s, except in Northern Ireland. The old Liberal Party did retain important power bases in the 'Celtic fringes' of Britain, in particular, the south-west of England. As we shall see in chapter 8, minority nationalist parties, committed to regional interests, cultural rights and constitutional decentralization, have become a significant feature of UK party politics over the past four decades.

It has also been suggested that contemporary society is divided by the values held by the public. As we shall shortly see, the erosion of the link between class and politics (what is called 'de-alignment') in the 1960s and

1970s is understood by some political scientists as being connected to the opening up of a new social cleavage based on 'materialist' and 'post-materialist' values. In an increasingly affluent society, it is argued, a shift has been taking place from materialist concerns with economic growth, public safety and national defence towards post-materialist concerns with individual rights, the environment and social equality. This has given rise to a reconfiguration of political cleavages, not least as post-materialists grew in number across the western world and their views tended to take them to the liberal left of the political spectrum.[8] While the majority of voters remain 'materialists', those who hold post-material values have been drawn to support green politics in particular, because of their concerns about the state of the environment.

To political sociology, all these social cleavages matter because, simply put, the more divided or pluralist a society is, the more political parties there are likely to be competing for power, gaining representation and having an impact on the shape of government. As we shall see, a more pluralist society has posed considerable problems for the established political parties in Britain, in terms of both their own organization and the threat they face from more niche-based political parties.

## Electoral systems and party systems

An electoral system is simply a way of counting votes and allocating seats or positions of authority. Different electoral systems sort votes and decide winners in different ways. Some systems count the votes in each electoral constituency once. The winner, usually the candidate who wins a seat in a parliament or assembly, is the person with the highest score. This is called single member simple plurality – or, more commonly, first-past-the-post. (For some local government elections in England and Wales, a system of multi-member simple plurality is used.) A variation on simple plurality is a majority system such as the alternative vote and supplementary vote systems, in which the winning candidate has to secure 50 per cent of the votes cast. In a majority system, there is a second round of voting between the top two candidates in the first round (e.g. for the French presidency) or the opportunity on the ballot paper to make a second preference, ensuring that one candidate wins half of the votes cast (e.g. for the London mayor). The majority-based alternative vote system has been put forward to replace straight simple plurality for UK general elections.

Proportional electoral systems differ by attempting to make the result of the election representative in the sense that the number of winning candidates for a party broadly reflects the number of votes cast for the party – hence the term proportional representation, or PR. Proportional systems come in a number of types. List systems involve multi-member constituencies and, as the name suggests, a list of candidates for voters to choose from. Seats are allocated to parties on the basis of the proportion of votes cast for that party in each constituency. Elections to the European parliament in England, Scotland and Wales use a list system and the country is divided into electoral regions. For national elections in the Netherlands, there is a single national electoral district, resulting in the Dutch parliament being particularly representative of votes cast for different parties (see figure 1.3, pages 10–11).

The mixed member proportional or additional member system combines elements of PR and simple plurality in an attempt to make up for the lack of proportionality in plurality systems. So, for example, in Germany and in elections for the Scottish parliament and the Welsh Assembly, voters cast a ballot for a candidate in the single member constituency, just as they would do under simple plurality. Voters have an 'additional' vote which they use to support a party in a larger multi-member constituency. The distribution of seats is largely determined by the vote in this second party vote. The final version of PR is the single transferable vote (STV). Voters are asked to list candidates in order of preference. When it comes to the count, candidates who reach a certain quota of first-preference votes are elected. Any votes in excess of this quota are re-allocated to other candidates. This method of counting voter preferences aims to bring greater proportionality to the voting system. STV was chosen for elections for the Northern Ireland Assembly to guard against any one community in the province dominating government and politics (see chapter 8). It is also used for European elections in the province, and for local government elections in Scotland.

Does the electoral system matter to the type of party system? According to the French political scientist Maurice Duverger, there is a relationship between the institutional arrangements of the electoral system and the pattern of results produced by the election (the party system, in other words). According to Duverger's law, electoral systems influence how people vote. Under simple plurality, the electorate are averse to 'wasting' their votes on smaller parties that have no chance of winning seats. By contrast, PR systems allow voters to match their political preferences more closely with what parties are on offer, knowing that their votes have a greater chance of counting. As a general rule, then, Duverger's law predicts that, where elections are held under proportional voting systems, multi-party competition and collaborative (coalition) government result. Under these institutional arrangements, smaller parties have more opportunity to compete in the political marketplace. Where elections use simple plurality or majority voting, political systems are dominated by two parties, and smaller parties tend to lose out, and there is very little cooperation (at least of a formal kind) between political parties during elections or in government.

In thinking about Duverger's law, there is something of the chicken and the egg: does the electoral system shape the party system or the party system shape the electoral system? In practice, where elections are held under simple plurality, it is harder for smaller parties to gain representation in parliament

except, as in the case of the UK, where small constituency sizes provide opportunities for regional parties to prosper (there are enough votes in the right
places for the Scottish National Party and Plaid Cymru to win seats). Across
Europe, where PR systems are the norm, it is by contrast easier for smaller
parties to gain representation because votes are more proportionately turned
into seats, although there are subtle differences between types of PR on this
and different threshold rules that set a minimum share of the vote a party
must reach before it can win a seat. The type of electoral system, then, can
act as a barrier to small parties gaining representation in parliament – and
therefore becoming 'effective' or 'relevant' parties. But political parties won't
prosper, whatever voting system is in place, without a critical mass of support
in the electorate generated by a social cleavage and nurtured and exploited
by those parties.

Things do change. In New Zealand, electoral reform overturned the country's traditional two-party system (see box 1.1). As we shall see shortly, the
British party system started to change before any reforms were made to

## Box 1.1 Voting reform and party systems: the case of New Zealand

The relationship between electoral systems and party systems was the subject of a
major comparative study of party systems by Arend Lijphart. This work established an
empirical relationship between voting systems and party systems. In four countries
using simple plurality, the UK, the US, Canada and New Zealand, the average effective
number of parties score between 1945 and 1980 was 2.1, indicating a two-party
system. By contrast, in fifteen other countries that used systems of proportional representation, there were multi-party systems with an average effective number of
parties score of 3.8.

New Zealand provides an interesting case study of the impact of institutional reform
on party systems. For years, New Zealand used the same first-past-the-post voting
system as the UK. And, just like Britain, New Zealand was a model of two-party politics.
Between them, the National and Labour parties dominated the party system. And,
just like the UK, the election results were highly disproportional. Pressure for change
started in the 1980s, and, by the 1996 general election, the country had a new
voting system. Simple plurality was replaced by the additional member (or mixed
member) system. The effect was dramatic. The dominance of the National and Labour
parties was ended. The number of parties in parliament jumped to between 6 and 8
(helped by a low threshold of votes needed to gain a seat). Single-party government
was replaced by coalition government. The effective number of parties in votes, already
creeping up before 1996 to 3.52 in 1993, averaged 4.1 in the 1996, 1999 and 2002
elections. In the same elections, an average ENP score for seats of 3.7 put New Zealand
in the camp of multi-party politics. In subsequent elections in 2005 and 2008, strong
performances by the National Party have taken the ENP scores for votes and seats back
to around 3.

*Source*: A. Lijphart, *Democracies: Patterns of Majoritarian and Consensus Government
in Twenty-one Countries* (New Haven: Yale University Press, 1984)

voting systems in the UK. But, as systems of proportional representation have been introduced – in European and devolved elections, for example – so the British party system has changed further. So, in answer to the question, does the electoral system shape the party system or the other way round: they influence one another; or to put it another way, the number of political parties created by society will be conditional on the electoral system.[9]

Political parties are also a factor in shaping party systems. Labour and the Conservatives don't simply work with pre-existing social cleavages. In the process of seeking power, parties mobilize groups of voters in a way that helps to shape the political divides that social approaches suggest exist outside the realm of politics. Parties do this by helping to structure the preferences of voters: what people think is important when they consider which party to support in an election. Parties, of course, don't work with a blank canvas. Voters are shaped by their social environments. But parties, through their activities such as running political campaigns, help to give definition to the interests, values and political commitment of voters. The political activities of the Labour Party in mobilizing voters, for example, served to reinforce the collective political identity and ambitions of the working class in Britain. In Scotland and Wales, this activism tended to work against other political identities, in particular nationalist attachments to place, that might otherwise have been significant – and which did grow in importance from the 1970s onwards.

Social and institutional factors, then, both play a part in shaping party systems. In the next part of this chapter, I want to examine how the British party system has changed since the post-war period.

## The changing British party system

Post-war British politics, as we have seen, was dominated by the Conservative and Labour parties in what was regarded as a classic example of a two-party system. What, then, has changed?

By the 1960s, the first signs of change were already on the political horizon. In the 1964 and 1966 general elections, which Labour won, the Liberal Party vote bounced back from the nadir of the 1950s. In 1955, fewer than three-quarters of a million voters supported the Liberals, just 2.7 per cent of the total votes cast. Liberal support went back up to over 3 million in 1964 (11.2 per cent of the vote); and, while it fell to under 2.5 million in 1966, the party increased its representation in parliament from nine MPs to twelve.

The result of the 1970 election appeared to suggest that two-party politics was still entrenched: Labour and the Conservatives remained the dominant forces in British politics, accounting for just fewer than 90 per cent of total votes cast; and the (unexpected) Conservative victory looked like just another swing of the two-party political pendulum. However, rather than a sign of a

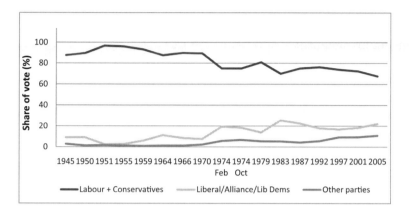

Figure 1.6 *The decline of two-party politics: general elections 1945–2005*

return to two-party politics as normal, it was the last result in which Labour and the Conservatives really held sway. In the two elections held in 1974, Labour and the Conservatives barely managed 75 per cent of the total vote. Both parties secured less than 40 per cent of the vote each – and Labour wouldn't get above this level again until 1997. The Liberal Party won 6 million votes in the February poll and nearly 5.5 million in the October poll, a share of just under one-fifth of votes cast. The number of Liberal MPs was now well into double figures and the party was a realistic potential coalition partner in government. This, at the very least, was moving Britain towards a two and a half party system.

Beyond the numbers indicating the decline of two-party politics, we can also see an ideological polarization in British politics in the 1970s and early 1980s that, as we shall see in chapters 3 and 4 of this book, took Labour to the left and the Conservatives to the right. Post-war consensus politics fast disappeared in the turbulent times ushered in by the end of the long post-war boom. Indeed, one view was that the British party system was contributing to the growing instability in government and to a crisis in the British state brought about by ideological extremes and the see-sawing of public policy-making.[10]

The political trends established in the 1970s continued into the 1980s and beyond. The result of the 1979 election, when the combined vote for Labour and the Conservatives went back above 80 per cent, was rather like a 'dead cat bounce' in the financial markets (even a dead cat will bounce when dropped from high enough . . . ). This was no return to traditional two-party politics. The Conservatives, however, continued to poll above 40 per cent of the vote under Margaret Thatcher and John Major. Indeed, the success of the Conservative Party led to suggestions that the UK was becoming a predominant party system as Major pulled off a fourth election victory in a row for the Tories in 1992. Conservative defeats in 1997, 2001 and 2005 put paid to this argument.

The real story in this period was the continued fragmentation of the British party system. In the 1983 and 1987 elections, Labour's claim to be the main opposition party was under threat from the Social Democratic Party (SDP) formed by a group of disillusioned senior Labour politicians. The SDP teamed up with the Liberals in an alliance that, for a while at least, looked set to 'break the mould' of Britain's two-party politics. While the merger between the Liberals and the SDP to form the Liberal Democrats was hardly pain-free, the new party would, under Paddy Ashdown in the 1990s, establish itself as a real force in British politics. In the 1992 general election, the Liberal Democrats were supported by just under 6 million people, winning 20 seats in parliament. Since then, the Lib Dems have consistently won a fifth or so of total votes. But this level of support, because it is spread fairly evenly across the country, is not turned into a similar proportion of seats in the House of Commons by the electoral system. In 2005 and 2010, 22–3 per cent of votes for the Lib Dems netted a little under 10 per cent of the representation in parliament (62, then 57, MPs).

Significantly, the Lib Dems have become the main opposition to the leading party in a growing number of constituencies across the country. Before 1970, the vast majority of seats on mainland Britain were straight fights between Labour and the Conservatives. From the seventies onwards, the political geography of Britain started to shift. There has long been something of a north–south divide in support for political parties: Labour did well in the north; the Tories far better in the south. The explanation for this regional variation in support goes beyond the different demographic mixes across the UK. There is something about where people live that shapes their political attitudes. In the 1980s, the north–south political divide became more pronounced with the uneven regional economic development of the UK. At the same time, the gap between Conservative-supporting rural areas and Labour-supporting urban areas also continued to grow.[11] This opened the door for third- and minor-party challenges to two-party politics, and led to the decline of one or other of the two main parties where they were in the weaker position (i.e. Labour in the south, the Conservatives in the north). What is particularly striking is the decline in the number of straight Labour–Conservative fights in British politics at a constituency level. By the 2010 general election, the Labour and Conservative parties were only really fighting each other in a little over half of all seats. And the key battlegrounds in the marginal seats were split three ways between Labour, the Conservatives and the Liberal Democrats. Today, all three main parties fight on different fronts, in different ways, in different places.

With the defeat of the Conservatives in the 1997 general election, it was all too obvious that British politics had changed. Labour's victory saw the combined vote of the two main parties slip back below 75 per cent – and it would continue to fall. By 2005, as we have seen, this two-party share was down to just under 68 per cent of the vote and it slid further in 2010. British electoral politics was becoming more competitive, beyond the revival of the old Liberal Party. Voters were increasingly looking beyond the usual political suspects. In growing numbers, the electorate were turning to the minor parties. This catch-all group included the nationalist and unionist parties in Scotland (the Scottish National Party), Wales (Plaid Cymru) and Northern Ireland (Ulster Unionists, the Democratic Unionists, the Social Democratic and Labour Party and Sinn Fein), as well as parties on the ideological edges of British politics, in particular the British National Party and the UK Independence Party on the right, and the Green Party, the Scottish Socialist Party and Respect on the left. Putting to one side votes for parties in Northern Ireland, the minor parties in British politics were, by 2005, attracting more than 8 per cent of the vote.

This fragmentation of British party politics can be measured, as we saw earlier, using effective number of parties scores. Just to recap, this can be measured either using the shares of votes won by competing parties or by shares of seats gained in parliament as a result of the election. Between 1945 and 1970, the effective number of parties in general elections based on voting shares was 2.36; after 1970, the average rose to 3.21. Using party shares of seats in parliament, the effective number of parties increased from 2.05 to 2.21. At the 2005 poll, the effective number of parties by share of votes rose further to 3.48; and by share of seats, to 2.44.[12]

What these numbers show is that the British party system has changed beyond the return of the Liberals. UK politics has seen a fragmentation and polarization of political support. In later chapters we look in more detail at what this means for politics on the far right, among socialist and green parties and in the devolved institutions established in 1998. The fragmentation of support for political parties at the polls has had less of an impact at Westminster, in part because of the voting system. This is shown by the lower figure for the effective number of parties by share of seats compared to share of votes. None the less, in the House of Commons, British politics has become a two and a half party system – and the result of the 2010 general election was a further continuation of this long-term trend.

## The new politics beyond Westminster

Beyond the world of Westminster politics, the decline of two-party politics is evident too. In local, devolved and European elections, not only are voters supporting a wider range of parties, but also these votes are being translated into seats in town and county halls, devolved parliaments and assemblies, and the European parliament. Greater political representation is further leading to shifting patterns of executive control across local and regional government. The forward march of the minor parties beyond Westminster has shifted beyond the electoral arena where votes are counted and reached the legislative and executive arenas where power is exercised. Indeed, British politics has moved away from a party system dominated by a two-party race for government at the national level to political competition across multiple jurisdictions and overlapping party systems with their own distinct patterns and characteristics.[13]

In local elections (including mayoral elections in London and other English cities) and elections for the devolved institutions and the European parliament, the number of parties in the political running is increasing. Labour and Conservative dominance over town and county affairs is over as the Liberals, later the Liberal Democrats, established themselves as a significant third force in local politics, with over 4,400 councillors in 2007 in Britain, controlling twenty-nine councils, 7 per cent of the total in Britain. Using estimates for the national equivalent vote at local government elections in 2007, the Conservatives and Labour together received 66 per cent of the vote, the Liberal Democrats 24 per cent. By comparison, in 1980, the combined share of the vote for the big two was 82 per cent, with the Liberals on 13 per cent.[14]

Local politics is also seeing the gradual advance of smaller parties and independents. In 2007, 'others' in local elections won over 2,500 council seats (including 546 for the Scottish National Party and Plaid Cymru) and a national equivalent share of the vote of around 10 per cent in Britain. The composition of non-mainstream groups includes – aside from the nationalists in Scotland and Wales – local branches of national parties, such as the Greens, Respect, the British National Party and the United Kingdom Independence Party; local parties active in just one locality; local political associations set up outside of party politics but which have entered local electoral politics; and individuals independent of local party or association. Significantly, the position of these smaller parties and independents in local politics is such that, in around 20 per cent of local councils since the mid 1990s, support for 'others' overwhelms the big three.[15] Not surprisingly, the role of independents in British politics has become the subject of debate.

In mayoral elections, non-mainstream candidates have also attracted support. In the first election for London mayor in 2000, the contest was won by the 'independent' Ken Livingstone beating the Conservatives, Liberal Democrats and the official Labour candidate. In 2004, Livingstone, now back in the Labour fold, won again, only to be beaten by the Conservative Boris Johnson in 2008. But, in the 2004 contest, nearly a fifth of first-preference votes were cast for minor parties. This fell to around 10 per cent in 2008. In twenty-two mayoral contests around the country between 2000 and 2007, eleven were won by Labour, two by the Conservatives, two by the Liberal Democrats and seven by independents, including H'Angus the Monkey, mascot of Hartlepool Football Club (a.k.a. Stuart Drummond) in Hartlepool in 2005.

Devolution has further embedded multi-party politics. Indeed, the more proportional voting systems for the Scottish parliament and the assemblies in Northern Ireland and Wales mean that multi-party political competition in elections is translating into more multi-party representation and into multi-party government. Since 1998, Scotland and Wales have both been run by coalitions. Following devolved elections in 2007, the Scottish executive was controlled by a minority Scottish National Party administration. In Northern Ireland, the combination of proportional representation and a power-sharing constitution ensures that governance in the province is by multi-party agreement. Until 2010, the commonly held view was that political parties didn't work together in government. In Scotland, Wales and Northern Ireland (as well as at a local level across the country), recent experience is that they do so more than was thought.

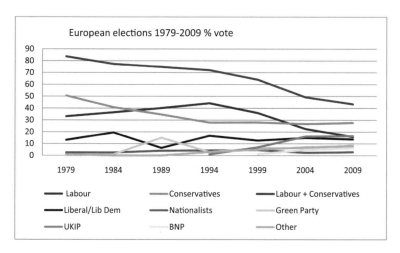

| | Labour | Conservatives | Liberals | Nationalists | Greens | UKIP | BNP |
|---|---|---|---|---|---|---|---|
| 1979 | 17 | 60 | - | - | - | - | - |
| 1984 | 32 | 45 | - | - | - | - | - |
| 1989 | 45 | 32 | - | 1 | - | - | - |
| 1994 | 18 | 62 | 2 | 2 | - | - | - |
| 1999 | 29 | 36 | 10 | 4 | 2 | 3 | - |
| 2004 | 19 | 27 | 12 | 3 | 2 | 12 | - |
| 2009 | 13 | 26 | 11 | 3 | 2 | 13 | 2 |

Table: European election results 1979-2009, seats won

*Source: House of Commons.*

**Figure 1.7** *European election results 1979–2009 100% vote. Note: results are for GB not UK; NI MEPs elected under different system; 1979–1994, elections from single-member constituencies, thereafter using regional list PR*

Elections to the European parliament have also seen two-party politics take a battering. The first direct elections to the European parliament took place in 1979 using single member constituencies in Britain and the single transferable vote in Northern Ireland. The election on the mainland was dominated by Labour and the Conservatives in both votes and seats – and little changed in 1984.

However, the 1989 poll saw the Green Party win 15 per cent of the vote, but no seats under simple plurality. Proportional representation was introduced for the 1999 election and the picture since has been the growing fragmentation of support. The Greens won two seats in 1999, holding on to them in 2004 and 2009. UKIP jumped from 7 to 16 per cent in 2004, winning twelve seats. In the 2009 poll, UKIP pushed Labour into third place winning one extra seat, although its share of vote barely crept up. The British National Party also won two seats in the 2009 election, although its share of the vote was up just 1.3 points to 6.2 per cent. The big story in the 2009 election was the collapse of the Labour vote – and the success of the smaller parties needs to be put in this context.

In summary, British party politics has changed significantly since the early 1970s. We have entered what Patrick Dunleavy calls 'a radically new era of party competition' in which five to six parties compete in elections, and there are clear political divides between these parties, offering voters the full range of ideological positions from socialist and green parties on the left across to nationalist and far right parties. The results from the 2009 European elections and the 2010 general election are part of a pattern that stretches back more than three decades. This shifting pattern of party politics has led to calls for electoral reform – and, as the 2010 election result confirmed, it has also dramatically increased the chances of a hung parliament even under simple plurality voting.[16]

But what has been driving this shift to more multi-party politics in Britain? This is what the final part of this chapter will examine.

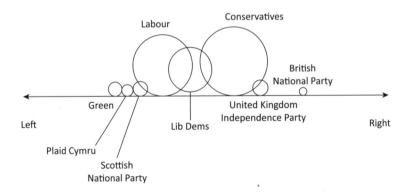

Figure 1.8 *The contemporary British party system*

## Social class and partisanship

Post-war political analysis took it as read that Britain was a two-party system – and this party system was rooted in the sociology of British society. General elections were little more than an organized class struggle. Broadly speaking, the middle classes voted Conservative – and the Tories represented the interests of these voters. The working classes voted Labour – and Labour represented the interests of these voters: enough said.

Voting patterns bear this out. During the 1960s, over 60 per cent of the manual working class voted Labour; and over 60 per cent of the non-manual middle classes supported the Conservatives.[17] To be sure, these patterns were always more complex. A sizeable proportion of working-class and middle-class voters didn't vote according to their social backgrounds. There were also other weaker political divides that had some influence on voting patterns. In the case of politics in Northern Ireland, as we see in chapter 8, religion, not class, was the dominant political cleavage. None the less, these voting patterns did show the majority of the white-collar middle classes voting Conservative; and the blue-collar working class lining up behind Labour. These numbers underpinned the idea that social class was the main factor in understanding British political parties – that there was an *alignment* between class and party.

Such an understanding of British politics was established in the work of two leading political scientists in the 1960s, David Butler and Donald Stokes. Their analysis was for more than a decade the established orthodoxy in the study of British politics. Butler and Stokes sought to explain why parties were supported by particular groups of voters. The core of their work was based on a theory of political identification or partisanship first developed in the United States at the University of Michigan. Political identification means a strong commitment by individuals to a particular political party. These partisans supported a party almost irrespective of what it said or did. These commitments were, moreover, long-term and shaped from a young age in the class background of voters and reinforced by community, school and work. As a result, the electorate was made up of large blocks of partisans committed, in the British case, to one party (the Conservatives) or another (Labour).

Furthermore, not only did around 90 per cent of voters associate themselves with a particular party, but around 40 per cent of the electorate were 'very strong' identifiers.[18] As a result, there was little switching of sides, especially between the two main parties. Indeed, the largest group of switchers (20–5 per cent of the electorate) in elections in the late 1950s and 1960s were those who moved between voting and non-voting. Hard-core partisans were very unlikely to switch sides – and they were also much more likely to vote.

According to Butler and Stokes, then, voting was not so much a political choice as the result of deeply embedded patterns of individual and social behaviour. Short-term factors, such as the political campaign, had little influence on election results. Indeed, it was thought, the electorate went to the polls without a great deal of political knowledge or understanding. Voting was more about group identity, much like supporting a football club. Partisan voters didn't listen either. Or at least, being a loyal group member made voters highly selective in the way they developed their political knowledge: they listened to things that reinforced their identity and ignored anything that challenged it. And where voters broke with their groups and supported another party, this approach assumed they were deviants from the basic partisan rule.

Such an understanding of voting patterns suggested that the two main parties in Britain had large core votes based on the class structure of society. Not surprisingly, perhaps, these parties spent most of their time appealing to their core votes. According to Butler and Stokes, the number of voters with a weak sense of partisanship – the classic 'floating voter' – was small. These votes were important to which party won an election. But their small number also meant that party campaign strategies were built around mobilizing core voters: getting the partisans, in other words, out to vote. The political activism of Labour and the Conservatives served, then, to intensify and entrench two-class/two-party politics in Britain.

So, if political change was going to happen, it would be glacial in timescale. In fact, within a couple of decades, this orthodoxy in political science had been challenged. Exactly how and why party politics in Britain changed is not without its controversies. There are important methodological debates on how to measure and analyse voting behaviour.[19] These controversies extend internationally to the question of whether or not class has disappeared from the electoral landscape across the developed world – including the strength of such alignments in the first place.[20] The influence of Butler and Stokes has in certain respects proved difficult to shake from everyday understandings of British party politics. However, there has emerged some degree of consensus on the scale and scope of political change in Britain and how this underpins the shift away from two-party politics. Key to this change is the idea of class and partisan de-alignment.

## De-alignment

Post-war political analysis, as we have seen, assumed there was a powerful relationship between class and party. The main evidence supporting this was the alignment between the two in patterns of voting. Contemporary political science acknowledges this relationship has, in different ways and to varying degrees, weakened or even broken down. The alignment between class and party has shifted. This is what is called de-alignment.

There are two broad views on de-alignment. The first is that class is a declining influence on politics and that other social divides have opened up to shape party politics. Society still matters, but political commitments have become re-aligned reflecting new or re-emergent social cleavages. This can be seen, for example, in the growing support for green parties reflecting value commitments to an environmentally sustainable society; and nationalist parties in Scotland and Wales tapping into shifting senses of national identity within the United Kingdom. A second view on de-alignment is that voters are less embedded in social relations and more able and more willing to make choices about which party to support, often on the basis of the performance of a party leadership in government or opposition and their perceived capacity to deliver public policy ('valence' politics).

Before looking at these perspectives, let us examine the evidence for de-alignment, in particular the weakening link between class and party.

As we have seen, back in the 1960s, around 60 per cent of middle-class voters voted Conservative – and about the same slice of working-class voters voted Labour. By 2005, less than 40 per cent of these middle-class voters supported the Conservatives; and just under a half of working-class voters voted Labour. Since the 1960s, then, the total amount of class voting (what is called 'absolute class voting') has fallen from around two-thirds of voters to around two-fifths. The decline in class voting, in particular among middle-class voters, has underpinned the success of the Liberals and the Liberal Democrats since the 1970s. Two further measures are traditionally used to measure the weakening relation between class and party: the Alford index and the odds ratio. Both these measures suggest that class voting has declined significantly in British politics since the 1960s. The Alford index, which is calculated by taking Labour's share of middle-class voters away from its share of working-class voters, has fallen from above 40 in the 1960s to around 20 after 1997. The odds ratio, which is a measure of the relative chance of middle-class voters supporting the Conservatives rather than Labour and of working-class voters supporting one or other of the two main parties, has also fallen from over 6 in the 1960s to under 3 after 1997.[21]

There is, to be sure, considerable debate about these measures of political change and what exactly they show. None the less, there is a broad consensus that the relationship between class and party has at the very least weakened, not least because class voting in Britain was, by comparison with other similar countries, so strong in the first place.[22] British party politics has become less partisan, – less tribal, as one study puts it.[23] It isn't so much that voters have stopped identifying with parties – the vast majority still do. But the key point is that the strength of these attachments has fallen. Back in the 1960s, over 40 per cent of voters were 'very strong' party identifiers – largely for either the Labour or Conservative party. Today, the pool of these hard-core partisans has fallen to around 10–15 per cent. Moreover, while over 80 per cent of voters identify with a party, only around two-thirds identify with one or other of the two main parties.

One of the important consequences of social and partisan de-alignment is a more volatile and contingent political scene. As voters have become less attached to a particular party, they have become more likely to defect; and once they defect, they are likely to keep switching parties. Back in the 1960s, the percentage of voters who switched parties was in the range of 10–20 per cent. After the 1970s, the range increases to 16–25 per cent. In the 2005 election, nearly a quarter of voters changed parties. Significantly, switching between the main parties and the minor parties is more common than between Labour and the Conservatives.[24] This volatility in voting patterns is, then, taking in a broader range of parties. Voters, in other words, have not only turned away from Labour and the Conservatives towards the Liberal Democrats, but also to parties including the Scottish National Party, Plaid Cymru, the Greens, UKIP and the BNP.

This, in turn, has consequences for the organization and political strategies of parties, as we examine in more detail in the next chapter. Where once the campaigns of parties were built around large core votes, those parts of the electorate that strongly identified with the party, parties have increasingly looked beyond these core voting blocks to those whose partisan attachment was weaker or non-existent. The electoral imperative to attract more voters in this less class-based context is at the heart of the shift away from mass, to what is called catch-all, politics.

## What has caused de-alignment?

If these are the indicators and the consequences of de-alignment, what has driven the weakening relationship between class and party in British party politics? To begin with, politics has changed because society has changed. Shifting patterns of work, away from unionized blue-collar manual employment – in particular, in heavy industry – to less unionized white-collar non-manual employment in the public and private sectors, have eroded and fragmented long-established working-class communities and identities. Furthermore, there has been a significant increase in the number of people, including the large number of women entering the workplace, who don't fit the manual/non-manual model of class classification. Since the 1950s, sociologists also traced the rise of the 'affluent worker' with their own home and car, taking foreign holidays, having more leisure time and generally living a more middle-class lifestyle. Social mobility in the 1960s and 1970s also played a part. A better-educated and more socially mobile population – in particular, through a growth in numbers going to university – has weakened the influence of class on politics. This 'modernization' of individuals and society is seen to have broken up traditional social relations (including class ones) and created a society characterized by greater 'individualization': meaning individuals actively shape their own lives, including making political choices, often on the basis of more immediate and personal concerns.

Another perspective pointed to how greater affluence brought about a culture of post-materialism. With their material needs having been met, more and more people look to political issues (such as the environment) that reflect particular values regarding what a good society should look like, values that were generally ignored by a left/right politics dominated by the ('materialist') question of the production and distribution of wealth.[25] This has contributed to a shift away from class politics to a politics revolving around identity and single issues such as the environment, the rights of women and minority groups, animal welfare and Europe. Other perspectives have focused on the political divides that have opened up, in particular between those working in the public and private sectors; and between those reliant on the consumption of public goods (e.g. social housing) and those with greater private sector consumption (e.g. private home ownership).

Taken together, these social trends have in different ways weakened the link between class and party and led, in certain cases, to a re-alignment of politics. Class is still one important factor in shaping politics, but it is, more and more, one of a number of such social influences.

Some political analysis points to an even more fundamental de-alignment of voting behaviour as the electorate break free of what Paul Webb calls their 'social moorings'.[26] From this perspective, party identification has declined and, in its place, voters have become much more active consumers of politics, making choices about which party to support. Elections are fought more or less on the basis of what voters think about political parties in relation to the issues they consider important. Voters have particular preferences, they understand where political parties stand on these preferences, and they vote accordingly – though it may be that institutional factors such as the voting system prevent voters from adequately expressing these preferences.

This rational choice approach to understanding the party scene challenges the social psychological approach taken by the Butler and Stokes model of party identification that focused on the social influences on individual and group behaviour. Voters make informed and rational decisions about the issues of the day and consider how parties best meet their preferences, just as they might do when buying a washing machine or an insurance policy. In this valence politics, the electorate vote on the issues facing them, not on the basis of whom their parents voted for. Party politics is more conditional, based on position and performance; and loyalty has to be earned, not inherited. Parties, in this potentially more volatile situation, have to get themselves into an electable state where voters not only agree with their policy priorities but also think the party leadership is competent enough to deliver them.

The idea of the informed, rational voter is fraught with as many difficulties as the informed and rational consumer trying to buy consumer durables or financial products – it's not so easy or so straightforward. Voters may have limited knowledge and may not always act in a way that is rational, given what they think or say. The valence model in politics tries to deal with this complexity by assuming that voters' choices at the ballot box are influenced by just three key things: the perceived competency of the party leader; which party best delivers on a voter's top-rated issues; and whether a party is thought to be able to manage economic affairs.

## Conclusion

In terms of thinking about the contemporary party scene, exactly how far the electorate have been freed from their social moorings, or exactly what balance of new social forces is shaping party attachment, can be put to one side. In the end, de-alignment has, political science broadly agrees, weakened the relationship between class and party. There are still, to be sure, plenty of partisans out there in the electorate. You might be one of them. Not everyone is switching parties between elections. And not everyone is voting on the basis of how well the party leaders are running or might run the country. But more voters are. As Dunleavy observes: 'There is a long-term trend, which shows no sign of easing up, for voters to support a wider range of parties more conditionally and more flexibly.'[27] This has broken up the stable pattern of two-party voting established in the post-war period in Britain and has led to a fragmentation of support away from Labour and the Conservatives. The major beneficiary has been the third party in British politics, the Liberal Democrats. But there has also been a significant increase of support for what have traditionally been viewed as minor parties – in particular, the national-ist parties in Scotland and Wales, the Green Party, UKIP and the BNP. The erosion of two-party politics has not only made the political marketplace more competitive, but has also increased the chance of hung parliaments – and parties working together in government. And, as we shall see in the next chapter, the de-alignment of class and politics has also had a signi-ficant impact on the structure, organization and electoral strategies of parties themselves.

## Further reading and research resources

The classic position on party systems comes from Sartori in *Parties and Party Systems*. Useful starting points for the contemporary shape of the UK's party system (or systems) are Dunleavy's 'Facing up to multi-party politics', and Webb's 'The continuing advance of the minor parties'. Webb's *The Modern British Party System* is a must for further study. David Denver provides a clear and informed guide to contemporary voting patterns in *Elections and Voting in Britain*. Generally, the Hansard Society is an important source for analysis of British politics (www.hansardsociety.org.uk/), not least through the journal *Parliamentary Affairs*; as is the body that regulates British politics, the Electoral Commission (www.electoralcommission.org.uk/); and the library of the House of Commons (see www.parliament.uk/business/publications/research/

research-papers/). The European Consortium for Political Research is a very useful source for comparative study (www.ecprnet.eu/). Aside from the general politics journals (including *Political Studies*, *British Journal of Politics and International Relations* and *Politics*, all published by the principal academic body for UK political science, the Political Studies Association), there are specialist journals for the study of political parties – in particular, *Journal of Elections, Public Opinion and Parties* (published in association with the specialist group in the field of party politics, EPOP (www.epop.org.uk/), and previously published as *British Elections and Party Review*) and *Party Politics*. Other important journals include *Political Quarterly*, *Comparative Political Studies* and *Western European Politics*.

# CHAPTER TWO

# Political Parties

## All change

In the last chapter we saw how the relationship between class and party weakened in the final decades of the twentieth century. This 'de-alignment' has seen a growing slice of the electorate become detached from traditional partisan politics, more likely to make individual choices about which party to support. Labour and the Conservatives, closely followed by the Liberal Democrats, remain the key players in national politics. But the class-based two-party system has fragmented. Voters are supporting a wider range of parties. The result is a more pluralist, multi-party politics across the United Kingdom.

The de-alignment of class and politics has significant implications for the structure, organization and electoral strategies of parties themselves. Twentieth-century politics in Britain rested on large blocks of committed voters unwavering in support for 'their' party. But, as this chapter examines, the decline in partisanship that has reduced the number of these political diehards – voters who, come hell or high water, vote for one party or another – has had important consequences for the organization of political parties and how they go about winning votes. In particular, politics has seen a shift in strategies away from nurturing these loyal supporters to attracting the growing number of voters not so loyal to any one party. 'Mass parties' have given way to 'catch-all parties', as we shall see.

To win over these less partisan voters, political parties have turned to professionals to help them on the campaign trail. The traditional foot soldiers of politics, local party members, have, to a degree, been sidelined, just as their numbers have declined. This professionalization of politics has handed party leaders greater powers. It has also made the business of winning elections more expensive than ever before – and all parties have had to look for new sources of funding to supplement their incomes. But is there a democratic price to be paid for the 'win at any cost' approach parties now take to elections? As the local voluntary side to politics is replaced by a far more professionalized and centralized approach, will parties still be able to play an effective role in stimulating interest and participation in the political life of the country? These are themes not just for this chapter but also for the rest of the book.

## The origins of modern British political parties

Eighteenth- and early nineteenth-century Britain was divided between the two opposing camps of post-civil war politics, the Whigs and the Tories (see box 2.1). But neither side was a political party in any modern sense. They were political factions, elite parliamentary groups, with little in the way of formal organization, either at Westminster or in constituencies across Britain. National politics had no grassroots, as we would call it today. There was no base of members active in local parties. Membership was not open to anyone to join. No one was a party member in the modern sense of paying a subscription and having a membership card and being subject to the rules of a national organization. The political factions that did exist at Westminster were characterized by their informal and rather fluid nature. Lines of division were unstable, unpredictable and as much about personal connection and loyalty as shared interest or political ideology. These elite parliamentary groups formed and sustained governments; and, from time to time, engaged in elections of a sort. With tight property rules restricting the electorate to around 300,000 voters in the 1700s (3 per cent of the population), these were not quite the party races that we know today.

Party politics in Britain, as we might recognize it, begins in the second half of the nineteenth century and was driven by two things: first, the extension of the franchise that created a new mass electorate; and second, economic and social change that led to new working-class political organizations.

As the first industrial nation, Britain was in many respects the most modern of European countries. But political change lagged behind. Liberal Whigs led calls for voting reform, as they also did for the abolition of slavery. Reactionary Tories opposed any extension of the franchise, as well as other reforms such as political emancipation for Catholics in Ireland. Parliament held out against political reform until 1832 when the Great Reform Act was passed. This extended voting in a limited way to about one in seven male property owners. It also dealt with some of the more notorious aspects of electoral practice – in particular, the 'pocket boroughs', where local bigwigs had voters in their pockets; and the 'rotten boroughs', where the local population had fallen to such an extent that the number of voters could be counted on the fingers of two hands. The Reform Act also marked a shift in politics that would be the making of the modern Conservative Party (see box 2.2).

The 1832 Reform Act was just a start. The Chartists and other political radicals campaigned for far more significant reforms of the British political system, including universal male suffrage. The People's Charter was signed in 1838, but the movement faded after 1848. By the 1860s, the new Liberal Party, bringing together Whigs, radicals and liberal conservatives, was in government and making proposals for extending the franchise further, in particular to the growing urban areas of Britain with little or no representation in parliament. The new rising star of the Liberal Party, William

## Box 2.1 Whigs and Tories

The origins of the Conservative and Liberal parties can be traced to older political factions that emerged during the seventeenth century in the aftermath of the English civil war between the king, Charles I, and parliament. After a decade of parliamentary government, the restoration of the monarchy under Charles II in 1660 led to increasing tension between supporters of the Stuart monarchy, the Tories, and parliament, the Whigs. Predisposed to believing that kings had the God-given right to be, well, kings, the Tories were the 'court party'. Whigs, by contrast, tended to think that monarchs were 'appointed' to serve their people (they were the 'country party'); and if they didn't do it well, the people had the right to change their head of state.

These divisions were never as clear-cut as they might appear at first glance to the contemporary eye, not least because many on both sides were getting cold feet over the royal succession of James II. Indeed, James's reign threatened not just the return of unchecked executive power, but also the supremacy of the Church of England, as James was a Catholic convert. British politics got behind the 'Glorious Revolution' that saw William and Mary become co-monarchs as James fled to France. But while this revolution may have established a 'constitutional monarchy' – i.e. the crown ruled through parliament – William, who reigned alone following the death of Mary in 1694, emerged with his powers enhanced by the choices he could make as king, among what were now groups of politicians competing in parliament for power, as to who should serve in government. Differences between Whig and Tory, country and court, blurred. What mattered, as the historian Derek Jarrett once wrote, was who was in – and who was out.

The Tories got off to a bad start in the eighteenth century. The party was split between those happy to be part of government (the court Tories) and those who weren't (the country Tories). There were also a hard core of Tory Jacobites, supporters of James II and the claims of his descendants (the Old Pretender and his son Charles, the Young Pretender) to the royal throne. Unable to shake off their Stuart sympathies, and split by personal rivalries, the Tories backed the wrong horse in the succession to the throne on the death in 1714 of the last Stuart monarch Queen Anne. With the crown passing to a distant German cousin, the Elector of Hanover and future George I – a man of sound Protestant upbringing, but no English to speak of – the Whigs, who had led the 'Protestant succession', were in the political driving seat. There followed what became known as the 'Whig supremacy'.

But all political tides turn and this one eventually did. The Tory revival came in the 1780s under the leadership of William Pitt the Younger: he first became prime minister at 24 in 1784. Pitt dominated late eighteenth-century politics – and while, confusingly for the modern student of politics, he did not regard himself as a Tory, Pitt's governments were conservative ones. Pitt supported economic, social and political reform, but only within the framework of the established constitution. In a period of growing revolutionary instability across Europe, Pitt had no qualms about doing what he thought was necessary in the national interest (including the suspension of habeas corpus in 1794). Whatever he thought of his own politics, modern conservatives claim Pitt as one of their own.

Derek Jarrett, *Britain 1688–1815* (Harlow: Longman, 1965).

## Box 2.2 Robert Peel, the Great Reform Act and the making of the Conservative Party

The 1832 Reform Act was the making of the Conservative Party under the new leadership of the 'liberal conservative' Robert Peel, a former home secretary and leading legal reformer. Once it was on the statute book, Peel drew a line under the reforms he and his party had resisted so fiercely – and made this position clear in his Tamworth Manifesto (he was MP for Tamworth), endorsed by his fellow Tories. Conservatives (and this is really the first time that the word 'Conservative' is used as a political label for the Tories), Peel argued, had to move on and offer strong and united leadership to the country in a time of growing economic, social and political instability. Reform was possible, but should be moderate and suit prevailing circumstances. The Tories in this period also got organized. In 1832, the Carlton Club was established as the headquarters of the Conservative Party. Out in the country, local Conservatives were also setting up their own political associations to register voters and campaign for Tory candidates. But Peel, in government after 1841, took the Tories in a direction that many Conservatives were uncomfortable with. By 1846, the Conservative Party was divided over economic reform, about how far market forces should be allowed to regulate society. The repeal of the Corn Laws that restricted imports of food into Britain split the party, leading many 'Peelites', in particular, William Gladstone, to switch to the newly forming Liberal Party. Today, the Conservative / Liberal Democrat coalition formed after the 2010 general election has brought back memories of Peel's 'liberal conservative' politics.

For more on the history of the Conservative Party,
see Robert Blake's *The Conservative Party from Peel to Major*
([1970] London: Faber & Faber, 2010 – the final edition of Blake's text).

Gladstone, a former Tory and protégé of Robert Peel, supported reform. In 1866, Gladstone became leader of his party. Previous Liberal attempts to extend the franchise had been defeated. But it was with the Conservatives briefly back in office, and with their own rising star in the House of Commons, Benjamin Disraeli, that a new reform bill was passed with cross-party support from Gladstone's Liberals.

The 1867 Reform Act gave the vote to 1.5 million house-holding and largely working-class men living in urban Britain. The Reform Act also redistributed parliamentary seats to the country's growth towns and cities, notably Liverpool, Manchester and Birmingham. As British society was being reshaped by industry and commerce, the movement for political reform became unstoppable. Despite opposition from Conservatives, Gladstone's Liberals extended the right to vote in 1884 to men living in rural areas. These extensions of the franchise transformed the British electorate. Working-class men had for the first time real power at the ballot box. Women, however, did not first win the vote until 1918.

These reforms turned elections into serious contests. Politicians had to start working for their votes, campaigning in ways far more familiar to us today. They took to the streets, knocked on doors, talked to voters, many of whom were not their natural supporters or even known to the candidate. This meant getting organized, certainly beyond the corridors of power at Westminster. The Conservatives had already set up the Carlton Club in 1832 as a party HQ. The radical Whigs in support of the 1832 Reform Act established their own London base, the Reform Club, becoming the centre of Liberal politics nationally. By the 1860s, Liberals were also setting up registration associations to organize support for Liberal candidates in elections. In the 1870s, the association in Birmingham led by Joseph Chamberlain was a fearsome political machine – and in 1877, the newly established National Liberal Federation held its first conference in the city. On the Conservatives' side, with the further extension of the franchise in 1867, the National Union of Conservative and Constitutional Associations was formed to act as an umbrella organization for local Conservative bodies that selected candidates for election, recruited members and ran election campaigns. The National Union would also in future organize Tory party conferences. Disraeli, as party leader, set up Conservative Central Office in 1870 – an office directly accountable to the leadership.

## From cadre to mass party

Constitutional reform in the second half of the nineteenth century prompted the development of more modern political parties with national and local organizations to recruit members, select candidates, fundraise and fight elections, and generally support the party's cause. The Liberal and Conservative parties remained elite 'cadre' parties in the sense that the focus of their activities, as well as the centres of power, remained with the leadership at Westminster. Internal party democracy was very limited. But in order to adapt to the new democratic order, these parties took on more formal constitutions and sought to establish organizations capable of mobilizing much larger numbers of voters at election time. What also changed the business of politics in this period was the emergence of 'mass' parties. These had their roots beyond the cloistered parliamentary world in the trade unions and other groups that had sprung up to express the interests of workers in civil society.

This distinction between 'cadre' and 'mass' parties is at the centre of the work of one of the pioneers of the study of political parties, Maurice Duverger.[1] Duverger characterized the cadre party as one revolving around members of parliament ('cadre', in this sense, means a group of political activists). Membership of these parties was restricted to MPs and other leading members of society, who Duverger dubbed 'notables'. These rich backers provided the finance and social connections to win elections in the era before mass democracy. According to Duverger, political reform after 1850 put pressure on these traditional cadre parties to modernize – in particular, to admit a wider membership to support electioneering. In the twentieth century, the Conservative Party proved very successful at attracting members into local associations, not least by the offer of social benefits through clubs and events. While local Conservative constituency associations enjoyed a good deal of autonomy from the national party, the leadership of the party, in theory at least, enjoyed wide-ranging powers over the party and its policies. The major constraint on these powers came from the cabinet or shadow cabinet and backbench MPs (through the 1922 Committee). (Chapter 3 examines how members now have greater powers over the selection of the Tory party leader, and how the selection of candidates has put the national party at loggerheads with local associations.)

According to Duverger, it is on the left of the political spectrum that fundamental change takes place as new mass parties emerge. These are organizationally different to traditional cadre parties. In particular, the mass socialist parties involved citizens in politics at a grassroots level through local branches of centralized national parties. If the elite cadre parties of the nineteenth century relied on the quality of their members to provide the connections and resources to win power, the mass party relied on the quantity of these members, as Richard Katz and Peter Mair put it.[2] These new parties required large numbers of people to supply both the financial and the human resources to engage in politics. Certainly, membership of European socialist parties grew significantly in the first part of the twentieth century. In Germany, party membership of the Social Democrats hovered around a million in the 1920s before Hitler took power and banned the party in 1933. Trade union membership in Britain took total Labour Party numbers to well over 3 million after the First World War, before falling to around 2.5 million during the depression years of the 1930s. Just before the outbreak of war in 1939, individual membership of the Labour Party was around 400,000. In Austria, France, Switzerland, Scandinavia and the Low Countries, growing membership of mass socialist parties was a significant feature of the political scene in the first half of the twentieth century.[3]

As we shall see shortly, there are significant problems with counting the membership of political parties. But, as Duverger pointed out, what made the new mass parties different was not so much the number of members, but what they did with them and what they got from them. Membership of these new parties was a rite of passage: a formal process of enrolment into local branches. The signing of a membership form resembled a sort of legal and psychological undertaking to the party to abide by its rules and its ideological commitments.[4] (Until Tony Blair changed Labour's constitution, the socialist commitment to public ownership was printed on every party membership card.) Membership was an integral part of people's social identity. The mass fascist parties in Germany and Italy in the 1930s and 1940s took this to the extreme with elaborate and rather sinister initiation ceremonies.

In the model of the mass party (and remember, we are looking at a model that might help us understand general trends in the development of political parties), local branches were the focal point for the activities of members in

## Box 2.3 Tension in the Labour Party's constitution

Political leadership in the Labour Party has long been a thorny issue. Unlike other social democratic parties in Europe, Labour was a party – as the historian Eric Shaw puts it – of '*interest* rather than ideas'. It was not a party driven by a Marxist-inspired ideology that pointed to revolutionary change in society. Rather, the Labour Party was formed by trade unions to increase their influence in politics. One clear sign of this is the position of unions within the decision-making processes of the Labour Party. The party's 1918 constitution, best remembered for Clause IV that committed Labour to the public ownership of property, embedded the power of the trade unions inside the party. As a federal party, individuals could join as members through constituency parties (CLPs); and, in theory at least, the Labour Party Conference was the supreme authority within the party. But the decisive influence within the party – at the annual conference and on the National Executive Committee (NEC) elected by the conference to run the party – was the unions, with their power deployed as blocks of delegate votes. The effect of this constitution was to marginalize individual party members, viewed by many in the leadership of the party as unreliable and a source of political extremism.

The constitutional position of the unions led to tensions as the parliamentary party grew in size. By 1922, Labour with 142 MPs was the official opposition to the Tories; and after the election in December 1923, following a split in the Conservative government, Labour under Ramsay MacDonald had its first brief taste of power as a minority government for nine months. As the number of Labour MPs increased in the late 1920s – in the election held in May 1929, the party emerged as the largest party in the House of Commons with 288 seats – so did the power and influence of the Parliamentary Labour Party (PLP) within the party. With Labour in government again, Prime Minister Ramsay MacDonald and his chancellor Philip Snowden made it quite clear that the British cabinet was accountable to parliament, not the Labour conference. But the position of the PLP was struck a huge blow when, in 1931, as the British economy sank into recession, MacDonald and Snowden agreed, after their budget had been rejected by the Labour cabinet, to form a National Government with the Conservatives and Liberals. In the general election that followed soon after, the MacDonald-led National Government won and the Labour Party was reduced to fifty-two MPs. In the years that followed before the war, the Labour Party, and the trade unions in particular, were eager to assert their political prerogatives over their MPs. The Labour conference made policy – and everyone else, including the PLP, had to abide by it. As we see in chapter 4, the battle between the 'party in the country' and the leadership of the party in parliament returned with a vengeance in the 1970s.

For more on the history of the Labour Party, see Eric Shaw, *The Labour Party since 1945* (Oxford: Blackwell, 1996).

the life of the party. Local parties recruited and enrolled new members and, critically, collected party subscriptions. They also engaged in a range of political activities, including organizing meetings and events, fundraising, selecting candidates for elections and delegates for party conferences, and planning campaign activities at election time such as leafleting, canvassing and ensuring that supporters got out and voted on the day. By taking part in these activities, party members received training in political activism, as well as an ideological education into what the party stood for. In this way, mass parties, by socializing and mobilizing political activists and voters, helped to consolidate the political divides upon which this form of mass politics was based in the first place. Mass parties shaped politics and society as much as politics and society shaped them. Their activities helped to make the already partisan-inclined voter come to think of themselves as aligned with one class or another.

Party members also, in theory, held the leadership of the party nationally and in parliament accountable for their actions. They had a big say in what kind of politics and policies the party adopted. Mass parties were not just about large numbers of people joining parties. Membership was also about becoming active in what the party said and did. The mass party was based on a model of democracy in which its leaders in parliament were held accountable to members; the leaders were delegates to be instructed by an active membership, not left to make independent decisions as representatives. And in this model of democracy, the policy programme of the party involved the mass participation of party members – in particular, through the national conference. As we see in box 2.3, as the number of Labour MPs increased in the inter-war period, the relationship between the party in parliament (and in power) and the party in the country was increasingly strained.

## The mass party – and the iron law of oligarchy

The idea of the mass party as a model of democracy has long been disputed. An early and influential critic was the German sociologist Robert Michels.[5] He argued that the mass party was run by its leaders, not its members. This was because, like other large organizations, political parties were subject to the same forces that generate bureaucratic hierarchy. Michels called this the 'iron law of oligarchy' (rule by the elite). In any complex situation, the imperative to create structure and organization to get things done meant power and authority in political parties shifted decisively to the leadership – the oligarchy. According to Michels, the mass membership was largely passive in this respect. And members had little option but to cede control of the party to the leadership if they were serious about winning power. Once parties had grown in size, leadership became something that required knowledge and expertise, something Michels believed the mass of members didn't possess. This served to widen the distance between leaders and the led. Indeed, the leadership came to enjoy the perks and privileges of leadership and sought to retain them. Threats to their position from more active members were ruthlessly put down. Moreover, according to Michels, the leadership of the mass party came to have interests over and above those of the membership of the party, interests that had more in common with other political elites in other political parties. This cast doubt on the idea that mass parties served to further the interests of their members or the political ideology they espoused.

Such a view was adopted by one leading analyst of post-war British politics: Robert McKenzie. In his 1955 study, *British Political Parties*, McKenzie argued that the Labour Party, in particular, far from being a party organized to further the interests of its working-class members or the political ideology of socialism, was dominated by a small group of leaders whose central motivation was their own power and position. Despite the formal differences between the Labour and Conservative parties in terms of leadership, the practice of politics was not very different. As with many things, it is easy to overegg the pudding: the idea that party members have no influence on their party leaderships can only be taken so far. Not only are members a valuable resource for parties – even today with dwindling numbers – but their views can constrain the actions of leaders. As we shall see in the following chapters, Labour struggled in the 1970s and 1980s with the power of its party activists, and Conservative members became more assertive following the party's disastrous defeat in 1997.

## The decline of mass party membership

In the second half of the twentieth century, membership of the main political parties in Britain fell. Before we examine this decline, a note of caution on the numbers is needed. Membership of political parties is notoriously difficult to measure. Part of the problem is that membership is self-reported – still the case today when British political parties are legally obliged by the Electoral Commission to submit figures. This can lead to all kinds of inaccuracies and omissions in data. The Conservative Party did not in the past keep central membership records. Local Labour parties before the 1980s were under pressure to exaggerate individual membership in order to reach a high threshold to ensure affiliation to the national party. Membership of the Labour Party also combines individual membership of local parties with membership of affiliated trade unions. Until the party stopped publishing these figures, only 10–15 per cent of Labour members were individuals, reaching a peak in 1952 when just over a million people (16.6 per cent of the total population) were on the rolls of the party. As we shall see in chapter 4, Labour has been anxious to maintain its formal link with trade unions not simply for the money it raises (£8 million in 2008, compared with £3.9 million in membership fees), but because the affiliated members bring a working-class dimension to what is otherwise a middle-class party.[6]

With these caveats in mind, membership of British political parties is generally thought to have peaked in the 1950s. The Conservatives claimed around 3 million members; the Labour Party 1 million. This is the period

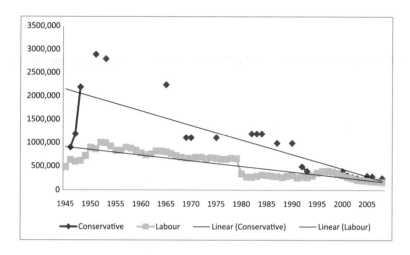

*Source: figures from table 1, Marshall,* Membership of UK Political Parties, *pp. 8–9 (data not continuous for Conservative Party).*

**Figure 2.1** *Individual membership of Conservative and Labour parties, 1945–2008*

when membership of a political party was still the dominant form of political participation beyond the ballot box, even if the 1950s may represent some highpoint in party political membership that is out of step with what went before and after. By the late 1960s, membership of the Labour and Conservative parties made up something like 5 per cent of the total electorate of around 40 million.

Membership of the Labour and Conservatives parties declined from this peak in the 1950s (see figure 2.1), just as it did in most developed countries. The decline in party membership in Britain was gentle, but sustained. In the 1980s, membership of the Labour Party dipped more sharply as the figures came to reflect more accurately how many people were on party lists. From time to time, membership of particular parties increased, for example when Tony Blair became leader of the Labour Party or in the early years of the Liberal Democrats under Paddy Ashdown. This suggests that political parties have some control over how many members they have. None the less, there is little getting away from the long-term downward trend in membership of the main political parties. Today, the Conservative Party has around a quarter of a million members, Labour around 166,000 and the Liberal Democrats 60,000. By comparison with the early 1980s, when membership of the main parties made up just under 4 per cent of the electorate, today it is under 1.5 per cent – very much at the low end of the European scale of rates of party membership. As the membership of political parties has fallen, so has the activism of those who remain.

What factors account for the decline in membership of political parties? There are two broad explanations. The first focuses on the supply of party members. The decline in party membership is in part bound up with the general decline in partisanship that we saw in the last chapter eroding the link between class and party at the ballot box. As society changed, people stopped joining political parties in such numbers, not least because the cost in terms of time and effort was becoming too high with changing lifestyles and the decline in people's attachment to parties. Potential party members could also obtain some of the benefits of joining a party from elsewhere (e.g. somewhere to drink (Labour), a husband or wife (the Conservatives)). The number of potential party recruits was also cut by structural shifts in society that saw a decline in traditional working-class jobs and communities, falling trade union membership, a blurring of employment-based class identities, and an increase in the number of women going to work (a trend that hit the Conservative Party hard). These social trends that weakened the link between party and class at the ballot box and on party rolls also drew people interested in politics to the growing number of single-issue pressure groups and new social movement organizations that sprang up around environmentalism, nuclear disarmament and identity politics more generally. With their narrower political offer, these groups are often seen as being better placed than political parties to attract the post-materialist but time-poor citizen interested in politics and seeking to influence government at a time when parties were seen not to be delivering in power. As chapter 9 explores, this growth in non-party political participation has provoked a fierce debate about the future of political parties and political activism.

The second set of explanations focuses on the demand for members by parties – and the incentives offered to individuals to join parties. As we have seen so far in this chapter, the cadre parties in the late nineteenth century needed members to get voters to the ballot box. The mass political party also depended on the membership for financial and human resources: parties on the left had no rich 'notables' to provide the money and connections to win power – save, that is, for the trade unions and their members. As we shall see shortly, the development of mass communications media brought about a shift in the demand for members as parties looked to radio and television to reach the electorate at large. These new forms of political campaigning increasingly relied on paid specialists, professional 'political consultants' practised in the dark arts of political spin, not members acting as volunteers to get the party's message across to voters. Having large numbers of members is also a cost (in terms of recruiting and maintaining local parties) with, potentially, lower benefits in terms of votes cast compared with other forms of political campaigning. Parties have also, as we see later, come to rely more and more on large donations to fund party activities. As a result, they have done little to put in place the kinds of incentives that might make membership of a political party an attractive proposition to politically minded citizens, however much parties might still think having members is important. Indeed, one factor that explains the success of single-issue pressure groups in attracting members is that they are easy to join and very little is expected in the way of activism. In recent years, parties have made it easier to join. For example, the Conservative Party has introduced a new category of 'supporter' to attract less committed citizens; and the Labour Party has allowed newer members to vote in leadership elections, thereby increasing the incentives to join. Nevertheless, membership of political parties is still generally viewed as something that requires time and effort – both in short supply among voters.

There are two points on party membership worth making. The first is that political parties have not given up on having members – for good reasons. Members continue to be a valuable resource for parties in terms of both financial resources and political activism. While political campaigning, as we shall see, has become centrally directed, local activism remains important to win elections in marginal seats across the country. The membership of parties also provides the stream of activists, workers and candidates that are needed to engage in electoral politics and representative government. And a party with no members does not have the same legitimacy with the wider voting public as one that does. The second point is that, if the number of Conservative, Labour and Liberal Democratic members is in long-term decline, since the 1990s there has been an increase in membership of smaller political parties. In the UK's more multi-party politics, these minor parties are attracting not just votes at the ballot box but also members on party rolls, as we shall see later in the book.

### The catch-all party

The post-war period is seen as a time when the organization and electoral strategies of political parties start to change; and the general decline in the membership of political parties is seen as an indicator of such change. Writing in the 1960s, the German political scientist Otto Kirchheimer suggested that political parties, as a consequence of the weakening link between class and party, turned their attentions away from their traditional sources of support in the electorate to a broader group of voters. Rather than Labour, for example, focusing on working-class voters already inclined towards the party, and turning these voters into committed supporters and members, it looked to gather votes from wider sections of society, including the middle classes. This 'catch-all' strategy was generally more pragmatic, less ideological and more focused on electoral considerations than the strategies that underpinned mass politics. In electoral terms, catch-all meant parties trying to win support, potentially, from all corners of the electorate, not relying on one large slice of society for votes. To be sure, from the start of mass democracy in the late nineteenth century, parties had to appeal beyond their narrow class base. In

Britain, the Conservative Party was particularly successful in this respect. But still mass politics was founded on a bedrock of committed partisan voters and activists. Once this core of support started to wear away, it is argued, parties had not only to broaden their political appeal, but also to find new ways to mobilize voters. The ideologically inflected appeals to class identity characteristic of mass politics wouldn't wash beyond the hard core of traditional voters.

As a result, catch-all parties have to temper the appeal to class interests. To catch all voters successfully, parties have to address and to connect with a broader range of interests and perspectives across society and to distance themselves from the partisan interest groups that had formed the base of the party's support. Coalitions of voters have to be built and re-built; and the connections with these voters are shallower and more contingent. As a result, catch-all politics inevitably placed limits on the ideological divide between the two main parties in British politics, contributing to the sense of an 'end to ideology' in the post-war period. Votes had to be won among parts of the electorate who could, potentially, swing both or even all ways. Little would be gained by pulling away to the ideological edges. This would put off too many other voters. Indeed, when Labour did in the 1970s and early 1980s, it found itself at odds with the general views of the electorate, as we see in chapter 4. So, as voters became less partisan, so did (or, at least in electoral terms, should) parties. And as parties dropped their class appeals, so this consolidated the decline in voter partisanship. Instead, parties turned to presenting the competency of their leadership team and the capacity of that team to deliver what voters wanted. The idea of a programme of policies shaped by the interests and ideology of a social class was redundant in this new catch-all era of politics. This led to concerns that the social roots of political parties were being cut as parties became more professionalized campaign machines with power shifting decisively to the leadership. The catch-all party didn't need members – or, as we shall see shortly, at least not in the same way.

## Electoral campaigning and political communication

The shift from mass to catch-all politics can be seen in how political parties campaign in elections. If catch-all politics was about parties presenting a less partisan message, it was also about finding new ways to deliver that message. Election campaigning was set to become much more organized and more professional in ways that would have important implications for the distribution of power in political parties. Three stages in political campaigning have been identified that we can map onto the changing shape of political parties – and these stages are seen as an 'evolutionary process of modernization'.[7]

A first 'pre-modern' stage in election campaigning dominated the world of politics before television. During this era of mass politics, running up to the

1950s, party campaigns weren't planned a long time in advance and were not hugely costly. The role of the national party was limited. Party leaders might go on tours of the country, but much of the organization of these campaigns was left to local parties. The localism of political campaigning relied heavily on the unpaid activism of the large numbers of party members communicating directly with voters. The politicians running campaigns listened to what was heard on the door step. Canvassing and public meetings and the traditional print media aimed to reinforce established partisan views and to motivate supporters to get out and vote. There was little serious attempt to change minds. The strategy was aimed more at reassuring those whose hearts were already in it. This approach was, essentially, defensive.

The combination of declining partisanship and the spread of radio and television across society led to a second 'modern' stage in election campaigning, starting in the early 1960s. If the mass party walked the streets, catch-all parties were more likely to be found in broadcast studios. In the early 1950s, there were around a million households in Britain with a television set – a radio was already a standard fixture in homes around the country. By the late 1960s, there were over 15 million TVs. Political parties continued to use the traditional print media to reach voters, in particular newspapers, leaflets and advertising hoardings. But political campaigning also took to the airwaves. At the same time, and in part as a consequence of the broadcast media, the organization of election campaigns by parties was increasingly done nationally and well in advance. Mounting election campaigns also started to get more expensive. A year or more before a big poll, internal groups of leading party politicians and officials, assisted by outsiders with specialist knowledge of media, advertising, marketing and public relations, worked on campaigns. Where once party members were integral to political communications, now these professional 'communicators' took greater control of getting the political message from the party to the electorate. This form of campaigning was driven from the centre, not left to local parties. While the politicians leading the campaign would still listen to voters on the campaign trail, parties increasingly looked to their hired professional consultants to gather the views of the public, using opinion polling.

This modern stage in political campaigning and communication was aimed not just at the partisans, but at all voters. The daily press conferences and stage-managed events were put on to change voters' minds: to convince the less socially attached voter that the party understood what issues really mattered to the man and woman on the street; and that the leader was up to the job of being prime minister. The party's policies and its team of leaders had to be sold to the electorate. Parties had to go on the offensive. Local party activists, and less active party members, were as a result increasingly sidelined. National elections needed national campaigns run through the national media. The established authorities in political science in the 1960s and 1970s agreed. When politics swung from one party to another, this swing was uniform across the country. Since there was little local variation in election results, constituency campaigning was not worth the effort. What could be done was to identify core partisan supporters and get them out to the polling station. Otherwise, stick to the national picture. This would deliver votes all over the country.

By the 1990s, all this was set to change as a revisionist literature in political science offered a more nuanced geography of British politics. In recent decades, the swing in support between parties has become far less uniform across the country (this was clearly in evidence in the 2010 general election). This led to the view that intensive local campaigning relative to other parties could make a difference to the result in particular constituencies. Evidence from the 1992, 1997 and 2001 elections suggested that the 'effects of campaigning are not large, but they are clear and significant'.[8] As we shall see in chapter 5, parties such as the Liberal Democrats increasingly took a 'where we work we win' approach to campaigning that recognized that a more targeted approach, focusing resources on building local political reputation and campaign capacity, paid dividends come general election day. Labour was also ahead of the game on this, using the national machine to plan and coordinate local campaigns, to target resources on winnable seats, to use modern communication technology to target small groups of voters and to plan all of this well in advance. Under Lord Ashcroft's direction and funding, the Conservative Party in the 2000s also sought to target resources on winnable marginal seats.

This shift back towards more local and interactive strategies is seen to be a feature of the third stage in campaign communication, the 'post-modern' stage starting in the 1990s. On the one hand, the drivers of this third stage, the innovations in information and communication technologies (in particular, satellite and cable TV, the internet, digital radio and TV), have increased the dependency on professionals organized centrally to run what have in effect become permanent campaigns (and the costs of these campaigns have continued to rocket). On the other, the delivery of these nationally coordinated campaigns has been decentralized to grassroots activists and organizations. Political parties have to be marketed to the electorate, but this electorate is split into a more complex mosaic of people and places. The new communication technologies have enabled parties to develop more targeted campaigns aimed at particular slices of the electorate, not least because new digital technology has led to the fragmentation of the media. In the era of catch-all politics, campaign communication has turned into niche marketing. In this increasingly fluid and less partisan broadcast, cable and internet world, political parties compete madly for all the exposure they can grab. In an attempt, if not to control the medium, then to make sure their message gets heard, parties are driven further to professionalize their campaign party machines. This is not something that can be left to well-meaning volunteers, even if they are needed to deliver campaigns on the ground.

## Box 2.4 The Obama effect? Political campaigning and the 2010 general election

Is electoral campaigning in Europe moving inexorably towards the candidate-centred American model? Or will campaigning vary from place to place, shaped by local factors such as electoral and party systems and different rules on politics and the media that place limits on 'Americanization'? Certainly US politics is seen to be in advance of Europe in the use of digital technology and social networking internet sites. The presidential campaign by Barack Obama is seen to have blazed a trail for all political communications. Obama's 2008 campaign witnessed a step change in the use of the internet and social networking to fundraise, to organize local groups and events, to respond to the attacks of his opponents and generally to mobilize voters, especially younger people and others with poor voting records. The Obama campaign was much admired, but did British politics follow suit?

Certainly there were Obama-like features to the 2010 campaigns of the political parties. All of them were armed with web and email, text, Twitter and Facebook, online advertising, YouTube and campaign software to collate local information in national databases, manipulate web searches and invite public contributions to party activities ('crowdsourcing'). The parties also found the dangers of such campaigning as wonderful cyber spoofs hit the web and chats on mumsnet got out of control, to name just two. But what many thought would be a campaign won and lost on the post-modern battlefield of social networking sites turned out to be fought in the good old-fashioned television studio – and the even more old-fashioned street corner. Indeed, the two were horribly combined for Gordon Brown in 'bigotgate' following his meeting with Rochdale pensioner Gillian Duffy. Brown's private thoughts on the meeting were recorded on his lapel microphone as his car left the town, only to have them replayed to him on live radio and television, his head firmly in his hands. And while there were tweets and texts galore, the big events of the 2010 campaign were the 'prime ministerial' debates on television. The fact that Britain lagged behind the rest of the democratic world on this would always mean these live debates would take centre stage. That the first of these debates also propelled Nick Clegg and the Liberal Democrats into the political spotlight ensured their place in the 2010 campaign. There were similar TV debates as well between party leaders in Scotland, Wales and Northern Ireland, reflecting the demands of party competition under multi-level governance (see chapter 8). But while 2010 wasn't quite the internet election many thought it might be, post-modern technologies have become part of the normal business of political campaigning in Britain – and their influence will only increase in the future.

*Further reading*: Norris, *A Virtuous Circle*; R. Gibson, P. Nixon and S. Ward, *Political Parties and the Internet: Net Gain?* (London: Routledge, 2003)

## Political marking – or why political parties listen

Today, political campaigning by parties has come to rely more than ever on gathering information on what the electorate thinks and how it might vote. If the opinion poll came into its own in the age of television, the focus group, in which groups of voters sit in small groups and talk about what they think, has became the political tool of the contemporary campaign. Over time, political campaigning has become far more responsive to what voters say. This sense that voters know best is at the core of the idea of political marketing. This has shifted attention away from the 'sale' of political products (party leaders and their policies) to the marketing of parties in response to what the electorate want.[9] But are political parties now spending so much time finding out what voters think, so they can tailor their appeal to them, that they have stopped trying to convince them of what the party actually believes in? Do parties in this post-modern communication age adapt their message (and policy positions) to the audience, not try to change the audience to the message and their policies?

Politicians, as is often said, will say anything to get elected: conviction politics that actually believes in something has given way to something altogether more expedient. Parties adapt their programmes to the electorate, rather than trying to shape the views of voters to their programmes. Political science certainly agrees that 'preference-shaping' by political parties has given way to more 'preference-accommodation', even if political parties can't adopt any marketing strategy they want.[10] There is always an element of path dependency that limits how parties change. A party traditionally committed to cutting taxes for higher earners, for example, will find it difficult to turn itself overnight into a party that wants to market itself as being on the side of the poor. None the less, the changing political sociology of modern society forces political parties to find out more about groups of voters who might not otherwise support them. If not, they have little or no chance of getting elected. Certainly for the Labour Party in the late 1980s and early 1990s, 'Labour listens' was part of a process that led to considerable changes to the party's policy programme, as we see in chapter 4. For those committed to a more radical left political agenda, Labour listened to the wrong voters: not those parts of the electorate the party had traditionally represented and who made up the bulk of its trade union membership. Labour modernizers disagreed. The party had to listen to a far wider slice of British society if it was to have any chance of getting elected, in particular those more middle-class voters who often make the difference between winning and losing elections in marginal seats by and large in southern and middle England. For the Conservatives after 1997, it might also be argued that the party listened to the wrong voters – voters already committed to the party – and not enough to those parts of the electorate that had switched to New Labour and the Liberal Democrats in the 1990s and 2000s.

## The electoral professional party

In campaign terms, political parties have become rather good at winning elections in less partisan times. At the same time, they have, it is suggested, become rather cut off from those interest groups in society that gave rise to them in the first place. This growing divide between political parties and their social bases is one important theme in the study of political parties. The pressures of catch-all politics have turned political parties more and more into election machines, staffed by professionals and career-oriented politicos whose main objective is winning power by presenting the party to the electorate in the best possible way. The Italian political sociologist Angelo Panebianco called this rise of the political party driven by electoral considerations and employing directly, and as outside consultants, professionals to support the party leadership in winning power, the 'electoral professional party'.[11]

This professionalization of the party machine, sidelining both members and activists in the party, it is argued, weakens the linkages between parties and their social bases. It also reinforces the power of the leadership over the rest of the party. If knowledge is power, and those with the knowledge of modern political campaigning techniques are employed by the leadership of the party, then the growing reliance on hired guns further concentrates power and authority in political parties. Quite simply, political professionals are taken on by the national party and work for the national leadership in parliament and the national party office. Those pushed to one side are not just the membership of the party, but, perhaps more significantly, the party activists who traditionally have taken many of the key jobs inside the national party organization. The growth in state funding of political parties across Europe has also contributed to the increasing number of paid staff working for central parties (see below on the 'cartel' party).[12]

The battle for votes, then, is increasingly one undertaken by groups of people working for political parties as aspiring politicians, political advisors and political consultants, who are, in many respects, very alike. Politics, like other professions, has become a career, not a voluntary activity. These political professionals are all generally well educated. The knowledge and skills demanded by the job of election campaigning are more or less the same whichever party a professional works for. And the goal for all in the business of politics is the same: to win power. Inevitably this has meant that far less emphasis is placed on the importance of local branch members working in their spare time to advance the party's cause. Or at least, votes can be mobilized in a much more direct way, through political campaigns orchestrated by the national party leadership through the national mass media and, more recently, through social networking, and supported on the ground by local party activists under direction from the national party.

As party politics has become professionalized, so it has become more expensive. Those hired to give advice to the party on running campaigns need to be paid. More and more resources have been poured into increasingly expensive election campaigns. At the same time, traditional sources of funding have been drying up, not just for Labour with its trade union funding, but for parties in general as membership has declined. Political parties have increasingly looked to private sources of funding, from rich donors and business. This has further driven professionalization as political parties establish specialist fundraising units to gather donations. In other parts of the world, political parties increasingly looked to the state to fund their activities. Both routes have their problems, as we shall see shortly.

Catch-all politics, and catch-all parties, then, have come to rely on well-educated career-orientated professionals whose working lives are frequently spent in the networked worlds of the media, marketing, advertising and public relations. Social and demographic differences between parties in this respect have blurred. The shock troops of electoral class war are gone. But has the rise of the political professional meant that social background has become a declining feature of British party politics? Are those working in politics, as is popularly thought, really 'all the same'? Do sociological differences remain between the political parties?

## The sociology of political parties

Looking at the social characteristics of MPs in the post-war period, a number of features stand out. First, using a broad division between manual working-class occupations and middle-class white-collar working backgrounds, the Conservative and Labour parties at Westminster split as we might expect. The vast majority of Tory MPs between 1951 and 2005 were middle-class, with law and business being the most common occupations. By contrast, a greater number of Labour MPs, certainly up until the early 1990s, were working-class, ranging from a fifth to a third between 1951 and 1992. The other great provider of Labour MPs was the teaching profession. The backgrounds of Liberal and Liberal Democrats MPs are by and large middle-class. The educational backgrounds of MPs also show some differences. Between 1951 and 2005, a high proportion of Conservative MPs went to public school (falling from a peak of 81 per cent in 1966 to 60 per cent in 2005) and generally around half of those who attended university went to Oxford or Cambridge. By contrast, far fewer Labour MPs have attended public school (generally between 15 and 20 per cent); and while two-thirds of Labour MPs had attended university by the 1980s, the proportion going to Oxbridge was under 20 per cent.

However, the social divide between the parties is closing. This is largely as a result of the sharp decline in the number of Labour MPs from a working-class background, as measured by their previous occupation. In 1987, 29 per cent of MPs on the Labour side were from working-class occupations. By 2005, this had dropped to 10 per cent. At the same time, the late 1980s and 1990s saw a significant rise in the number of MPs whose previous occupations were as politicians or political organizers. In 2005, across the three main parties, eighty-seven MPs had such a background, third only to teaching and business as the most common occupations. In the Conservative Party, 10 per cent of its MPs were former politicians and political organizers; 17 per cent of Labour MPs; and 11 per cent of Lib Dem MPs. The 2010 intake of MPs reinforced this trend. Across the chamber of the new House of Commons, 20 per cent of MPs had political backgrounds, 15 per cent in business, 12 per cent in consultancy, 12 per cent in law, 10 per cent in financial services, 6 per cent in charities and non-governmental organizations, 5 per cent in education and 5 per cent in the media – all thoroughly middle-class.[13]

As we shall see in the following chapters, the individual members of political parties are also taken broadly from the middle classes. For the Labour Party, it is the institutional link to the trade unions that by and large delivers working-class members. Otherwise, surveys suggest that only around 13 per cent of individual Labour members have manual jobs. This research also shows that party members are, across all parties, older than the general population, more likely to be in retirement, be better educated (especially so for the Liberal Democrats) and be more affluent (Conservative members more so), have stronger partisan attachments and, in the case of the membership of Labour and the Liberal Democrats in particular, be white men.[14] Membership of political parties, not surprisingly, shows all the demographic biases seen in all surveys of political participation.

## Boys' own parties

The social background of MPs in parliament has become a hot issue for political parties as they seek to reach out to voters. Both Labour and the Conservatives, as we shall see in later chapters, have introduced measures in an attempt to make their candidates standing in elections more representative of British society – in particular, regarding women and black and minority ethnic groups. Given the background of most politicians, this is not surprising. MPs at Westminster are overwhelmingly male. The first woman MP to take her seat in the House of Commons was Nancy Astor in 1919. In the postwar period, the number of women in the chamber never exceeded 30. In the 1987 general election, 41 women were elected as MPs, increasing to 60 in 1992 and 120 in 1997 (101 for the Labour Party). In 2005, 128 women were elected, and in 2010 139. MPs at Westminster are also overwhelmingly white. The first black and minority ethnic MP was elected for the Liberals in London in 1892. Since the 1980s, the total number of black and minority ethnic MPs has risen from 4 to 15 in 2005, with the majority sitting on the Labour side. In 2010, 26 MPs were from black and minority ethnic backgrounds, including Westminster's first female Muslim MP.

Feminist political science seeks to explain these inequalities in women's participation in parliament through a wider understanding of how politics is gendered, like all other areas of social life. The number of women MPs immediately raises the question about how candidates for parliament are selected – and the degree to which political parties have become more 'feminized'. The feminization of party politics has two main aspects: first, the number of women becoming involved in politics, in particular in more formal roles involving policy and decision-making; second, political and policy debates increasingly addressing women's concerns and perspectives. A feminist party is one in which there is parity in elected representatives; women have a realistic chance to become party leader; and feminist perspectives are embedded in the party's policies and commitments. The last of these dimensions is significant. A party might be open to women but hostile to feminist arguments.[15]

As we shall see in later chapters, British political parties have to a certain extent become less boys' own parties. The increasing number of women MPs is one indicator of the feminization of British party politics. The Labour Party, as we shall see in chapter 4, has sought to bring more women into politics through changes to party structures and roles, the adoption of an equality agenda for women and the selection of candidates in local constituencies. Feminists in the Labour Party, such as Harriet Harman, have been prominent in this respect. When David Cameron became Conservative party leader in 2005, he too sought to increase the number of female candidates, as we shall see in the next chapter. The Liberal Democrats have also introduced measures to increase the representation of women – for example, alternating men and women on the party list for European elections (so-called 'zipping'). More generally, the feminization of party politics has brought women's concerns and perspectives into policy debates and into the strategies parties pursue to win over female voters. At the very least, political parties are more open to these concerns and perspectives, not least because of their vote-winning potential among women voters. However, there remain concerns that political parties need to go beyond a headcount approach to women's representation ('critical mass'). Political parties, feminist political science argues, need 'critical actors', whether people or institutions, that not only seek to advance women's interests in the political sphere, but also inspire other women to participate in politics.

## Funding political parties

The decline in membership of political parties has hit their in funding. Like any other organization, political parties need money to carry out the work they do. But the question of how to fund this work is a tricky one. On the one hand, political parties are private, voluntary organizations. They are not part of the state. If parties cannot raise enough cash from members and supporters to run election campaigns and all the other things they do, some argue, then they shouldn't be in business. The political marketplace will fund parties. On the other hand, political parties perform a public role. They provide a vehicle for political expression and representation and form governments and oppositions to run the country. It is only reasonable, others argue, that they receive public funding for the work they do for the nation as a whole. Left to the market, political parties might be unable to perform this public role effectively – in particular, those parties that do not have the support of wealthy individuals and corporations.

If parties need funding, then, and democratic government needs parties, how can the funding of parties be assured in a way that supports rather than distorts democratic governance?

There are four main sources of funding for political parties: party members, private individual donors, corporate bodies (largely businesses and trade unions) and taxpayers. The funding mix varies from country to country. In the UK, the amount of financial support from the public purse is very limited. MPs are paid a salary; during election campaigns, political mailing is free; and opposition parties receive a special allowance, known as 'Short' money after the MP who proposed it, to carry out their parliamentary duties. In many other countries, by contrast, the level of funding from the state is far higher. The growth in public funding across Europe and in countries such as Canada and Australia reflects concerns that, with the decline in party membership and the growth of private donations by individuals and corporations, political parties are both less able to act as 'intermediaries' between citizens and the state and more open to the corrupting influence of private finance on public policy-making.[16] Using taxpayers' money to pay for politics is seen as a way of both supporting parties as they play their role in democratic life and helping them to avoid the potential tarnish of private interests buying influence from those in power.

Political parties in Britain, as elsewhere, have come under pressure to diversify their sources of funding, particularly in the face of declining party membership. As the expert on party funding Justin Fisher shows, both the Conservatives and Labour have moved away from their big traditional institutional sources of money.[17] During the 1980s and 1990s, personal donations to the Conservatives increased considerably, as did income from commercial activities such as conferences and financial services. The Labour Party too sought funding from other sources. Historically Labour relied on the trade unions to bankroll its activities, not just with affiliation fees but also in other ways such as the sponsorship of local candidates and MPs and the use of physical and human resources. The economic transformation of Britain in the 1980s led to a decline in trade union membership; and the Conservative government introduced new rules in 1984 regarding political donations by trade unions that required unions to ballot their members before making a donation. Still, as recently as the early 1990s, 90 per cent of Labour's funds came from the unions. But as union sources of funding decreased in the 1990s, Labour looked to more private donations, and events such as high-profile dinners, to fill the funding gap.

The reform of the funding of parties has become an essential part of the debate about how to restore trust in political institutions, as we shall see in the final chapter. But one area is worth exploring at this point in the book: the sustainability of political parties. As Fisher points out, party spending has risen as the costs of doing politics have gone up and political operations have become more professionalized and bureaucratized. Traditional sources of income for political parties, by contrast, have become less secure and the debts of parties have spiralled. The financial stability and sustainability of political parties have become more acute issues as parties go on a more or less permanent campaign footing as the number of elections has risen, while the main sources of funding remain tied to general elections. The evidence, according to Fisher, points to the need for more public funding for parties to play their proper role in democratic politics, because an effective market for political funding does not exist.

The funding of political parties does, then, raise some big questions about the state of democracy in Britain today and the role of political parties. Political parties have been integral to the democratic state since the extension of the franchise in the second half of the nineteenth century. They connect individual citizens to the state. In casting a vote for a party's candidate, the electorate take part in a process that leads to the formation of a representative government. Whatever failing parties might have, the recruitment of politicians at all levels is done by political parties – a fact that makes how and whom they recruit such an important and controversial issue. Because political parties are seen to have a necessary and desirable role in democratic government, so the state has, in many countries, become more and more involved in their funding. But as the state's role in party funding has grown, this has, according to Ingrid van Biezen, 'contributed to a transformation of parties from traditional voluntary private associations towards parties as public utilities'.[18]

The consequences of this may be to weaken, rather than strengthen, democratic governance. As political parties have moved closer to the state, the linkages between parties and the rest of society have weakened and become harder to sustain. This is, of course, a mutually reinforcing process: as party membership declines, for example, so parties look to the state for more support; and as state support increases, so parties see less need for a mass membership. The more political parties become 'public utilities', the less able they are, potentially, to carry out their roles as providing a bridge between the citizen and the state and acting as a mechanism to integrate citizens into the democratic political process. And the more political parties become part of the state – and public funding may reinforce this process – the more distant they become from citizens and the more disconnected voters become from the political process.

## Back to the future?

As we saw earlier in the chapter, the old elite cadre parties in the nineteenth century had little need for grassroots members. Before mass democracy, elections were won by having rich, well-connected friends (Duverger's 'notables') to deliver the votes needed to get into parliament. By contrast, mass parties in the first part of the twentieth century not only were better organized than the cadre party, they also depended on a mass of members to provide the resources to win power. The ratio of members to voters was relatively high. These members were (or at least, some of these members were) active in the party, shaping its policy programme and its campaigning activities. Mass parties were, on the face of it, democratic organizations in which leaders were held to account by the active membership. There was as a result more of a balance of power between the central party, in parliament and the national headquarters, and the party out in the country.[19]

The declining influence of party members over party affairs has been the source of some concern. The shifting balance of power towards the central party is seen to have marginalized the local party and the party membership. Membership of mass parties was seen to be significant beyond its importance at election time. The mass party had deep roots in civil society: it was, in certain respects, one important way large groups of people were given the opportunity to participate in the political life of the country. In this way, mass membership connected the parties in government to citizens in civil society in a direct and accountable way. Parties were part of the political education of the country – and without such an education, political participation would decline. This would weaken the legitimacy and effectiveness of government, giving more space to well-organized lobby groups to promote their own special interests.[20]

The rise of catch-all politics re-wired these connections between political parties and civil society. As Katz and Mair argue, if the mass party was the agent of social interest groups intent on capturing state power, the catch-all party is better seen as a broker between the plural and fragmented interests of contemporary civil society and the state. In taking on this role, the roots of political parties have become shallower and less permanent – to use a gardening metaphor, more like annuals that need planting out every year than the perennial plants that keep growing year-in-year-out with just a bit of green-fingered tending. The catch-all party seeks power on behalf of a temporary coalition of interests and opinions in society. To do this, it needs to broker a political platform that will attract enough votes to win power – rather as in the pluralist model of democracy. Once in power, the party in government must be able to deliver on its promises to those groups of voters that elected it. The danger, of course, is that political parties as brokers may have interests (in seeking power) over and above both the interests of the social groups they seek to represent and the national government.

This shifted the balance of power away from local parties and the membership towards the leadership and the central offices of the party – and increasingly to the party leader and his or her personal office outside of traditional party structures. This leadership, if it was to play this role as political broker, needed to distance itself from particular groups in civil society, even at the expense of cutting the special ties between the party and the social groups that formed the party in the first place. Indeed, in order to free itself from the constraints imposed by the party in the country, the leadership of political parties – in particular the Labour Party, as we shall see in chapter 4 – has sought to empower the inactive members through periodic plebiscites of its decisions, as a means to exert their authority over the party and to do what was necessary, in the way of programme and policy changes, to win power. Membership remains, but is a more an individual choice and may be one of many memberships, rather than a badge of social and group identity. Members become, in Katz and Mair's terms, 'organized cheerleaders' for the party with little real power over what the party says or does. Some have even suggested that political parties have become like franchise businesses, where local parties 'deliver' the product produced by the central leadership (these are known as 'stratarchical parties').[20]

To be sure, the idea that political parties can do without members is an exaggeration. Political parties need members not just to deliver national campaigns locally, but also still to provide financial resources and a wider sense of legitimacy for the party and its leadership. But a tension remains between having active members to play these roles and not allowing them to become so active that they challenge the power and authority of the leadership.[21] The selection of candidates is one area, as we shall see in later chapters, in which this has become an acute problem.

Still, concerns persist that, behind what some view as a façade of mass participation (and mass democracy), political parties in the late twentieth century have became modern versions of the old elite cadre parties of the nineteenth century. Indeed, Katz and Mair suggest the development of political parties has taken a further twist: catch-all parties are, in certain countries such as Austria, Denmark, Germany, Finland, Norway and Sweden, becoming 'cartel' parties. If the mass party was firmly rooted in civil society, a 'delegate' for particular social interest groups, and the catch-all party took up a position as an entrepreneurial broker between civil society and the state, then the cartel party is part of the 'state apparatus'. The decline of party membership forces parties to look not only to rich backers and business to finance political activities, but also to the state. Political parties, in particular where national political cultures are collaborative rather than competitive, seek to use the offices of the state to gain resources and access to the media – even those that are not officially in government. Political parties collude to secure these resources and this privileged access and politics become ever more 'self-referential'. Politics becomes a profession, and what competition there is between parties is, more or less, about who can manage government most efficiently. The purposive goals of previous political eras, largely involving varying degrees of social reform, are lost.

The Katz and Mair thesis does not, as they acknowledge, fit British politics very well. The adversarial institutions and culture of British politics limits inter-party collaboration and the state provides very little in the way of financial support. The result of the 2010 general election will not change this overnight. None the less, there is a shifting relationship not just between the party and civil society, but also between the party and the state. As the final chapter of this book explores, in a time when there are real concerns about political trust and participation, the role of political parties in the democratic life of the country is coming under close scrutiny. Democratic government and politics have relied on political parties to recruit political activists and politicians, run election campaigns and take over the levers of power. As parties have become professionalized, no one would doubt their extraordinary capacity to mount such campaigns and to organize the business of government and opposition. But, as Paul Whiteley has argued, the decline in party membership may be a real concern.[22] As the more voluntary side to their organizations' activities has declined, political parties have in other respects become weaker, more dependent on other sources for funding, and less able to play their role in promoting and supporting political activity in wider society – all activities crucial to the democratic health of the country as political participation falls, the legitimacy of government is called into question and the power of special interest lobby groups rises. The public may have fallen out of love with politics, but democracy needs parties not just to run the country but also to stimulate voters and engage them in debate in how the country is run.

### Further reading and research resources

The starting point for the study of political parties is Duverger's *Political Parties*. Katz and Mair's 'Changing models of party organization and party democracy' is a key article for contemporary debates on party organization. The 'electoral professional' party is analysed in Panebianco, *Political Parties*. Research by Pat Seyd and Paul Whiteley (see bibliography) is essential to understanding current trends in the membership of political parties. How parties address the world of political de-alignment is explored in Dalton and Wattenberg's edited collection *Parties without Partisans*. Norris's *A Virtuous Circle* is an important guide to politics in the contemporary media world. The question of women and politics is explored by Childs in *Women and British Party Politics*. Justin Fisher is a source of expertise on party finance (see bibliography); and voting patterns in parliament are covered by www.revolts.co.uk, led by the academic Philip Cowley.

# CHAPTER THREE

# The Conservative Party Post-Thatcherism

### 'The Conservative century'

The Conservative Party is the most successful political party in British history. In the twentieth century, a century described by one study as 'the Conservative century',[1] the Tories were in power alone for forty-seven years. Conservative MPs also provided most of the support for nine years of National Government in the 1930s, as well as two prime ministers, Stanley Baldwin and Neville Chamberlain, between 1935 and 1940. Another twelve years were taken up by wartime coalitions, the second led after 1940 from the Tory benches by Winston Churchill. Labour, by contrast, managed just twenty years of single-party government in the twentieth century. Before the Labour Party won the 1997 general election, the Conservative Party appeared to be the 'natural party of government'; and Britain's two-party system looked like one in which a single party predominated.

This extraordinary record is put into further perspective by what happened next. Just as the Labour Party did after 1979, the Tories endured a lengthy spell in the proverbial political wilderness. Following the governments of Margaret Thatcher and John Major, the Conservatives were out of office for more than a decade. In search of political power, three leaders followed in quick succession: William Hague, Iain Duncan Smith (who did not even get the chance to fight a general election) and Michael Howard. But the great vote-winning machine had stopped working. Following defeat in the 2005 election, the party turned to David Cameron who insisted his party had to change.

In this chapter I want to examine first how the Conservative Party under Margaret Thatcher came to dominate British party politics after 1979 and then how the party lost its way after the triumphant years of the 1980s and early 1990s. The focus of the chapter will be on how the party struggled with the legacy of Mrs Thatcher; and whether, under David Cameron, the Conservatives have successfully found a politics after Thatcherism.

### Conservative politics in un-conservative times

The ('swinging') 1960s were never going to be easy for the Conservative Party. Having won the 1959 general election easily ('You've never had it so good',

**Table 3.1**   The long 'Conservative century': British government 1900–2010

|  | Party (ies) in power | Type of government | Prime minister (s) |
|---|---|---|---|
| **1900–5** | Conservative | One party (majority) | Salisbury/Balfour |
| **1905–8** | Liberal | One party (majority) | Campbell-Bannerman |
| **1908–15** | Liberal | One party (majority) | Asquith |
| **1915–16** | Lib/Con/Lab | Coalition | Asquith |
| **1916–22** | Con/Lib/Lab | Coalition | Lloyd George (Lib) |
| **1922–4** | Conservative | One party (majority) | Bonar Law |
| **1924** | Labour | One party (minority) | MacDonald |
| **1924–9** | Conservative | One party (majority) | Baldwin |
| **1929–31** | Labour | One party (majority) | MacDonald |
| **1931–5** | Con/National Labour/Lib | Coalition | MacDonald |
| **1935–40** | Con/Lab | Coalition | Baldwin/Chamberlain (Con) |
| **1940–5** | Con/Lab/Lib | Coalition | Churchill |
| **1945–51** | Labour | One party (majority) | Attlee |
| **1951–7** | Conservative | One party (majority) | Churchill |
| **1957–64** | Conservative | One party (majority) | Macmillan/Home |
| **1964–70** | Labour | One party (majority) | Wilson |
| **1970–4** | Conservative | One party (majority) | Heath |
| **1974–9** | Labour | One party (minority/ majority/minority) | Wilson/Callaghan |
| **1979–90** | Conservative | One party (majority) | Thatcher |
| **1990–7** | Conservative | One party (majority/ minority) | Major |
| **1997–2007** | Labour | One party (majority) | Blair |
| **2007–10** | Labour | One party (majority) | Brown |
| **2010–** | Con/Lib Dem | Coalition | Cameron (Con) |

*Sources*: D. Butler and G. Butler, *British Political Facts 1900–1994* (Basingstoke: Macmillan, 1994, 7th edition); D. Butler and G. Butler, *British Political Facts since 1979* (Basingstoke: Palgrave Macmillan, 2006).

campaigned Prime Minister Harold Macmillan), by 1962 the Tories were in trouble. The economy was shaky; the party was divided over Europe; opinion polls were unfavourable; and the tide was turning against government by rich men in tweed suits. A by-election defeat to the Liberals in the leafy London suburb of Orpington did little for the mood inside the Conservative Party. As disaffection grew, Macmillan sacked six cabinet ministers in the 'night of the long knives'. Worse was to follow. War minister Jack Profumo was found to be sharing a lover, Christine Keeler, with a Soviet military attaché. The party of power had become the party of scandal. Macmillan resigned, ill and exhausted, in October 1963. The 'magic circle' of Tory grandees picked as leader the 14th Earl of Home, who then disclaimed his peerage, fought a by-election as Sir Alec Douglas–Home and became prime minister. (Since then, all Tory leaders have been elected.) Home was a unity candidate for a party divided between its big beasts, including Quinton Hogg and R. A. Butler, jostling to succeed Macmillan. But Home, very much a man in a tweed suit, was hardly a prime minister for the times; but then, frankly, the times had tired of the Conservative Party after thirteen years of government. In general elections in 1964 and 1966, the Tories lost to Harold Wilson and his Labour Party, which seemed more in tune with the 1960s. Luckily for the Conservatives, Labour's six years in government were tough ones, however much the country swung.

By the time of the 1970 general election, an election Labour was expected to win, the Conservatives had a new leader, Edward Heath. Heath was different. For a start, he had been elected in a ballot of MPs. He was also middle-class. And, like Wilson, Heath was something of a modernizer, determined to take the United Kingdom into the European Economic Community, as it then was. When Heath won the 1970 election, there was an expectation of something radical happening to British politics. The expectation was in part generated by a pre-election meeting of the Conservative shadow cabinet in a hotel in Croydon, south London. The Selsdon Park Hotel has entered the footnotes of British political history as the place where the Conservative Party turned against the post-war political consensus. 'Selsdon Man' – and the subsequent general election manifesto – marked a change in direction for the party, one that pointed towards the Thatcher years.

To be sure, the post-war consensus was never as clear-cut as it is sometimes made out to be. In government in the early 1950s, the Conservative Party sought a balance between market-led economic growth and the provision of welfare by the state. This post-war Conservative line was led by the One Nation Group who wanted to break with the interventionist economic policies of Conservatives before the Second World War and establish a more free market approach to the economy. But these one-nation Tories also acknowledged that Labour's welfare state was here to stay: freedom should be balanced with community – and here the group drew inspiration from Benjamin Disraeli whose politics inspired their name (see box 3.1). Until Harold Macmillan became prime minister in 1957, economic policy was steered by this more free market approach. But with growth faltering in 1958, government interventionism was once more on the cabinet agenda, to the dismay of advocates of economic liberals such as Enoch Powell, a contributor to the work of the One Nation Group.

By the 1970s there was a growing weight of opinion within the party that Conservative politics needed to change. Some, like Heath, believed the party and the country had to modernize by becoming more European. Others on

## Box 3.1 Disraeli's political legacy

Benjamin Disraeli was one of the leading Conservative politicians of his generation. He was prime minister in two governments: for a few months in 1868 and then between 1874 and 1880. His legacy is an enduring one. Back in the mid nineteenth century, Disraeli wanted his party to appeal to a broad range of voters. There were sound reasons for this. Electoral reform was transforming politics. The Tories could no longer rely on a narrow base of landed voters to win power in an increasingly urban and enfranchised society. For Disraeli, the Conservatives had to appeal to middle- and working-class communities by making themselves the party of the nation and of reform. Social issues mattered. The gap between rich and poor was too great. Government should work to bring these two sides of the nation together, as he talked about in his 1845 novel *Sybil* (and there is in Disraeli a somewhat romantic vision of a grand Tory alliance between the aristocracy and the noble working man against the more rapacious individualism of the new Victorian middle class). While critics often accused Disraeli's Conservatives of not going far enough in their social reforms, Tory governments in the second half of the nineteenth century continued the broad trend of public policy-making that sought to temper the worst excesses of the market economy, for example by the extension of the Factory Acts covering the employment of children. With Disraeli's death in 1881, Robert Cecil, Lord Salisbury, who had been a harsh critic of Disraeli, successfully led the party in the closing years of the Victorian era. Salisbury was an old-school Tory who liked to give the impression that politics was about doing as little as possible. This reflected his sceptical conservatism that doubted the power of governments to achieve very much, and a fear that mass democracy would undermine the rights of property and Britain's traditional institutions. In fact, the legacy of Disraeli lived on under Salisbury, and his governments continued to take forward social reform. This was also a period when Liberals struggled, following the party's split on devolution for Ireland. In 1886, a group of unionist liberals led by Joseph Chamberlain, opposed to Gladstone's policy of home rule, left the Liberal Party, eventually joining the Tory benches (the Conservatives becoming the Conservative and Unionist Party). This influx of liberals reinforced the reform-minded and liberal conservative strand of British Conservative politics.

the right of the party favoured more aggressive free market policies. What substance there was to Selsdon Man pointed to a move away from the economic interventionism that had come to characterize political economy in the 1960s. This had embedded trade unions and employers' organizations into a formal framework of public policy-making – what is called the corporatist state. Heath was taking government in a more free market direction; and this included joining the Common Market, as well as a tighter rein on monetary and fiscal policies.

But the honeymoon for the Heath government did not last long and soon the Conservatives were in trouble. By 1972, with economic growth stagnating, the chancellor Anthony Barber performed a U-turn on economic policy that stimulated a mini-boom in the short term, but did little for Britain's longer-term economic prospects. With industrial relations worsening, and Britain on a three-day week, Heath called an early election in 1974, asking the country, 'Who governs?' The answer that came back was far from clear. Heath, having won the popular vote but not a majority of MPs, tried to stay in office and engineer a coalition with the Liberals. This came to nothing and Harold Wilson's Labour Party was back in power as a minority government. A second election was held in October and Labour got just enough seats to form a majority government.

## Margaret Thatcher and the remaking of the Conservative Party

The knives were out for Heath. The battle for control of the Conservative Party began. Political change was about to take a dramatic turn. Traditionally the Tories are seen (and see themselves) as the party of statecraft: the art of managing the affairs of the nation (or, as Norton puts it, the 'party of governance'). Back in the mid 1970s, they were quickly becoming a party racked by ideological dispute. Political pragmatism was giving way to philosophical abstraction. The man at the centre of it all was Sir Keith Joseph.

With the Tories defeated in October 1974, Joseph challenged Heath for the leadership. The former health and social services minister in Heath's cabinet was a pivotal figure in the rise of Thatcherism. Disillusioned with the direction the party was taking under Heath, Joseph set up the Centre for Policy Studies (CPS) in 1974 to promote free market solutions to Britain's economic and social woes (which it still does today). Joseph was a clever but complicated man who, by his own admission, was probably not cut out for the strains of being party leader or prime minister. A controversial speech in Birmingham on lone parents effectively ended his campaign. Margaret Thatcher, who had supported Joseph, stood in his place and beat Heath, who resigned as party leader, forcing a second round of voting among Tory MPs. This time, Thatcher defeated Willie Whitelaw, the establishment candidate.

Margaret Thatcher was the surprising choice of leader of the Conservative Party in 1975. She certainly didn't have the party grandees on her side. Like Heath (and John Major after her), she wasn't born to rule. The daughter of a grocer, Alfred Roberts, from Grantham in Lincolnshire (he was also a nonconformist Methodist and a liberal), Margaret Roberts studied chemistry at Oxford on a scholarship in the mid 1940s and became chair of the university Conservative Association. She then worked as a research chemist in the private sector; stood as the Tory candidate in the safe Labour seat of Dartford in 1950 and 1951; married a wealthy businessman, Denis Thatcher, before training as a barrister. Now Margaret Thatcher, she was eventually elected to the House of Commons in 1959 for the safe Tory seat of Finchley in North London. As an MP, she rose quickly through Conservative ranks, the bright, but token woman in the male-dominated world of Conservative politics. During Heath's government after 1970, she was secretary of state for education.

The significance of the leadership election that toppled Heath cannot be overestimated. British politics in general, and Conservative politics in particular, would not be the same again. The election became, in effect, a debate about what a Conservative government should do in power; and, more conceptually, what role the state should take in society. Those backing Mrs Thatcher took an old-fashioned liberal view of the state (what became known as neo-liberalism). Voters had come to expect too much from government; politicians were promising more than they could reasonably deliver; and this was leading to what political scientists called government overload. As a result, these proto-Thatcherites argued, government should be limited. Too much state intervention in the economy undermined the capacity of the private sector to generate wealth and employment; too much welfare provision created a 'dependency culture' that sapped individual responsibility; and the trade unions threatened not only the economic prospects of the nation, but also the very principles of representative government through their extra-parliamentary activities. Britain could arrest its decline, but only by getting government off people's backs.

This was all controversial stuff – and most of Mrs Thatcher's senior colleagues in the party did not share her views. In opposition, the new Conservative leader continued to draw on the CPS as a source of ideas, more so than her own party's research department. The 1979 manifesto certainly contained themes that would become all too familiar in the 1980s – the fight against inflation, trade union reform, privatization, strong defence – but it was far from being Thatcherism fully formed.

## Mrs Thatcher's 'temporary' electoral coalition

In the end, it probably didn't matter very much what the Tories promised to do in government. Throughout most of 1977 and much of 1978, the Conservatives were ahead of Labour in the polls (Labour had a small window of political opportunity in the autumn of 1978, but one Callaghan failed to take). Events then served the 1979 general election to the Conservatives on a plate. The Labour government was in disarray. The 'winter of discontent' could not have been more advantageous to the Tories if they had organized it themselves. Mrs Thatcher's Conservatives won 45 per cent of the vote to Labour's 38 per cent. Crucially, the party attracted voters from across the social spectrum – in particular, considerable numbers of working-class voters critical to winning marginal seats across Britain. Indeed, while the Tories continued to poll above 40 per cent in 1983, 1987 and 1992 general elections, only around 9 per cent were hard-core Tory identifiers.[2] The remaining support for the party was drawn from those parts of the electorate increasingly likely to cast their votes in less partisan ways. This 'temporary coalition', as David Denver describes it, would serve the party well over the next decade or so – until, that is, 'New Labour' came along.

The British Conservatives were not alone in tacking to the right in the late 1970s and early 1980s. A similar political passage was taking place in the United States. Republicans, tired of their own post-war consensus politics, were articulating an equally small-state message. Ronald Reagan, one-time Hollywood movie star and Democrat supporter in the 1930s, had switched parties (in the 1950s) and changed careers to become the Republican governor of California in the 1970s. In 1982, following four years of the Democrat president Jimmy Carter, Reagan was elected president. Like the British Conservatives, he attracted parts of the electorate usually hostile to the Republican Party – the so-called 'Reagan democrats'. These were working-class voters who generally voted Democrat but supported Reagan's Republican Party, just as working-class voters were drawn to Mrs Thatcher's model of Conservative politics.

## One of us? Tory party lines in the early 1980s

Conservative governments dominated British politics for over a decade. But there were few true believers in Margaret Thatcher's first cabinet. Those she would later describe as 'one of us' were in short supply around the table in Downing Street. The key economic jobs, however, did go to believers: Geoffrey Howe was made chancellor (with John Biffen as his chief secretary at the Treasury) and set about putting monetarist theory into practice; and Joseph was appointed secretary of state for industry and started the groundwork for the privatization of the nationalized industries that would become one of the hallmarks of Thatcherism.

But the early years of the first Thatcher government were difficult ones and exposed sharp divisions within the party. The lines of division between the so-called 'wets' and 'dries' had their roots deep in Conservative Party politics and British conservatism. They went back at least as far as the giants of late Victorian Tory politics, Benjamin Disraeli and Lord Salisbury. The division was in part a left–right split on economic and social affairs: between Keynesian Tories who promoted state intervention in the economy and society for the good of business and social cohesion; and free market (and often convinced monetarist) Conservatives not only sceptical of the power of governments to achieve very much but fearful that an expanding state would threaten the rights of property. The wets represented that strand in conservative thinking hostile to economic liberalism and its dogmatic application in government. Leading Tory critic of Mrs Thatcher, Sir Ian Gilmour, argued the party had become un-conservative: too ideological, too destructive of established ways of doing things and far too attached to the interests of business, not the whole nation.[3]

Mrs Thatcher's economic experiment, as the journalist William Keegan called it,[4] was not going down well – and not just with the usual suspects of Tory wets, Labour politicians, Keynesian economists (who wrote a mass letter to *The Times* condemning government policy) and *Guardian*-reading social workers. British society was falling apart. Unemployment was rising steeply; businesses were going to the wall; whole communities stopped working; and rioting spread across urban Britain. The Conservative government, opinion polls suggested, would be short-lived. Few were taking bets in 1981 that Mrs Thatcher would last into the New Year. But survive she did. Events came to her rescue. The invasion of the Falkland Islands by the military junta running Argentina (the Argentines claimed sovereignty, and the British government appeared to have been prepared to negotiate on who controlled this rocky and very British outpost in the South Atlantic) threw the Thatcher government a lifeline. The government response was swift and successful. Victory in the Falklands War restored British rule to the islands – and the popularity of Mrs Thatcher's administration. The Conservatives won the 1983 election victory at a stroll, helped enormously by an unelectable Labour Party and a divided opposition. The scene was set for Thatcherism proper.

## Conservatism and Thatcherism

Conservatives profess a deep distrust of ideology – of politicalisms. One of Margaret Thatcher's own ministers, William Waldegrave, once suggested that 'natural conservatives, like elephants, are difficult to describe; but we know one when we see one'.[5] No little blue book of conservatism, then. Conservatives certainly place great emphasis on the pursuit of power, not for its own sake (though some may claim they do), but because they see themselves as best placed to govern the country and to defend the interests of the nation. Conservatives may believe certain things to be important but, they claim, theory shouldn't come before practice. Politics is a craft, needing wisdom and experience; politics is not the application of abstract reason to public affairs.[6]

Whether they like it or not, however, conservatives have always believed in something called conservatism. To be sure, just as those on the left have different takes on what constitutes socialism (and liberals, liberalism), conservatives are divided on the balance of ideas that should inform their politics. Conservatives in the liberal or Whig tradition have generally placed greater emphasis on individual liberty and free markets; Conservatives in the Tory tradition, on established institutions and communities. These divisions have political consequences. Conservatives divide over the role of the state in the economy and in providing welfare and other collective services. They also divide on what institutions (and what values) are integral to social cohesion and to the building of 'one nation'. Conservatives have, generally, looked both ways: backwards to the importance of traditional ways of doing things; and forwards to the dynamism and wealth-creating possibilities of free enterprise. These strands in Conservative thinking do not always sit comfortably together: social provision by the state to support 'one nation' inevitably threatens the rights of property (whatever public good it might bring); and the 'creative destruction' (Joseph Schumpeter's term) of free markets rarely shows much respect for established institutions or settled communities.

The idea of a radical shift in Conservative politics in the 1980s – the birth of Thatcherism – came from the left. The sociologist Stuart Hall, drawing on the ideas of the Italian Marxist Antonio Gramsci, suggested this was no ordinary Conservative government. Rather, Mrs Thatcher was at the head of a new ideology seeking, in Gramsci's terms, hegemony. This ideology had been shaped by the political right in response to the economic and social crisis facing the British state. Indeed, the success of Thatcherism, Hall suggested, was its capacity to tap into the 'common sense' anxieties and concerns of ordinary people in difficult and uncertain times. There was, Hall admitted at the time, a little bit of Thatcherism in us all.[7]

But what did Thatcherism amount to? There is always the danger, to borrow Tim Bale's words, of using the 'sacred texts' of the New Right (in particular, those of the free market economists F. A. Hayek and Milton Friedman) as a substitute for the 'slightly less saintly actions' of Conservative ministers when looking back at the Thatcher and Major governments in the 1980s and 1990s.[8] A rather too literal reading of Thatcherism equates it simply with free markets and neo-liberalism. Certainly the neo-liberal *side* of Thatcherism pulled Conservative governments in this period towards free market solutions to public policy questions. In particular, there was an attempt by ministers – not always successful, it has to be said – to reduce the role of the state in the economy, in particular through privatization; to deregulate the economy by cutting back on the controls in place on business and management; to tame the power of the trade unions; and to put in place a macro-economic strategy that put low taxes and the fight against inflation, not full employment, at the forefront of the government's objectives. In the end, there wasn't much Thatcherism didn't think was better done by the market. Indeed, this urge to bring in market-based solutions to public sector reform put Conservative governments in the 1980s and 1990s on a collision course with established institutions in health, education and public administration. Doctors, teachers and civil servants all found themselves confronted with a government hell-bent on radical reform that brought a new 'managerialism' into public life.

There was also a more conservative side to Thatcherism – what Stuart Hall called, critically, its 'authoritarian populism'. The free market, as Andrew Gamble put it, came with a 'strong state': the discipline of the invisible hand of the market required the firm hand of the rule of law.[9] Thatcherism used the power of the state in an attempt to roll back government. This newly expanded market order needed policing, especially where state monopolies such as the utility suppliers or British Telecom became dominant private sector companies. Thatcherism also used the power of the state to try to force market-based solutions in the private and public sectors (and this included taking on the power of the trade unions). Thatcherism was also traditionally conservative in the sense that it saw a strong state as a necessary guarantor of social stability and the nation state. This more orthodox conservative side to Thatcherism was – or certainly liked to sound – tough on crime, tough on immigration and tough on national defence. During the 1980s, there was a rise in police numbers; the introduction of more restrictive immigration laws; and vocal support for the armed forces, even if defence spending fell after its peak in the mid-1980s. Thatcherism was also, rhetorically at least, strong on (married) family values. And when it came to gay rights, the Conservative government added a clause (number 28) in the 1988 Local Government Act prohibiting local authorities from promoting homosexuality as a 'pretended family relationship'. More socially liberal Thatcherites just had to bite their tongues.

This New Right mix of economic liberalism and more traditionally conservative ideas brought with it its own tensions as, sometimes, the free market pulled the Conservative government in one direction and the strong state in another. The Conservative case for education reform, for example, came from both market liberals and supporters of traditional ways of schooling. As a result, the landmark 1988 Education Act took a belt and braces policy approach: an internal market that handed power (in theory) to schools and parents *and* a national curriculum that gave the secretary of state for education Napoleonic authority over what was taught in classrooms across England and Wales.

But events, as they always do, made Mrs Thatcher's governments (and Thatcherism) a more pragmatic political project than is often imagined. 'Lame ducks' in the British economy were not always put out of their misery (both British Steel and British Leyland received state aid during Mrs Thatcher's first term); and the promise of radical reform of the welfare state constantly hit the buffers of what was politically possible.[10] Indeed, some believe the -ism that bears Mrs Thatcher's name was a bit of a mess. The historian Mark Garnett suggests that, while the word 'Thatcherism' will endure, 'it denotes an odd assemblage of unoriginal ideas, rather than a novel and coherent approach to the business of government'.[11]

Coherent or not, at the core of Thatcherism was that enduring tension in Conservative thinking and practice between liberal commitments to individual freedom and the market economy and a more conservative sense of community. All political parties are, to a greater or lesser extent, coalitions. Parties encompass a broad range of interests and viewpoints, and their political appeal must be sufficiently wide to have any chance of attracting enough votes to win power. Going right back to the debate over the repeal of the Corn Laws in the 1840s, economic liberalism and the interests of business have been significant drivers of modern conservatism over two centuries. Indeed, it was the party's capacity to appeal to the property-owning liberal (and usually unionist) interests in society that proved its strength in the twentieth century in the face of the newly founded Labour Party. The poor old Liberal Party had its base of support cut from both sides. Mrs Thatcher and her supporters were in many respects simply drawing upon this Whig or liberal conservative strand of politics.

But other strands of Conservative politics were also drawn into Thatcherism's ideological mix. In particular, traditionalist Tories who put social order and defence of the nation state at the core of their politics also got behind Mrs Thatcher. Marginalized in the post-war years with the end of empire, traditional Tories abhorred the threat to national sovereignty posed by Britain's entry (under a Conservative government) into the European Community. It wasn't so much the economic liberalism, however, that attracted these Conservatives to Mrs Thatcher, though they shared her dislike of what seemed to them little more than state socialism. Rather, it was her broader narrative about reversing Britain's national decline. Economic liberals, not surprisingly, saw this decline largely in economic terms. Traditionalists viewed it much more in moral and cultural terms. They wanted a leader to stand up for Britain and the nation's institutions and traditions. National sovereignty mattered in a visceral manner often incomprehensible to the more rationally minded (and often internationalist) neo-liberals. So when Mrs Thatcher controversially suggested in the run-up to the 1979 general election that Britain was being 'swamped' by immigration, traditionalist Conservatives knew exactly what she meant. As we shall see shortly, the move towards greater European integration in the late 1980s would serve to drive a wedge through the Conservative Party – and Thatcherism's governing coalition in the party.

In summary, Thatcherism marked a reconfiguration of the Conservative Party in the late 1970s and 1980s, with a greater emphasis on economic liberalism and social conservatism. But this was a far from stable mix. The new Thatcherite camp was made up of free market neo-liberals, social liberals and social conservatives. On the important question of Europe, they did not speak with one voice. The Thatcher governments in the 1980s also depended on the support of more socially liberal, pro-European and more economically interventionist figures such as Michael Heseltine.[12] By the end of the 1980s, these tensions in Conservative politics were coming to the fore over the issue of Europe. But before we examine the fall of Margaret Thatcher, it is useful to see how deeply Thatcherism touched the Conservative Party in the country. Did Tory members turn Thatcherite in the 1980s?

### True blues?

Like other parties, membership of the Conservative Party started to fall from the late 1950s. According to a major study of these 'true blues', after 1960 the Conservatives lost something like 64,000 net members per year – a loss that inevitably had important financial implications for the party.[13] As we saw in chapter 2, the decline in partisanship was a major driver of falling party membership. The demands of modern lifestyles also made joining a political party less attractive; and those who did join did not have as much time to devote to politics, thus leading to lower levels of political activism. The Conservative Party was also hit hard by the main source of their activist base, women, going out to work. These factors cut the supply of party workers just at the same time as the demand for such workers fell as a result of the growing reliance of parties on paid professionals and political communication strategies built around the mass broadcast media.

This professionalization of Conservative politics in the late 1970s and 1980s was continuing a trend dating back to the 1950s. In the post-war period, the Conservative Party led the way in using opinion polling and the broadcast media (and radio was just as important as television in the early years) to reach voters, especially the increasing number of those less partisan in their support. Mrs Thatcher's leadership continued the professionalization of the party. In 1978, she appointed the television producer Gordon Reece to run the party's publicity machine. For the 1979 election, the Conservatives appointed the advertising agency Saatchi & Saatchi – famously producing the campaign poster 'Labour isn't working' against a background of a snaking dole queue. Directed by Reece and Saatchi's Tim Bell, the Conservatives in 1979 and 1983 brought the world of politics far closer to the worlds of advertising and marketing. Mrs Thatcher's Conservatives had a brand – and it needed selling. The professionalization of party affairs also rather suited Mrs Thatcher's style of leadership, which saw a further erosion of cabinet-style government and a growth in a more presidential form of British political

---

### Box 3.2 Where did the true blues stand in the 1980s?

Looking from the Conservative Party grassroots in the 1980s, it is clear that Thatcherism did not hold sway in the minds of Tory activists. Using three dimensions of conservative thinking and politics – traditionalism, individualism and progressivism – which, more or less, map onto the traditional, economic liberal and one-nation strands in Conservative Party politics respectively, the authors of *True Blues* examined the attitudes of Conservative Party members to a range of issues that can be taken as indicators of ideological groups in the party. So, for example, 'A future Conservative government should encourage repatriation of immigrants' could be considered indicative of traditionalist conservatism; 'unemployment benefit should ensure people have a reasonable standard of living' of progressive conservatism; and 'when someone is unemployed, it is usually their fault' of individualist conservatism. Clearly, Thatcherism, if it represented anything, was a shift away from the progressive Tory view towards the individualist and traditionalist perspectives. But did the party follow her? According to the *True Blues* study, the party in the country in the 1980s remained 'rather anti-Thatcherite'. While there was clear support in the survey for traditionalist and individualist policy positions among party members, there was also significant support for progressive one-nation positions. Indeed, when asked where they placed themselves on a left–right ideological spectrum, 41 per cent of members chose the centre left of the party and only just over 20 per cent the right.

*Source*: Whiteley, Seyd and Richardson, *True Blues*

leadership. Moreover, with the appointment of Marks & Spencer boss Sir Derek Rayner to head an efficiency unit in the cabinet office to reform the civil service, all of this added up to a growing reliance on private sector management in place of traditional public administration.

On party membership, there is some evidence that Thatcherism itself may have contributed to the continuing fall in the 1980s. Or, at least, Mrs Thatcher divided the party in the country just as much as she divided the party at Westminster.[14] Many party members thought very highly of her and what she was trying to achieve. But many other members didn't like her at all – and these were more often than not members whose views coincided with the progressive one-nation Tory view.

Mrs Thatcher's impact on her party, then, was, in the shorter term, limited. She worked with what she found. But in the longer term, as we shall see later, she left a more lasting impression. However, the manner of her departure from the political scene was to leave deep scars on Tory politics.

## The lady vanishes

Despite thumping victories at the ballot box, by the late 1980s the wheels were coming off the Conservative government – and voters were turning against the Tories. The disastrous episode of local government finance reform, the 'poll tax', did little for the government's and the party leader's credibility. By the summer of 1989, the Tories were behind Labour in the polls and losing a string of by-elections. Divisions in the government and in the party were opening. Chancellor of the Exchequer Nigel Lawson resigned in opposition to the government's refusal to join the economic exchange rate mechanism. The following November, all hell broke loose. Geoffrey Howe, former chancellor, foreign secretary and now deputy prime minister joined Lawson on the backbenches where his stinging criticism of Mrs Thatcher's handling of European policy further weakened her premiership. A growing number in the parliamentary party saw Mrs Thatcher as a political liability. Michael Heseltine, the leading figure on the pro-European centre left of the party, lit the touch-paper. He challenged Mrs Thatcher for the leadership, gaining enough votes in the ballot of MPs to force her resignation. In the second round of voting, John Major, who had the support of the Thatcherites, did just about enough to win. Heseltine conceded – and the lady had gone.

The coup against Margaret Thatcher in the autumn of 1990 may in the short term have been the action of a party with a keen eye on power. Despite opposition to many of Mrs Thatcher's ideas in parliament and in the country, most Tory MPs were happy to go along with her government as long as the party kept winning power. Once it appeared that she couldn't deliver at the polls, her exit was nasty, brutish and short. In the longer term, however, the removal of Margaret Thatcher did lasting damage to the Conservatives as a governing party, not least because it did nothing to soothe the wounds of

division festering at Westminster and beyond. It was a trauma with consequences that would last more than a decade.

## Europe and the Conservative Party in the 1990s

While John Major won the 1992 general election mid-recession, he was lucky
to face a Labour Party the electorate still had doubts over. But the Major years
proved difficult ones for the Conservative Party in parliament. The question
of European integration had long divided the Conservative Party. But it wasn't
until the final years of Mrs Thatcher's premiership that Europe seriously began
to destabilize her party and her government. As we have seen already, both
Nigel Lawson and Geoffrey Howe, two of Mrs Thatcher's most loyal supporters,
resigned over Britain's relationship with Europe. The signing of the Treaty on
European Union – better known as the Maastricht treaty – in 1992 brought
the simmering discontent in the party to the boil. Hardcore Thatcherites
committed to free markets and the sovereignty of nation states (and the sense
of national identity that went with this) lined up to oppose the treaty.

Major believed he had delivered a good deal for Britain by negotiating
various opt-outs to the treaty, including on the single currency. But backbench
opposition surfaced as the government attempted to ratify the treaty in the

### Box 3.3 Tory 'tendencies' turning factional?

Traditionally, the Conservative Party is seen as a party of tendencies, not factions. The
distinction was made by Richard Rose in the 1960s. Tendencies are 'fluctuating alignments on specific issues'; factions, 'group[s] of individuals who seek to further a broad
range of policies through consciously organised political activity'. Importantly, factions
are organized into political groups; tendencies are not. They are far more temporary
in character. Factionalism, then, requires evidence of MPs both thinking alike and
acting together as groups. So, did the Conservative Party become a party of factions
in the 1990s? According to research by Cowley and Norton, the Parliamentary Conservative Party was not particularly rebellious between 1992 and 1997; and the rebellions that did take place were by and large over Europe, as we might expect. But,
according to this research, the lines of division over Europe did not to any great extent
cut across traditional ideological divides in the party. Those on the right tended to be
opposed to Europe, while those towards the left were more likely to be pro-European.
And despite the appearances of organized cabals, the Conservatives remained a party
of tendencies not factions during the Major years. This should not for a moment
distract us from the hugely destructive impact of these rebellions on the Tories as a
governing party. But the party in parliament in the 1990s did not radically change in
character.

*Sources and further reading*: P. Cowley and P. Norton, 'Rebels and rebellions: Conservative MPs
in the 1992 parliament', *British Journal of Politics and International Relations*, 1 (1999),
pp. 84–105; T. Heppell, 'The ideological composition of the parliamentary Conservative Party
1992–97', *British Journal of Politics and International Relations*, 4, 2 (2002), pp. 299–324;
Cowley and Norton, 'What a ridiculous thing to say! (which is why we didn't say it): a response
to Timothy Heppell', *British Journal of Politics and International Relations*, 4, 2 (2002), pp. 325–9.

House of Commons. Both Labour and the Liberal Democrats supported the Maastricht treaty, but Labour was willing to vote against it to defeat the government. On 22 July, 23 Tory MPs voted with the opposition – and the government lost by 8 votes. The next day, the prime minister made the vote on the treaty a confidence motion in his government. He won by 40 votes. But Conservative divisions over Europe intensified. The 'bastards', as Major not so privately dubbed the Tory hard-line Eurosceptics, made his government increasingly unstable. As by-elections eroded the Conservatives' slim majority in the Commons, the government found it more difficult to get some of its business through (the privatization of the Royal Mail, for example, was shelved). In May 1993, Norman Lamont, chancellor during the exchange rate crisis in 1992 that had seen the Tories' reputation as sound managers of the British economy shredded, was replaced in the Treasury by Kenneth Clarke. In a speech from the backbenches, Lamont stuck the boot in, accusing Major of being 'in office, but not in power'. As the popularity of the government plummeted, Major called his critics' bluff. In June 1995, he resigned as party leader (but not as PM) and challenged his opponents to 'put up or shut up'. Arch Eurosceptic John Redwood put up, resigning from the cabinet, and lost – 219 Tory MPs to 89, with 22 abstentions. Major was safe, just, until the next election.

## The Conservative fall

By 1997 not only was the Labour Party fit for power, but voters were ready for change. The Conservative defeat in the 1997 election was comprehensive – and came as no surprise. Results from local elections over more than a decade were the signs of an impending political storm for the Tories. Back in 1979, the Conservatives triumphed in national *and* local elections. By 1997, according to election experts Rallings, Thrasher and Johnston, the party was at a low ebb locally, down to 4,550 councillors and in control of just one in twenty local authorities.[15] Local party organization is important to success at a national level. The long slow eighteen-year decline of the Conservative vote in local elections was a harbinger for what would come at the national general election in 1997. Thatcherism's electoral success was built on an alliance of middle- and skilled working-class voters. By 1997, however, it was New Labour that was winning the battle for the floating – or at least, less partisan – voter, as we shall see in the next chapter.

What was the significance of defeat for the Conservative Party? And what, crucially, would be the legacy of Thatcherism once the party was in opposition?

Certainly, the Conservative defeat in the 1997 election exposed deep divisions within the Conservative Party. While the question of Europe dominated these divisions, just as they had done during John Major's premiership, divisions in the party went deeper. The Conservative Party, as we have seen, has drawn on competing understandings of politics: both liberal conceptions that place great store on individual freedom, limited government and free markets, and conservative ones that put greater emphasis on traditional institutions, values and ways of doing things. Thatcherism's uneasy alliance of free market liberals and more traditional conservatives was founded on a shared dislike of what was seen as the encroachment of the state into (traditional) civil society. By the 1990s, this alliance was showing signs of strain.

At the heart of the matter was Thatcherism's radicalism. The question of change is a tricky one for conservatives (small c or big C). Any conservative party worthy of its name believes politics should be founded on continuity with the past. To be a conservative is to feel a sense of connection with what has gone before. Conservatism is in part to conserve ('if it ain't broke, don't fix it'; and if it is broken, try to mend it in a way that is sympathetic to how it was before). This can lead the party to defend the status quo with all its privileges. But even the most die-hard of Tories have recognized that change is sometimes necessary, and often see the advantages of managing reform in ways that divert more radical proposals. Indeed, nineteenth-century party leaders Robert Peel and Benjamin Disraeli were both what today would be called modernizers. They believed that Conservative governments had not simply to move with the times but to take the lead in making what were often quite radical economic and political reforms. Not for nothing was Disraeli's view that sound Conservative governments were 'Tory men and Whig measures'. Interestingly, though, while both Peel and Disraeli remain icons of Conservative politics, in their time they were controversial and often divisive figures; Mrs Thatcher was no less so.

By the mid 1990s, the Conservative government was getting flak from its own side not simply on Europe, but for its obsession with free markets as well. Conservative philosophers Roger Scruton and John Gray shared a view that the party had developed a one-track (rationalist) mind that valued individual freedom above the common bonds of community and civil society. Scruton urged the party to be more traditionally conservative; Gray gave up and became a supporter of New Labour.[16] Both echoed Gilmour's perspective that Conservative governments had become anti-conservative in their (neo-liberal) radicalism.

One legacy of Thatcherism, then, was a sense that the Conservatives had become the 'economics party' with little to say on social affairs.[17] Or at least, when it did talk about social affairs, the emphasis was on individual responsibility for welfare, and the introduction of markets and the private sector into the provision of public goods such as health, education and housing. The party had lost that Disraelian capacity to talk about issues such as poverty without sounding harsh and uncaring. The memory of the great Thatcherite Norman Tebbit's view that the unemployed should, like his father in the 1930s, get on their bikes and find work was hard to shake. This, allied with Margaret Thatcher's much misunderstood line that there was 'no such thing as society', gave the impression the Conservatives had become the party of greed and self-interest. That Mrs Thatcher simply wanted to remind people that the state was not the same as society was lost. It would take David Cameron's more polished finish to get this message across in 2010 with his talk of the 'big society'; and the equally polished Tony Blair to understand the mood of voters in the 1990s with New Labour's mantra of 'economic efficiency and social justice'.

This period also saw open up in the Conservative Party something of a cultural divide that Thatcherism had papered over. Many of Mrs Thatcher's supporters were not only economic, but social, liberals as well. They were sympathetic to the legalization of drugs and to other social questions which were, they believed, ones of individual responsibility and choice.[18] By contrast, more old-fashioned Thatcherites were all for economic freedom, but drew sharp lines in the sand on a whole host of social questions that touched, they believed, on traditional sources of authority in society. While all sides acknowledged the party needed more of a social agenda, including support for the public services, there were important divisions about the substance of that agenda. Modernizers, unsurprisingly, felt more in tune with contemporary patterns of social life, including gay relations, women's rights and the diversity of modern society. The Conservative Party, they believed, had to change to reflect this society by becoming more representative and socially liberal. Traditionalists, by contrast, felt far less comfortable with these social trends – regarding them more as a modern malaise, root cause of the problems facing British society. Traditional social relations – in particular, marriage and family life – should be supported. Post-Thatcherism, the Conservative Party should stick to what it believed in, not cave in to trendy ideas.

## A question of leadership: Hague, IDS and Howard

Could a new leader revive Tory fortunes in opposition? The election of William Hague following his party's defeat in 1997 did little to bring to an end the internecine warfare inside the party. The election, dominated by the question of the European Union, saw the centre right of the Conservative Party get behind Hague against the old warhorse of the pro-European centre left Ken Clarke. Hague, a politician embracing the Thatcherite economic legacy, was supported by some modernizers inside the party, including Alan Duncan who acted as his campaign manager. The leading modernizer, Michael Portillo, did not stand. Initially Hague appeared to draw inspiration from the revival of centre right politics in the US under the banner of 'compassionate conservatism'. Hague attempted something similar in the UK. He appointed Portillo as shadow chancellor who performed a U-turn on the party's opposition to Labour's minimum wage. But with little movement in the opinion polls, the Hague Conservatives turned inwards with their 'common sense conservatism'; and, when all else failed, to 'saving the pound'. The centre-ground issues of the economy and public services were left to Labour – and nothing could save the Tory party going down to a heavy defeat in the 2001 general election. Hague resigned and his place as leader was taken by Iain Duncan Smith (IDS).

Duncan Smith was elected under new rules introduced by Hague. These rules, on the face of it, gave grassroots Tories more power over the choice of party leaders. The rules split the process into two stages. Stage one would see MPs voting for the candidates, with the top two put forward to a ballot of party members in a second stage. The election of Duncan Smith, in many respects an outsider in the race to be leader, was taken by many as an example of new membership power in the Tory Party. However, while the new rules did give members what appeared to be the final say on who would become leader, MPs retained considerable power over the process – far more, indeed, than in the other major parties. None the less, the new procedures did allow Duncan Smith to become leader in a way that alternatives might not have done.[19]

The choice of Duncan Smith was also viewed by many as a consolidation of the Thatcherite revolution inside the Conservative Party. The traditionalists in the party (quickly dubbed the 'rockers' by the media) had defeated the modernizers (or 'mods') supporting Michael Portillo, who quit politics. Duncan Smith's background is important. He was a Tory on the right wing of the Conservative Party (a member of the Thatcherite No Turning Back Group), and the man who filled Norman Tebbit's shoes as MP for Chingford in north-east London ('if you think I'm right-wing, you should meet this guy', Tebbit is reported to have said). Duncan Smith was a traditional conservative who blended Thatcherite free market economics with a deep commitment to the nation state, national sovereignty (he was an original Maastricht rebel, for which many MPs never forgave him[20]) and established institutions such as the family, church and armed forces.

But in certain respects, IDS played a different hand from the one many expected. While his stumbling leadership left the party more or less where it started in the polls – and he was unceremoniously sacked in 2003 – under Duncan Smith, a signal did go out that the Tories should govern for 'the whole country': in particular, by shifting attention to social issues under the banner of 'A fair deal for everyone'.[21] One indication of change was the appointment by Duncan Smith of a leading modernizer, Theresa May, as party chairman in 2002. In this post, May famously delivered the Tories some home truths: 'Our base is too narrow and so, occasionally, are our sympathies', May told delegates to the annual conference; 'You know what some people call us: the nasty party.' Much of the focus of May's speech was on questions of representation – and how the party, accurately or not, was seen to 'demonize minorities'. To have any future, May argued, the Conservatives had to develop a more inclusive politics in tune with modern society.[22]

This included talking about poverty. Much has been made of Duncan Smith's Damascene conversion on a visit to a rundown housing estate,

Easterhouse in Glasgow, in April 2002.[23] The point was that Duncan Smith as party leader made some attempt, if not always consistently, to reposition the party in such a way that it had something to say, beyond free markets and defence of the nation state, to questions of poverty and deprivation that many communities continued to suffer despite the general prosperity of the country. The message was: the Conservatives did believe in society (and always had done) and had policy ideas to prove it.[24] Later, from the backbenches, IDS went on to found the Centre for Social Justice that was instrumental in developing the party's 'broken society' arguments for David Cameron.

Changing political parties is never easy. The Parliamentary Conservative Party remained split, and most MPs had little faith in their party leader. Divisions surfaced over Labour's Adoption and Children Bill, which included a clause allowing 'gay adoption'. Duncan Smith made the question of the vote on the bill in the House of Commons into one of confidence in his own leadership. This proved to be in short supply. The Conservatives then turned to the old stalwart of the Thatcher/Major years Michael Howard to limit the damage at the next election by digging up some old favourites of the Tory faithful: immigration and crime. To a certain extent, Howard's way worked in 2005 to limit the size of Labour's victory, helped enormously by the Blair government and the unpopularity of the war in Iraq. The Tories were once more in the political frame. But could they seriously challenge for power, not least by fighting Labour on the state of the public services?

## David Cameron and his electoral challenge

In the aftermath of the Conservative Party's defeat, controversial Tory treasurer Lord Ashcroft urged Conservatives to 'smell the coffee'.[25] With this in mind, perhaps, the party turned to an old Etonian to lead the party back to power – except that David Cameron wasn't very old, just thirty-nine at the time (Tony Blair became Labour leader aged forty-one). And it didn't feel much like 'Dave' was an old-school Tory toff – or, if he was, he wore it well. Certainly Cameron was part of that new breed of professional political operator: a former advisor to Norman Lamont and director of corporate affairs at Carlton Television.

There is, as the commentator Peter Oborne observes, something of a contradiction to David Cameron. On the one hand, he is a throw-back to a past age of Tory politics – 'he will be the first prime minister who was born to rule in half a century' – far more like Harold Macmillan or Alec Douglas Home than Margaret Thatcher or John Major. On the other, he is a modernizer in the mould of Tony Blair ('I am a child of my time', Cameron told the party's annual conference in 2008).[26] Indeed, Cameron went as far as telling media executives shortly after becoming leader that he was the 'heir to Blair'. The Conservative Party, Cameron insisted, had to change. With his advisor Steve Hilton, a successful marketing man, at his side in the leader's office, Cameron set about 'decontaminating the Tory brand': to make voting Conservative less of an embarrassment in polite company. With die-hard Tories waiting to pounce on any slip-up, this wasn't going to be an easy ride.

The electoral challenge facing Cameron was a steep one. While the twentieth century may have been the Conservative century, the party's old winning ways hid two uncomfortable electoral trends. The first is one the Tories face with Labour – a shrinking vote. In the eight elections between 1945 and 1970, the Conservative Party had a mean vote of 45.3 per cent. In the nine elections between 1970 and 2005, the average Tory vote fell to 37.8 per cent. As we saw in chapter 1, since 1970 the combined share of the vote won by the Conservative and Labour parties has fallen as the British party system has shifted away from two-party politics. On top of this, the core part of both the Tory and Labour vote has shrunk back. In these more volatile and contingent electoral times, Cameron's Conservative challenge – just as for Blair's Labour challenge which we examine in the next chapter – was to appeal to wide sections of the electorate (and certainly not to assume that voters were secret Thatcherites). Nothing else would get them into power and keep them there. The decline of two-party politics also made a hung parliament more likely. Could Cameron take his party far enough ahead of Labour to win outright victory? Given where the Tories were in 2005, this was always an unlikely prospect.

The second worrying trend in Conservative election results was the regionalization of its support. Since 1974, the Conservative Party has increasingly become an English party, in general, and a party of southern England, in particular. This trend can be seen in terms of the share of the vote in different parts of Britain and, in an even more pronounced way, the distribution of seats. In 2005, the Conservatives won a majority of the vote in only three out of eleven regions of Britain: south-east England, south-west England and eastern England. The party was a close second to Labour in the East and West Midlands. Otherwise, the party trailed Labour (and in the case of Scotland and north-east England, the Liberal Democrats) in all other regions of Britain in terms of votes cast. This north/south split is even more pronounced in the distribution of seats: the Conservatives have gone from being a party that won seats across Britain, to one where its support in the House of Commons is dominated by MPs elected for constituencies in southern England.[27] Just as Labour needed a bit of 'southern comfort' in the 1990s, so the Conservatives under Cameron needed some northern soul.

It should also be added that the electoral system does not do the Conservative Party any favours. It gives Labour a clear advantage at the polls. This is because the Tory vote has become more concentrated in seats the party already holds, leading to more 'wasted votes'. Labour support, by contrast, is more evenly and therefore efficiently spread; and Conservative seats are generally larger in population than Labour ones. As a result, in 2005, the

Conservatives won 92 fewer seats than Labour in England although they polled more votes.[28]

## Cameron's political strategy

By 2009, the Conservative Party was riding high in the opinion polls. The new Labour Prime Minister Gordon Brown had blown his chance in the autumn of 2008 to go to the country with any hope of winning. Tories were quietly confident about their chances at the forthcoming election. So, what had Cameron done right, where Hague, IDS and Howard had gone wrong? Philip Norton, academic and Conservative parliamentarian, suggests that Cameron's success was based on doing things differently.[29]

To start with, he got the Conservatives talking about ideas and values, including social justice. British society was 'broken' – and the Cameron Conservatives wanted to do something about this. Cameron also moved the party onto new territory on issues such as the environment; and fought to lose the 'nasty party' tag by being for things (the NHS, gay relationships and the rights of minorities) rather than against things (notably immigration and Europe). The new Tory leader in his early days also avoided policy commitments. Instead, Cameron farmed policy out to specialist groups that not only included a range of views within the party, but also brought in well-known outsiders, like Bob Geldof. Critically, none of the policy ideas developed by these groups would be binding on the leadership. This all helped Cameron take the Conservatives back to the centre ground of British politics, appealing to the kind of voters who had turned to New Labour in the mid 1990s. The strategy was inclusive, not partisan. The message was: the Cameron Conservatives were social liberals not just economic ones; and they understood the everyday concerns of voters.

Cameron was also a brilliant communicator – and great debater in the House of Commons. This led to accusations that, like Blair, Cameron was all style and no substance. But this is to miss the point of what the new Tory leader did after 2005. Cameron had to establish the party as a credible alternative to Labour in government with a broad range of voters, only some of whom were loyal Conservatives. Simply churning out policy proposals without a broader narrative about what a new Conservative government would be like had been tried and failed. Cameron also had to prove himself a leader, not least over a parliamentary party that had become dysfunctional since the Major government. When Tory MPs were caught paying for duck houses and cleaning moats in the expenses scandal that rocked parliament in 2009, Cameron's response was tough and decisive. He acknowledged the public's anger, made clear his apology, and told his MPs to do as he said – or get out.

But where was Cameron taking the Conservative Party? Was he taking the Tories back in the direction of Thatcherism or moving his party on from the legacy of the 1980s and 1990s?

## The ideology of Cameron conservatism

Cameron's Conservatives continue to operate within the broad framework of political economy established in the 1980s under Margaret Thatcher. There is always an element of pragmatism in a government's dealings with business. But free markets have become a given in British economic policy-making over nearly three decades. Indeed, as the recession hit Britain in 2008–9, Cameron promised a 'government of thrift', suggesting the Tories might return to their hair-shirt days of Austrian economics in which public spending was, by default, bad and state intervention always an inhibitor of market innovation. In the depths of the downturn, the Conservatives said they were better placed to deal with the mountain of government debt Britain faced by aggressively cutting public spending. A new Conservative government would also look to communities and the private and voluntary sectors to deliver public goods (the so-called 'big society'). While this rather ignored how Labour, as it increased spending, had looked to non-state bodies to provide public services, there did appear to be an important ideological dividing line in the run-up to the 2010 election. All suspiciously Thatcherite.

This anti-state message should not hide, however, the shift in Conservative politics post-Thatcherism and, as one writer put it, 'after Blair'.[30] To start with, Cameron and his shadow chancellor George Osborne have resisted calls from the right of his party to put tax cuts at the top of the Conservative agenda. There was also a commitment on funding for the public services: the Cameron Conservatives would stick to Labour's spending plans (an echo of Labour's pre-1997 pledge to do the same with Tory ones); and the NHS, Cameron could almost have said, really was safe in his hands (the passport out of the NHS idea, a policy Cameron had written into the 2005 manifesto under Howard, was quietly dropped). These public services would need to be reformed – and there is something of the Major Conservatives and New Labour in this respect. On schooling, for example, the 'free schools' agenda marks a clear continuity with Labour's academy schools programme outside traditional local government control.

To be sure, by 2010 the scale of Britain's fiscal deficit made nonsense of the early commitments on public sector spending. In government, George Osborne's first budget as chancellor unveiled swingeing cuts to public spending as the Conservative/Liberal Democrat coalition attempted to steady the public finances. The comprehensive spending review that followed in the autumn confirmed that this would be an age of austerity with substantial cuts to planned spending in the years to follow, in particular for many on welfare. Health spending, however, remained a protected budget. Indeed, this ring-fencing of NHS funding concerns not just those who see it as fiscally illogical, but also those who have supported Cameron in reforming Tory policy on the public services but who would like alternatives to the NHS model of healthcare provision to be considered.

Welfare is another area where Cameron's political economy marks a break with the old-style safety-net policies that, rhetorically at least, dominated the politics of Thatcherism. On the 'broken society', Cameron's Conservatives insisted that market forces alone could not provide the necessary social fix. Problems of poverty and social breakdown required government working with other agencies in the private and voluntary sectors to support more personalized welfare-to-work programmes. The broad thrust of welfare policy under the Cameron government will continue the reforms started by Labour and recommended by the banker David Freud, brought in by Blair to advise Labour on welfare in 2005–6 (Freud subsequently joined the Cameron team in the House of Lords). The reforms, which include a simplification of welfare benefits and tougher penalties for those not taking work, will struggle to deliver lower public spending and shorter dole queues in times of sluggish growth. Having said this, the economic good times in the 1990s and 2000s did little to cut levels of welfare dependency. Fixing the broken society is going to be a long-term project whichever party is in power.

So, on a range of social policies, in particular health, education and social security, there is in Cameron's version of conservatism not only a positive commitment to the state (however much it might be in 'partnership' with the private and voluntary sectors as part of the 'big society'), but also a re-engagement with questions of poverty and social justice. Having moved the party on, and as his position became stronger, Cameron was able to combine these progressive political messages with more traditional Conservative ones, notably on support for marriage in the tax system and cutting inheritance tax. During the 2010 election, the party also campaigned hard on crime and immigration. None the less, Cameron Conservatives mark a shift away from the mix of economic liberalism and social conservatism that characterized Thatcherism to one in which the interests of property and enterprise are balanced with a more liberal and progressive social policy. This mix of social and economic liberalism provided the ideological opportunity for the 'liberal conservative' coalition with the Liberal Democrats – a party, as we shall see in chapter 5, that became more economically liberal under its leader Nick Clegg. But it is a mix too that potentially causes problems for Cameron with the right of his party, who do not like his modern and modernizing ideas; and who view with horror the coalition with the Lib Dems.

## Remaking the Conservative Party

In reforming his party, David Cameron relied on a laid-back, conversational style in public. But he was also accused of being a control freak: of centralizing power and authority in the party.[31] So, how has the party fared under Cameron?

As we saw in chapter 2, while the Conservatives took on some of the features of mass politics, card-carrying members had little say over the leadership of the party or its policies. The Tories were a 'hybrid party' welding mass twentieth-century politics to the elitism of the nineteenth-century scene. Party democracy was very limited. The leader in particular had wide-ranging powers over policy and political strategy, though these powers were always limited by the constraints imposed by cabinet and the parliamentary party organized through the backbench 1922 Committee. While the annual party conference in the 1990s became more of an opportunity to express dissatisfaction with the leadership of the party in areas such as European integration, it remains a tightly controlled media-driven event.

On the face of it, the selection of the party leader is one area in which the Conservative Party has become more democratic. Until the 1960s, a group of senior party figures picked the leader. In 1965, new rules were introduced giving MPs the choice of who led the party. In the 1970s and early 1990s, the size of the threshold of the number of MPs needed to force a leadership contest was increased from two members to 10 per cent of MPs. In 1998, this threshold was raised again to 15 per cent and, after an initial ballot of MPs, if there were more than two candidates, the final decision over who became leader would be made in a ballot of all party members, as we have seen. But the jury remains out on whether these new rules will stick. After Iain Duncan Smith's brief tenure of office, this Tory experiment in party democracy was not thought a success. Indeed, following IDS, Michael Howard became leader almost by proclamation. But Howard's attempt at removing the final decision on the leadership from members was defeated by, unsurprisingly, local members. The 2005 contest that saw David Cameron emerge triumphant over David Davis in the ballot of members was seen as a great advertisement for the Conservative Party. Whether future contests with less polished performers would be an equal success is a moot point.

Certainly these changes to the rules governing the leadership of the party reflect pressure from the Tory grassroots after the débâcle of the 1990s. Following the Conservative defeat in 1997, William Hague introduced other reforms in an attempt to unite the party. The Conservative Party has three parts: the political section made up of MPs and peers in parliament; the professional section of paid party officials and the central office in London; and the voluntary party consisting of the National Union of Conservative Associations (the local parties and members). Hague's reforms to the organization of the party created a new board to manage Conservative affairs, with particular responsibility for raising funds, membership and the policy of selecting candidates. Membership of the board is drawn from all three sections of the party, but only five are elected by grassroots members.

Party policy is also an area that appears to have more input from the membership. Under Hague, new policy forums were introduced to give members an opportunity to have their say. In 2002, this consultation was reworked under the party's 'policy renewal' process. The basic idea was that the leadership of the party could canvass the views of the grassroots on policy development through local meetings. Under David Cameron, as we have seen, policy development was given out to specialist groups that appeared to offer a more open and inclusive approach to policy-making. However, these groups were appointed by and accountable to the leadership of the party; and the leadership were under no obligation to accept their recommendations. So, while Conservative members appear to have more input into the policy-making process, the leadership of the party, as it always did, retains a firm grip. This top-down organizational structure of the party should, in theory, have made it easy to turn the Tories around after 1997. The fact it took more than a decade is a puzzle. In the end, the party still looked too ideological and split by warring factions – and the party leadership and its supporters in the media just didn't understand why this was so.[32]

In government, Cameron also sought to exercise greater control over his parliamentary backbenches. A proposal to change the rules of the 1922 Committee of backbenchers, to allow all Conservative MPs – including those holding ministerial posts, who are traditionally excluded from the committee when the party is in government – to be members, provoked uproar among his MPs. Backbenchers promptly voted Graham Brady, noted for his independence of mind, as chairman. Since 2005, Cameron has also sought to intervene more directly in the process of becoming an MP. Candidate selection is one area of Tory politics in which local parties long ago secured dominion. These powers are, in part, the result of the capacity of local parties to fundraise for the national party. But if Cameron wanted to widen the appeal of the party by broadening the backgrounds of Tory candidates, he would have to increase the power of Conservative Central Office over local parties. If the 'nasty party' was to become a little more inclusive, then white middle-class men might have to give way for more women and black and minority ethnic candidates representing the Tories in elections. Cameron was caught rather between two goods: more representative candidates and more active local parties.

Before the 2005 election, the Conservatives had gone some way to reforming the approval of party candidates by its Parliamentary Assessment Board in order to find new talent rather than just traditional Tories. Cameron took this a step further by establishing a 'priority list' – better known as the 'A list'. Essentially, this sought to find the top 100 new candidates, and should include a balance of men and women, as well as people from black and minority ethnic communities. Local parties, especially those in winnable seats, were expected to take their candidates from this centrally approved priority list. What impact did this policy have on the kind of person being selected as a Conservative candidate under David Cameron? According to one study,[33] the A list did work by 'substantially' increasing the number of women candidates selected for winnable seats. However, when the A list was replaced by a simple 50/50 rule requiring an equal number of men and women at all stages of the selection process, the number of female prospective parliamentary candidates dropped, largely because of the under-representation of women on the approved list of candidates. Still, while only 69 of the 331 prospective parliamentary candidates were women in 2009, a quarter of the party's top 100 target seats had a woman candidate; and half the seats where a sitting Conservative was standing down had a women candidate. This raised the prospect that, at the 2010 election, the number of women Tory MPs could jump from 17 to 50-plus.[34] In the end, 48 of the new intake of Conservative MPs were women. Still, at the 2009 national conference, Cameron got into difficulty with his all-male economics team – and the largely men-only feel of his leader's office. There remains a sense that the Conservative Party has a way to go to 'end the scandal of under-representation of women in the party', as Cameron put it in 2005.

But if Cameron had made some progress in the area of representation, the legacy of Mrs Thatcher was revealing itself in a survey by the Conservative website ConservativeHome in April 2009. The survey of 148 Conservative candidates in the most winnable seats suggested that the Cameron leadership of any new Tory government would face a new cohort of MPs on the right of the party on most issues. Indeed, as Cameron has taken the party to the liberal left on social issues and turned it greener on the environment, his parliamentary party has become more socially conservative, pro-business and, perhaps unsurprisingly, Euro-sceptic.[35] As Fraser Nelson, editor of the conservative weekly the *Spectator*, noted after the election, the typical new Tory MP was the type 'who has posters of Thatcher on the wall' – and who think they were elected 'despite David Cameron, not because of him'.[36]

## An uneasy alliance

After all the hard work of the previous five years, the result of the 2010 general election was a disappointment to the Conservatives. They were seen as a credible party of government – just not by quite enough voters. On a national swing of 5 per cent away from Labour, the Conservatives increased their share of the vote by 3.8 per cent on 2005 to 36.1 per cent; and seats by 97 to 307, 19 short of the winning post. But the result was not unexpected. The Tories had a proverbial mountain to climb, with a peak made so much tougher by the rise of multi-party politics. A hung parliament was always on the cards.

The post-election deal struck with the Liberal Democrats was something made possible, as we have seen in this chapter, by the ideological shifts the Conservatives have made post-Thatcherism. While the Conservative/Liberal Democrat coalition was the only option that had any kind of political legitimacy (the combined total of 364 seats comfortably held an overall majority in the House of Commons), there was an underlying philosophical rationale to the new government beyond all the talk of a 'new politics'. With David Cameron taking the Conservatives back towards the centre ground of politics with a mix of economic and social liberalism, and the Liberal Democrats, as we shall see in chapter 5, shifting to the right with their 'Orange book' liberalism, there was the opportunity for a realistic deal between the two parties.

This will not, however, be an easy ride for the Conservative Party, just as it won't be for the Liberal Democrats. With the ink barely dry on the coalition document agreed between the two parties in the days after the election, the blogosphere (and the *Daily Telegraph*) was full of 'real conservatives' venting their anger at what was seen as betrayal of true Tory principles. The government backbenches are not short of dissenting voices. Economic circumstances in 2010 demanded a fiscal conservatism that Cameron's critics in the party found hard to disagree with. But with the pro-European Liberal Democrats having put electoral reform on the coalition government's agenda, these are likely to be interesting times for the Conservative Party in the 2010s. As we shall see in the next chapter, Labour underwent more than a decade of change that fundamentally re-shaped the party. The question remains whether political change in the Conservative Party under David Cameron is skin-deep or not.[37] Only time will tell.

## Further reading and research resources

On the history of the Conservative Party, see Blake's *The Conservative Party from Peel to Major*. For the classic analysis of Thatcherism, see Gamble's *The Free Economy and the Strong State*. The leading Conservative politician David Willetts offers an excellent introduction to Tory thinking and practice in *Modern Conservatism* (Harmondsworth: Penguin, 1992). Norton's edited *The Conservative Party* helps in understanding the challenges facing the party in the 1990s. Bale's *The Conservative Party* is the essential guide to the rise of David Cameron. See also the *Political Quarterly* (80, 2, 2009, pp. 165–315), largely devoted to the prospects for the Conservatives before the 2010 general election. The Conservative Party can be found online at www.conservatives.com/; and the best place to start exploring the Tory blogosphere is http://conservativehome. blogs.com/. How the Conservative/Liberal coalition is faring in government is explored in Simon Lee and Matt Beech's edited collection, *The Cameron–Clegg Government: Coalition Politics in the Age of Austerity* (Basingstoke: Palgrave, 2011).

# CHAPTER FOUR

# 'New Labour' and the Labour Party

All political parties change – and in the 1990s, the Labour Party changed more than most. The old Labour Party became 'New Labour'; and under the leadership of Tony Blair it came to dominate party politics in Britain for more than a decade. This was quite a turnaround. For a while it had looked like Labour might never get a chance again to run the country. Defeat in the 1992 general election led some analysts to doubt the party's long-term chance of success.[1] So, what led to this transformation of political fortunes? And in becoming a party that won – not lost – elections, was Labour still a *labour* party – a party on the centre left of British politics?

This chapter will examine how the Labour Party fell apart in the 1970s and 1980s, particularly in the face of Margaret Thatcher's resurgent Conservative Party. The chapter then explores how Labour responded to the challenge of Thatcherism and, under the leadership of Tony Blair and Gordon Brown, managed successfully to find a politics after Thatcherism – 'New Labour'. With defeat in the 2010 general election, the end of the chapter assesses the future prospects for Labour as it faces another spell in opposition.

## Defeat from the jaws of victory

The 1990s started well for the Labour Party. The Conservatives ditched their leader Margaret Thatcher, and Labour was well ahead in the opinion polls: a ten-point lead for most of 1990. Approaching the general election in April 1992, Labour still led in the polls. With the economy in recession, expectations of a Labour victory were high. A week before the election, in a mood of triumphalism, the party held a rally in Sheffield. Neil Kinnock, the Labour leader, arrived by helicopter, cheered on by banner-waving activists. The shadow cabinet were introduced as the 'government in waiting'. Hubris. The polling organizations had got it wrong. Voters, it was discovered later, were embarrassed to admit they might support the Tories. As the election results started to come in after the polls had closed, the call of 'Conservative hold' in Basildon, Essex, a key marginal seat – and bellwether, as Americans say, for Thatcher's Britain – was enough to signal that this wasn't going to be Labour's night. John Major's Conservative Party won more votes than Mrs Thatcher's had ever done (nearly 14.5 million). The Tories took 41.9 per cent of a high-turnout vote (nearly 78 per cent). Labour managed just 34.4 per cent – more or less where it had been on average since 1974.

Defeat for the Labour Party, as one critical study put it, had been snatched from the jaws of victory.[2] Kinnock resigned. He had done much as leader since 1983, as we shall see in this chapter, to pull his party back from the political brink. But as John Smith, the shadow chancellor, took over as leader, the future of the Labour Party as a serious political player was in the balance. Would 'one more heave' be enough to take the party into government? After all, Labour had fought two reasonably good election campaigns and was within touching distance of the Conservative Party in terms of parliamentary seats. Or would political change in the Labour Party have to go further and deeper?

## The pressures of catch-all politics

The political problems facing Labour in the 1990s were neither new nor ones that could be addressed easily. As we saw in chapter 1, British society was changing – and with it the country's political sociology. Old patterns of male, unionized, manufacturing employment were in long decline. The political loyalties and identities attached to these patterns of work were disappearing too. Class attachment of voters to parties, while not disappearing entirely, was eroding. Partisan de-alignment was re-wiring political behaviour. Voters were becoming more likely to shop around between political parties. And those parts of the electorate that mattered in the marginal seats of Britain, in particular the lower middle and skilled working classes, that had been drawn to Thatcherism in the 1980s and kept the Conservative Party in power for over a decade, looked like staying put. Labour somehow had to get to these voters.

The new political sociology of modern Britain was stacking the deck against the Labour Party. Labour activists might find comfort (usually in defeat) in election results that showed more people supporting Labour and the Liberals than the Conservative Party. This is a dangerous solace as it assumes that Labour and Liberal voters are interchangeable, when they are not, as we see in chapter 5. The electoral base of any 'progressive alliance' between the two parties is fragile at best. The hard truth in the early 1990s was that Labour faced an electorate with more core Conservative voters than Labour ones. These electoral numbers meant that if Labour was to have any chance of winning outright, the party would have to perform at the very top of its post-war range and the Conservatives at the very bottom of theirs. To form a government, in other words, the Labour Party had to mobilize its own supporters, shrinking in number and changing in character, and appeal beyond its class roots to non-Labour voters, especially in those parts of the south of England where the Conservatives were dominant. No wonder party reformers urged Labour to find a bit of 'southern comfort'.[3]

Labour, in other words, would have to stop being a mass party rooted in the working class and become a catch-all party capable of building a coalition of support from across the social spectrum. 'One more heave' would not be enough, these modernizers argued. More radical change was needed.

Wind forward five years. Tony Blair is the new Labour prime minister standing on the steps of Number Ten with his young family waving to the cameras and crowds of party workers. The Labour Party had just won a stunning victory in the May general election. With 43 per cent of the popular vote, Labour secured a 179-seat majority in the House of Commons. As James Callaghan, the last Labour prime minister before Blair, put it: 'This is like 1945 – but in space.'

The comparison with Clement Attlee's post-war Labour government was an obvious one. In 1945, Labour won by a mile (nearly 48 per cent of the vote and a 146-seat majority in the House of Commons). But the rapid collapse of the Labour government after the 1950 general election, which it won narrowly, makes the political success of Blair's Labour Party even more remarkable. The 1997 election victory was followed by the equally decisive win in 2001. Labour romped home with 41 per cent of the vote and a 167-seat majority. The Conservatives managed to gain just one extra seat. And while at the 2005 poll Labour's majority was slashed by 100-odd seats and its share of the vote fell to 37 per cent (an all-time low for a winning party in contemporary British politics), the party won what it had never won before: a third consecutive term in government.

So how had the Labour Party become a serial winner of general elections after being such a serial loser? How had it managed to overturn the political dominance of the Conservative Party? To begin to answer these questions, it is worth going back in time to when the Labour Party came close to tearing itself apart.

## The seeds of discontent

Labour's defeat at the hands of Margaret Thatcher in 1979 sparked a no-holds-barred factional fight inside the party. The seeds of this discontent had been sown in the previous decade. The late 1960s and 1970s were difficult times economically, socially and politically for Britain as the long post-war boom came to an end. Under its leader Harold Wilson, prime minister between 1964 and 1970 and again in 1974 until his resignation in 1976, the Labour Party first grew restless, then rebellious. Labour lost the 1970 election when many thought it would win. The party outside parliament pressed its claims for more power over party affairs. A growing number of left-wing members on the party's ruling body, the National Executive Committee (NEC), and a new generation of more militant trade union leaders, such as Jack Jones of the Transport Workers, supported these claims. Wilson had already alienated many in the trade unions with his government's proposals, in the 1969 white paper *In Place of Strife*, for the reform of industrial relations. The document was an attempt by Wilson's government to create a more manageable framework for employers and employees. In the end, all it did was expose how unmanageable the Labour Party was becoming. Wilson couldn't get the policy past the NEC or even his backbench MPs. Tony Benn, who for the next ten years or more would be the pivotal figure on the Labour left, led the calls for the NEC to be given control over not just the party's internal affairs, such as overseeing the selection of candidates and election campaigning, but also the development of policy.

As a result Labour went into the first of the 1974 general elections with a left-wing manifesto that put nationalization back on the party's political agenda, for the first time really since 1945. The influence of the left over significant areas of policy-making was made possible by the divisions on the right wing of the party on the question of the European Economic Community, which Britain joined in 1973. The February poll, called by Prime Minister Edward Heath in the face of growing union unrest, was more or less a draw. The Conservatives won more votes, Labour more seats. Heath hung on hoping for a pact with the Liberals, but, in the end, only Labour could claim any sort of majority in the House of Commons. But this couldn't hold and a second election was called for October. Labour, still led by Wilson, managed an overall majority of just four.

Labour's term in government, first under Wilson, then James Callaghan, was increasingly unstable. By 1976 Britain's economic situation was deteriorating rapidly. Chancellor of the Exchequer Denis Healey announced cuts in public expenditure for the following year. At the autumn party conference, Prime Minister Callaghan renounced the Keynesian economics that had underpinned Labour's post-war social democratic politics. As the pound fell on world markets, Britain applied to the International Monetary Fund for a loan to support sterling. The condition for the loan was a further cut in public expenditure and a ceiling on public borrowing and the money supply. This horrified both the radical left in the party led by Benn, and the old-style Keynesian social democrats such as Tony Crosland on the right who had done so much to shape Labour politics since the 1950s. By the spring of 1977, the government had also lost its working majority in the House of Commons and Labour negotiated a formal agreement with the Liberal Party for support in parliament. This 'Lib–Lab pact' would last until July 1978.

The Labour government faced other problems as well. It had been elected in 1974 partly because it offered voters peace with the trade unions. The support – or otherwise – from trade union leaders, however, became increasingly irrelevant as militancy on local shop floors grew. Callaghan's government struggled on through 1978 when it should have called a general election it had some chance of winning – it was ahead in the opinion polls. Instead, a 'winter of discontent' saw unions striking – in particular, poorly paid public sector workers. Infamously, rubbish was left uncollected on the streets, and the dead in Liverpool unburied. This was the final nail in the coffin for Labour as a governing party – at least, for nearly two decades. 'Labour isn't working' claimed the Tories on their election posters. The Keynesian social democratic era that Labour had done so much to shape was unravelling fast. Thatcherism would finish it off.

Labour's defeat by the Conservatives in the 1979 general election nearly finished the party off as well. The election saw a significant swing of support from Labour to the Tories. Not only was the electorate at large turning against Labour (this was the third successive poll when it gained less than 40 per cent of the vote), but so too were the working class (only 48 per cent supported Labour in 1979). As we saw in the last chapter, Margaret Thatcher's Conservative Party was attracting voters from across the social spectrum – in particular, considerable numbers of skilled working-class voters critical to winning marginal seats across Britain. The Labour Party was out of touch with voters in Britain.[4] But with the economy nose-diving, the popularity of the new Tory government was short-lived. Despite this, Labour turned in on itself. The party's ideological factions went to war with each other. Left-wingers accused the leadership of selling out: of failing to implement the radical 1974 manifesto agreed by the party as a whole. The Labour right responded that the left's programme was not only economically illogical but also politically insane. It made the party unelectable.

These were not dry academic arguments about the relative merits of competing political ideas. This was about power and ideology: who controlled the party and what Labour should do once it held power. Central to these debates were the main players in Labour politics: the MPs at Westminster, the activists in local parties and, above all, the trade unions who bankrolled the party and who dominated the party's decision-making processes.

## Party, power and ideology

The Labour Party was founded by Britain's well-established trade unions in 1900 as the Labour Representative Committee to advance the interests of working-class people in parliament (see box 4.1). The new party brought the trade unions together with socialist societies (in particular, the Fabians) and the Independent Labour and Cooperative parties into a federal structure. Labour's founders were by and large reformers, drawing heavily on the Fabian political tradition. This rejected revolution and sought to build socialism through progressive social reform organized through parliament. Trade unions – and what is often called the labour movement – are fundamental to studies of the Labour Party. To use the distinction made by H. M. Drucker, if the Fabians and other socialist thinkers provided the 'doctrine' of the Labour Party – the ideology that shaped what the party wanted to achieve in government – then the trade unions and the working-class communities in which they were rooted provided the party's 'ethos', the 'myths

## Box 4.1 Origins of the Labour Party

The Labour Party, founded in 1900 as the Labour Representative Committee, was in part rooted in radical politics dating back to the Chartists in the 1830s. Socialist activists (including Karl Marx's daughter Eleanor) formed the Marxist-inspired Social Democratic Federation and the Socialist League in the 1880s. In 1888 the Scottish Labour Party was founded, followed by the Independent Labour Party (ILP) in 1893. But unlike socialist activists in other parts of Europe, British activists such as Keir Hardie, a leading figure in the ILP, found the going rather harder (the main social democratic party in Germany today, the SPD, was founded in 1875). Trade unions were not only legal in Britain but also well established, often with close connections with the Liberal Party. Union leaders looked to these Liberal links in parliament to advance the interests of working-class people in government. By the end of the century, however, the political mood was changing. The expansion of trade unions in the 1880s and 1890s shifted the balance of interest and power away from the highly skilled and well-paid craft workers to more semi-skilled and unskilled workforces. A new generation of trade union leaders was becoming more militant in their demands for those they represented. As a consequence, by the turn of the century, many unions were looking for a more direct influence in parliament, including the election of working-class MPs.

*Further reading*: Shaw, *The Labour Party since 1945*; Donald Sassoon, *One Hundred Years of Socialism: The Western European Left in the Twentieth Century* (London: I. B. Tauris, 1996).

and memories' of a shared exploitation and struggle for recognition. In this sense, the Labour Party looked forward to a New Jerusalem *and* backward to a shared history.[5]

The importance of trade unions to the Labour Party is shown by their position within the decision-making structures of the party – in particular, at the annual conference and on the National Executive Committee (NEC) – even if they have rarely exercised these powers to the full.[6] The trade unions also provide the bulk of the party's funds and the organizational capacity to mobilize voters at election time. For much of the post-war period – during the Attlee government after 1945; during the reforming leadership of Hugh Gaitskell in opposition in the 1950s; and during Wilson's government in the 1960s – Labour's trade union barons tended to side with the party leadership: their main concerns were to maintain the unions' legal privileges (such as free collective bargaining in wage negotiations) rather than advance a more radical socialist agenda. When the Labour leadership looked like reneging on these rights, union leaders dug their heels in. Otherwise, party and trade union leaders alike shared a similar world view that was anti-communist and supportive of a mixed economy. This, perhaps, was not surprising given that many unions, such as the electricians and engineers, were rooted in private sector businesses. They opposed nationalization and wanted to work with, rather than against, management.

However, during the 1960s and 1970s there was a shift to the left among trade unions, in particular the transport workers and the miners, as well as an upsurge of local trade unionism that union leaders could do little to control. By the end of the 1970s, the left-wing block of unions had been considerably reinforced by public sector unions. This block had grown in the post-war years on the back of the expansion of local government and the welfare state. Some of these public sector unions represented the many poorly paid and generally unskilled workers in the public sector. Other unions, not always affiliated to the Labour Party, were made up of public employees in often highly skilled occupations in teaching, public administration and the health service. These union members, joining the party as individuals, saw Labour as a vehicle for extending welfare rights.

To summarize, the Labour Party had sprung up to represent and articulate the interests and opinions of working-class people. In the post-war period, Labour also came to represent the interests and opinions of a broader group of people working in Britain's ever-expanding public sector. But cutting across these social cleavages were ideological divides about what the Labour Party should be doing once it got into power. Broadly speaking, the party divided on left/right lines on political economy: what role the state should take in the economic affairs of the country. The left believed a Labour government should, through state planning and nationalization, take a controlling interest in the main sectors of the economy. The right, by contrast, thought a mixed economy should be based on a thriving and profitable private sector; and the role of a Labour government was to manage demand in the economy according to Keynesian principles and to promote investment in industry through an industrial policy and commercially run state corporations. During much of the post-war period, Labour politics was dominated by the trade union right and Fabian-inspired social democrats, in particular, led by Hugh Gaitskell and Tony Crosland. But during the 1970s and 1980s, Labour politics was increasingly influenced by the combined weight of the trade union and welfare state left. It was around the question of leadership that the battle between left and right focused following defeat in the 1979 general election.

## A question of leadership

Defeat in the 1979 general election left the Labour Party and its leadership weakened and demoralized. In its aftermath, the question of party democracy dominated Labour's internal power struggle. The left wanted the leadership of the party in parliament to be held to account by the wider party, as represented at the national conference and in local constituency parties – the CLPs. Labour's new leader Michael Foot had a long history on the left. But he now desperately sought to bring peace to the party. Foot was elected under the old rules that left the vote to the parliamentary party. The national party then agreed a new set of rules for leadership contests in early 1981. An electoral college would be set up that gave 30 per cent of votes to MPs, 30 per cent to the CLPs and 40 per cent to the trade unions. Sitting MPs would also be subject to mandatory re-selection by their local parties.

All this was too much for some on the right of the party who saw these new rules as consolidating the power of what they viewed as unrepresentative local activists and left-wing trade unions over the party. The founding of the Social Democratic Party (SDP) by Roy Jenkins, Shirley Williams, David Owen and Bill Rodgers, all senior Labour figures, opened a new chapter in British party politics (see also chapter 5). This so-called 'gang of four' looked across the Channel to a more European model of social democracy. They believed the centre left in Britain had to re-think the mixed economy, the provision of welfare and the role of the private sector in driving economic growth. The formation of the SDP, and its alliance with the Liberal Party, created an electoral headache for Labour. With the new party attracting massive attention in the media, Labour found itself competing with the SDP (and the Liberals) for the anti-Conservative vote. Almost immediately the SDP was polling in the teens; and an alliance with the Liberals later in 1981 brought a combined poll rating of well over 40 per cent. There were many in the Labour Party who complained bitterly that the SDP was keeping the Tories in power; but whether voters who supported the Alliance would have otherwise voted Labour at the time is another matter.

Back in the Labour Party, with the new leadership election rules in place, Tony Benn challenged Denis Healey for the deputy leadership of the party. Healey was the standard-bearer of the Labour right, a stalwart of the Manifesto Group of MPs, but not the easiest of characters. The election was then – and looking back now – crucial to the political development of the Labour Party over the next decade or more. It was for two reasons. First, Benn lost – though only just. Second, some on the left didn't vote for him. In the longer term, the result contributed to what became known as the 'realignment of the left': a split between a 'hard left' of MPs, party activists and trade unionists who had supported Benn; and a 'soft left' who didn't, or, in the future, wouldn't. Those for Benn were led by the Socialist Campaign Group of MPs that had been set up to support him. The group was a rival to the traditional home of left-wing politics in the party, Tribune. Significantly, one leading member of Tribune, Neil Kinnock, opposed Benn's move to become deputy leader.

Despite Benn's defeat, the 1983 general election manifesto was militantly left-wing. Based on the party's Alternative Economic Strategy, Labour's campaign supported nationalization, economic planning, the extension of welfare rights and withdrawal from the European Community. The party also was committed to unilateral nuclear disarmament and a shift away from NATO. It was, said the right-wing Labour MP Gerald Kaufman famously, the 'longest suicide note in history'. The result of the 1983 general election, a win by the Tories on the back of victory in the Falklands War, was a humiliation for Labour. The party only narrowly missed being pushed into third place by the Liberal/SDP Alliance. Support for the Labour Party was rapidly becoming a rump: a party whose support had shrunk back to its urban heartlands in the north of England, Scotland and Wales. If Labour was ever going to challenge the Conservatives again, something had to change.

## The road from 1983

The reform of the Labour Party that ended with Tony Blair's victory at the 1997 general election more or less begins in 1983. Labour's next leader was Neil Kinnock – a politician, like Foot, from the Tribune left. His deputy was Roy Hattersley from the Fabian wing of the party, whom Kinnock had beaten to the leadership. Hattersley, a protégé of Tony Crosland, had stuck around in 1981 when his fellow social democrats jumped ship. Kinnock had also beaten, by some margin, the candidate from the Bennite wing of the party, Eric Heffer. Kinnock and Hattersley promised to be a dream team for party reformers that cut across party divides. Indeed, as time passed, the hard left Campaign Group of MPs became increasingly isolated. Significantly, while the question of reform divided Tribune, the group came to represent the soft left, willing both to work with a reforming leadership and to countenance policy changes. Tribune was also the chosen group of newer MPs such as Tony Blair, Gordon Brown and Jack Straw who had little in common with the old left. As Eric Shaw argues, the polarization between left and right that had dominated Labour politics during the 1970s and early 1980s looked set, by the mid 1980s, to 'unravel'.[7] This might not be peace, but it did offer Labour a chance to move on.

However, the early years of Kinnock's leadership were not easy ones. The events dominating Kinnock's first period in office did much to shape Labour politics in the mid 1980s. The first was the strike in 1984–5 by the National Union of Mineworkers (NUM) against the planned closures of pits by the National Coal Board, a nationalized industry. The dispute had widespread support on the left; it was seen by many as a government-orchestrated assault on the whole labour movement. Kinnock, however, did not see it quite this way. Reformers in labour circles believed the kind of extra-parliamentary politics represented by the NUM was causing huge damage to the image of the Labour Party and to its legitimacy as a party that could represent the nation as a whole. None of this was helped by the fact that the NUM leader, Arthur Scargill, refused to hold a strike ballot that might itself have given some legitimacy to the strike in the eyes of the wider public. Kinnock, for political reasons, was wary of speaking out. His position was precarious. But the defeat for the miners, though ostensibly a defeat for the left, in the longer term played into Labour reformers' hands by discrediting the political tactics employed by the NUM.

What further played into Kinnock's hands was the question of the Militant Tendency. Militant, as we see in chapter 7, was a far left Trotskyite group who operated, in effect, as a party within the Labour Party. Michael Foot had attempted without much success to tame Militant by changing the rulebook on organizations permitted to operate inside the party. Kinnock took on Militant. When the Militant-controlled Labour council in Liverpool handed out redundancy notices to council workers in the hope this would force the government to back down on its attempts to control local government finance, Kinnock seized the moment. He gave an electrifying speech at the 1985 Labour Party conference on the 'impossible promises' of the left, denouncing Militant and its tactics, that drew applause from virtually all sections of the party. It was Kinnock's finest hour as party leader.

These two events contributed in the longer term to the reassertion of the power of the leadership within the party; and the organizational changes, including the new rules to expel party members, supported this. To Kinnock, this increasingly empowered leadership was about presenting Labour as a moderate, modern 'democratic socialist' party. And to help this presentation of what would one day be called 'New Labour', Kinnock turned to help from outside politics to reform the party's campaigning and communications operations.

## The power of spin

Defeat in the 1983 election had sent shock waves through the party leadership. Labour was clearly out of step with public opinion in large parts of the country. The party machine, many thought, had to become more professional. With the appointment of Peter Mandelson as the party's communications director in 1985, Labour discovered the power of spin. Before his appointment, Mandelson worked for the old ITV franchise London Weekend Television. As we saw in the last chapter, this was not the first time a major British political party had looked to television for help: Margaret Thatcher employed another TV producer, Gordon Reece, to run her party's publicity machine in 1978. But Mandelson was no hired gun. He had a Labour Party pedigree as a grandson of Herbert Morrison, a senior minister in the Attlee government.

With Mandelson, the Labour Party became an increasingly effective and professional campaigning and communications machine, using techniques drawn from the worlds of advertising, marketing and the media. The party started doing rather simple things such as commissioning research on public opinion and finding out whether campaigns might work with voters before they were finalized. Labour also became far more conscious of the image of the party across the electorate, especially with those voters with little or no partisan attachment to it. If Labour was ever going to win over those parts of the electorate which had lined up behind the Conservatives in 1979 and 1983, the leadership believed, it needed not only to understand these voters but also to be much more careful (and controlling) about how it used the mass media to get its message across. This meant hiring more guns with some background in the communications world.

All this strengthened the hand of the party leadership by centralizing control over how Labour put its message across to voters. The political professionals answered to the party leadership, through the Shadow Communications Agency, and had the resources and expertise to give the leadership what it wanted. The poor old party activist was sidelined. Professionalization also drove reform. Policies and campaigns were road-tested with voters. Those that failed this test, especially after defeat in the 1987 election, could more easily be dropped as voter-losers – and who in their right minds wanted more of these? Those in the party rather attached to these policies were, not unreasonably, aghast. All this market-testing was eroding Labour's traditional commitments to building socialism.

The Conservative victory in 1987 – after a communications campaign many thought Labour had won – was the final straw. Beautifully crafted party political broadcasts needed to be backed up by something more substantive: a serious review of party policy.

### Policy review

Between 1983 and 1987, there were few real substantive changes to party policy. But Labour's third election defeat in 1987, massive in terms of seats in the House of Commons and only marginally better on the share of the vote, marked a turning point in the party's search for the centre ground in British politics. A policy review was begun that led to significant shifts in policy in the 1992 general election manifesto. On the economy, the party became increasingly pro-market, limiting the role of government to the enforcement of competition and to mitigating market failures by policies in areas such as training and regional development. Labour's commitment to the renationalization of the privatized utilities – or, for that matter, public ownership at all – disappeared. Increased spending on welfare was to be financed from economic growth, except for pensions and child benefits, for which top tax rates would be increased. Trade union legislation would remain largely in place. And what was perceived as the party's albatross during the 1987 election, unilateral nuclear disarmament, was buried.

The policy review also saw the disappearance of Keynesian demand management and the withdrawal from the European Community. In their place the Labour leadership, in particular the shadow chancellor, John Smith, advocated stable macro-economic management and membership of the European exchange rate mechanism. Such fiscal conservatism caused division inside the reform camp between Smith and his shadow treasury team (including Gordon Brown) and older-style Keynesians, such as Bryan Gould, who also wanted the party to develop a more interventionist industrial policy. Gould's later defeat by Smith for the leadership of the party after the 1992 general election represented the growing ascendancy within the party of arguments that saw the defeat of inflation and the creation of stable economic conditions as the central goal of macro-economic policy, whether or not (and it proved to be the latter) Britain adopted the euro.

The policy review transformed the Labour Party's 1992 manifesto – and paved the way for New Labour. It didn't, however, prevent the party going down in defeat to John Major's Conservatives, as we saw at the start of the chapter.

## Tony Blair, Gordon Brown and New Labour

Following Labour's defeat in 1992, Kinnock resigned and John Smith won the election to be leader. The political tide started to turn against the Tories. The old adage that oppositions don't win elections, governments lose them, was proving right. Having won an election mid-recession, the Conservatives threw away their reputation for sound economic management on 16 September 1992 (Black Wednesday) when Britain was forced out of the European exchange rate mechanism (ERM). The fact that Labour also supported Britain's membership of the ERM was lost on voters who increasingly saw the Conservatives as untrustworthy and out of touch. While the pound's exit from the ERM proved the making of the British economic revival in the 1990s, Major's government never recovered. The Conservative Party was divided over Europe, mired in scandal and behind in the opinion polls. Under John Smith, Labour looked increasingly like a government in waiting.

The sudden death of Smith in May 1994 propelled Tony Blair into the national spotlight. At only forty-one, Blair appealed to those parts of the British electorate that Labour needed to win over if it was to have any chance of forming a government. This was partly a question of background. Tony Blair just wasn't very Labour Party. His father, Leo Blair, was a lawyer and a Conservative. Despite family setbacks due to his father's ill health, Tony Blair went to private school, then Oxford. This was hardly unusual in a Labour politician. But it is the manner of Blair's political choice, as he himself has emphasized, that makes Blair different. He was not particularly political at school or university – more famous for being in a band, Ugly Rumours. One of Blair's biographers, John Rentoul, suggests the future prime minister got into politics not as a career move but 'as the vehicle for his moral commitment'.[8] Christianity and Christian socialism at St John's College Oxford took Blair to the left, though not immediately into the Labour Party or the university Labour club. Even many of the future prime minister's contemporaries at Oxford were unaware of his political awakening. Blair did join the Labour Party – in 1975, the year he left university.

Before Blair could be elected leader of the Labour Party nineteen years later, he had to deal with his great comrade – though it is unlikely that Blair would have ever called him such – Gordon Brown. The two of them were, as the late Tory diarist Alan Clark dubbed them, Labour's 'two bright boys'. Under Kinnock and then Smith, Brown and Blair had been given ever more senior jobs in Labour's opposition government. By 1994, Brown was shadow chancellor; Blair, shadow home secretary.

But as Brown's star waned ever so slightly as shadow chancellor after 1992, Blair's was on the up. The shadow home secretary's claim that Labour would be 'tough on crime, tough on the causes of crime' struck a chord with voters. Blair had a knack of not sounding like a Labour politician, something Gordon Brown found far harder. Again, there is the question of background. Unlike Blair, Brown had never chosen Labour, Labour had chosen him. He was born and bred to the party. Brown was a student politician at university and embroiled in the devolution debates in Scotland during the Callaghan government (Brown was pro-devolution). In 1976 at the age of twenty-five he was selected as prospective Labour candidate for Edinburgh South, losing at the 1979 election. But Gordon Brown had already done enough to mark himself out as a man with a big political future.

The death of John Smith in May 1994 turned Gordon Brown and Tony Blair into rivals. Certainly Brown would have expected to succeed Smith: to lead the Labour Party and then become prime minister. This was Brown's ambition when he entered parliament in 1983; and it was still his ambition in 1994. But the political realities of the mid 1990s meant that it was Blair who was chosen, not Brown. Blair was not just the rising star. He was a Westminster politician who could reach out to the electorate in the country at large, especially to those voters who were not natural Labour supporters. But, whatever tensions were created between the two rivals and their camps that would surface again and again over the next decade, there was now a unified ticket for the modernizers in the party. What brought Blair and Brown together was the sense that Labour could reform its politics and its policies without compromising its fundamental principles. The party could draw on its stock of political traditions, ethical socialism, Christian socialism, social liberalism, revisionist social democracy, and values (principally equality and social justice) and rework them to suit the contemporary world.

## Clause IV

On 21 July 1994 Tony Blair was elected leader of the Labour Party. Three months later at the party's annual conference in Blackpool, 'New Labour' was unveiled. The Labour Party was about to acquire a new name by constant repetition. The message was that Labour had a new leader and a new party – and that, by implication, they weren't 'old Labour' (whatever that might be). Blair's first target was Clause IV of the party's constitution (Clause IV, part four, to be precise). Printed on the back of every membership card, the clause committed Labour to the traditional socialist goal of common or public ownership. To most party members, it represented a vague aspiration of creating a different kind of society: one that put people's needs before the profits of private business. Exactly what this meant in terms of public policy had long

### Box 4.2 The old Clause IV

To secure for the workers by hand or by brain the full fruits of their industry and the most equitable distribution thereof that may be possible upon the basis of the common ownership of the means of production, distribution and exchange, and the best obtainable system of popular administration and control of each industry or service.

been a matter of fierce debate on the left. There was, none the less, a nostalgic attachment to the clause, like singing 'The Red Flag' or calling other party members 'comrade'. In his first conference speech as party leader, Blair insisted that Labour had to 'stop saying what we don't mean and start saying what we do mean'. Clause IV had to go. It committed Labour to something it didn't believe in or have any intention of putting into practice.

In the new constitution, agreed by the party at a special conference in April 1995, Labour abandoned the idea that the role of the left was to replace the market with public ownership. Both private and public sectors had their place in ensuring a society that balanced wealth creation and social justice. The new Clause IV committed the party to 'common endeavour' in pursuit of the realization of individual potential; and declared that power, wealth and opportunity should be 'in the hands of the many not the few'.

This was all too much for left-wingers inside the party and out. Values were not enough to define the left. Socialism challenged the capitalist market order or it was nothing. The change of constitution, critics argued, simply consolidated the party's drift towards Thatcherism and its neo-liberal politics.

No doubt the rewriting of Clause IV is important in the sense that it is a moment of confession – Labour's 'There Is No Alternative' to market capitalism. With the collapse of the Soviet Union in 1989, such a statement was inevitable. It was also, arguably, not before time: the German social democrats, for example, had adopted markets and private ownership at their 1959 Bad Godesberg congress. The British Labour Party was certainly not alone in revising its political vision in the 1990s. Across Europe, social democrats debated what model of capitalism could best serve the political ambitions of the left. After the fall of communism, these 'neo-revisionists', as Donald Sassoon called them, believed there was no suitable socialist economic model, only a form of capitalism that could combine efficiency, prosperity *and* social justice.[9]

It is also misleading to think that Clause IV encapsulated what the Labour Party – and social democracy – stood for. It overstates the importance of the old Clause IV, and the critique of private property it expresses, to the Labour Party. Labour has traditionally been a social democratic party. This means Labour was committed to liberal democratic forms of political action to reform, not abolish, market capitalism. This is best expressed in terms of a mixed economy, Keynesian economics and the provision of public services and redistributive income transfers as part of a welfare state. Labour's modernizers, as well as a number of political commentators, see New Labour firmly within this revisionist social democratic tradition. Critics of New Labour insist the party has been taken beyond the bounds of social democracy to some kind of neo-liberal or conservative politics. But simply getting rid of the old Clause IV did not mark some crossing of a socialist Rubicon for the Labour Party. It misrepresents what 'old Labour' was and what New Labour was to become.

## 'Old Labour', 'New Labour'?

While it is tempting to see the unveiling of New Labour and the abolition of the old Clause IV as marking something new – the start of a great divide between 'Old Labour' and 'New Labour' – such a view is a mistake. Certainly the idea of 'New Labour' proved a key weapon in Labour's armoury of political communications. It allowed the self-styled modernizers to project to voters an image of a future Labour government that would not be like any old Labour government. Labour's record in government in the 1960s and 1970s was air-brushed from the political debate. Only the 1945–50 Labour administration – 'the greatest peacetime government this century', Blair said in 1995 – could safely be evoked in the spirit of New Labour. With political memories of the 1970s still reasonably fresh, Labour had to send a signal to voters that a Labour administration led by them would not make the same mistakes as past Labour governments, especially in terms of its management of the economy.

All this juggling of political language led some to suggest that New Labour was all style and no substance. Certainly, the rebranding of the Labour Party is part of the professionalization of politics in which image and presentation have become more and more important to party competition. The Labour Party in the 1990s, building on the work of the Shadow Communications Agency, took political communications to new levels. The exploits of the spin-doctors in the party's Millbank Tower headquarters in Westminster – led by Alastair Campbell (for Blair) and Charlie Whelan (for Brown) – have entered British political folklore. As we saw earlier in the book, the professionalization of parties has made such figures, as well as the hired guns more generally, much more powerful in politics. But whatever Labour's spin-meisters got up to before (and after) the 1997 general election, there were important shifts in the party's thinking on key areas of policy. New Labour did have substance, whatever your views on its merits.

The novelty value of New Labour in the 1990s, of course, served to exaggerate the divide between Labour, new and old. If there is a 'New Labour', there must, by logical argument, be an 'Old Labour'. In the cut and thrust of Labour politics, Old Labour became short-hand for what were thought to be the sins of post-war Labour governments. Being Old Labour meant an attachment to too much state intervention; to tax-and-spend public policy; and to a social liberalism that put rights above responsibilities. Being New Labour meant having a critical attitude to the power of governments to intervene in the economy and society; proposing limits on taxation and public spending; and asserting that the rights of citizens (especially to welfare) should be balanced with responsibilities (in particular, to find work). Time would prove New Labour just as keen on spending public money as Old Labour – and almost as interventionist. But back in the mid 1990s, the Labour Party had to prove it had changed.

So while binary distinctions between old and new served the cause of Labour reformers in the 1990s, they have limited explanatory power. To begin with, the idea of there being a single Old Labour – even if this is limited to the post-war years – is flawed. On the key issues of state intervention, fiscal policy and welfare rights, as well as other areas of defence, European and foreign policy, there have long been important debates within the Labour Party about the best way forward. Labour, past and present, is an organization with a complex mix of cultures and traditions that resists simple classification.[10] Moreover, as Tim Bale argues, what so-called Old Labour said and what it actually did are not necessarily the same thing – and the same can be said of New Labour.[11] The old/new dichotomy serves to exaggerate the coherence of New Labour, just as it does past Labour governments. New Labour is better thought of as a political composite than as a unified 'project'.

## The New Labour electoral coalition

At the heart of New Labour's political strategy was the building of a political coalition between working- and middle-class voters capable of tearing away the Conservative Party's grip on power. This consolidated Labour's shift from a mass to a catch-all party, drawing support from a wide slice of British society.[12]

The results from the 1997 general election show how successful this catch-all strategy was. To a certain extent the Conservatives lost simply for being Tories – and for being the party that had been in power for eighteen years. The electorate was ready for a change.[13] But Labour was also remarkably successful at winning over English Conservative and swing voters, especially in the marginal constituencies where the election battle would be won. It was these votes that Labour won in 1997 – or, at least, it was these voters who deserted the Conservative Party for Labour or the Liberal Democrats (tactical voting playing a small part in the scale of Labour's win) or who didn't vote at all. Compared with the 1992 election, Labour's overall vote was up 9 points and its share of the vote among all demographic groups was up, as figure 4.1 shows.

The 2001 election confirmed the success of New Labour's electoral strategy of welding together a coalition of working- and middle-class voters. Indeed, the voter in the middle chased by all mainstream parties felt closer to Labour

| | Conservative | Labour | Lib Dems |
|---|---|---|---|
| **Men** | 31 (41) | 45 (35) | 17 (18) |
| **Women** | 32 (44) | 44 (34) | 18 (18) |
| **AB (middle class)** | 41 (56) | 31 (19) | 22 (22) |
| **C1 (lower middle class)** | 37 (52) | 37 (25) | 18 (20) |
| **C2 (skilled workers)** | 27 (39) | 50 (40) | 16 (17) |
| **DE (unskilled workers)** | 21 (31) | 59 (49) | 13 (16) |
| **Age 18-24** | 27 (35) | 49 (38) | 16 (19) |
| **Age 25-34** | 28 (40) | 49 (37) | 16 (18) |
| **Age 35-44** | 28 (40) | 48 (36) | 17 (20) |
| **Age 45-54** | 31 (47) | 41 (31) | 20 (18) |
| **Age 55-64** | 36 (44) | 39 (35) | 17 (19) |
| **Age 65+** | 36 (48) | 41 (34) | 17 (17) |
| **All voters** | 31 (43) | 44 (35) | 17 (18) |

*Source: Ipsos MORI: How Britain voted in 1997, www.ipsos-mori.com/
researchpublications/researcharchive/poll.aspx?oItemID=2149&view=wide*

*Figure 4.1 The politics of catch-all: 1997 general election share of vote by
demographics (1992 in brackets)*

than to the Conservatives.[14] Labour's 413 seats in the House of Commons, a
majority of 167 over all other parties, were won with nearly 41 per cent of
the popular vote. Four years later, the 2005 election showed that the Labour
Party continued to attract voters from across the social spectrum. But the first
signs appeared that the New Labour electoral coalition was beginning to
crumble. Voters angry at the government's decision to go to war in Iraq
turned against Labour. More generally, middle-class voters, especially in key
marginal seats in the Midlands and southern England, where Labour and the
Tories battle it out, were beginning to defect. Labour also lost support from
lower-middle-class voters and the skilled working class – again both key
groups of voters for the party. At the 2005 election, the main beneficiaries of
Labour's losses were the Liberal Democrats. However, the Lib Dems did not
always attract the votes where they mattered: in the seats where they were
fighting the Conservatives, not Labour.

## New Labour, new party?

Was New Labour's catch-all politics indicative of wider changes in the party?
And if the party had changed, how significant were these changes to wider
questions about the structure and organization of political parties?

Power in the Labour Party has rested for much of its history with the party
leadership in parliament (and certainly not with the membership in local
parties). But this parliamentary party machine, as Patrick Dunleavy once
observed, is 'housed in the shell of an older and larger labour movement
which grows less relevant as the years go by'.[15] Mass unemployment, the
decline of manufacturing industry and tough labour laws introduced by

the Conservatives in the 1980s saw a sharp fall in the number of trade union-ists, a cut in union funds and a loss of confidence in industrial action as a means to advance working-class interests. None the less, the unions remained – and remain – powerful players in Labour Party politics.

Labour's defeat in the 1992 general election brought the question of the Labour Party's relationship with the trade unions to the fore.[16] In particular, the sight of union leaders casting preposterously large block votes at the Labour conference to make important decisions appeared not only undemo-cratic but quite outdated. It hardly fitted with the image of a new, modern Labour Party. During John Smith's period as leader before his death in 1994, three key reforms to Labour's relations with the unions were introduced. The first introduced 'one member, one vote' for the selection of the party leader and parliamentary candidates. The second ended the union block vote and cut the size of the union share in decisions at the national conference. The third required unions to ballot their members during party leadership elections.

These were important changes, although they were essentially compromise positions that left the unions with an important role in Labour affairs. Many modernizers wanted the party to go further in terms of distancing itself from the trade unions. The more traditionally minded, in particular John Prescott, believed it was important to keep these union links. They were what made Labour Labour. How, after all, could the Labour Party claim to be a labour party if it didn't have the trade unions to deliver a mass working-class mem-bership, regardless of the actual day-to-day involvement of these members in party affairs?

Academic studies of Labour's grassroots made depressing reading: party membership was in long decline (down from around a million in the 1950s to under 350,000 in the 1980s); levels of activism were falling; and individual members were likely to be older and more middle-class (Labour was more a party of teachers and lecturers than manual workers).[17] The trade unions affiliated to the party delivered large numbers of largely working-class members via the political levy paid by trade unionists who didn't opt out of paying it. Despite the fact that most of these members did very little for the party, it allowed Labour to claim itself to be a mass party, especially as indi-vidual membership fell below 300,000 in the 1990s.

By the time Blair became party leader in 1994, then, the drift of Labour's party reforms was towards giving individual party members more power at exactly the time when individual party membership was in sharp decline. Blair, like Kinnock before, went on a recruitment drive for new members. The Labour leader used these new members to drive forward key reforms, such as the rewording of Clause IV and agreeing a draft of what would become the 1997 election manifesto. At the same time, Blair built on earlier reforms to the machinery of party policy-making in a way that drove a final (and rather formal) nail into the coffin of 'delegatory democracy'. Under the party's general secretary, Tom Sawyer, the 'party into power' reforms in opposition, and subsequent Partnership in Power procedures in government, made it clear that the party leadership in parliament were not delegates of the party's membership – individual or trade union. The new procedures brought together the existing joint policy committee, the national policy forum and eight policy commissions in a bi-annual round of consultation. The bottom line was that the powers of the NEC and the annual party conference over policy-making were weakened significantly. These reforms reinforced the power of the leadership and allowed it to exert even greater control over the party. The annual party conference was to be a 'showcase' event; and the party leadership in government looked beyond the usual party suspects to road-test its ideas, notably in the People's Panel and the Big Conversation. This was 'plebiscitary democracy' that subjected the policies of the leadership to periodic review.[18]

Alongside this strengthening of the leadership's direction of policy-making was a continuing professionalization of the party, as the national party sought to exert control over local parties. The staffing of central offices of all the main political parties had been increasing for decades. In the run-up to and aftermath of the 1997 victory, the number of staff working in Labour's London and regional offices rose significantly. Research provides evidence of this professionalization of the party. At Millbank there were specialized roles based on areas of expertise; 'substantial if qualified autonomy' in the roles party workers played; and a 'fairly widespread commitment' by these paid activists to 'political entrepreneurialism'. This new generation of party workers generally had academic and vocational qualifications; experience from other workplaces that they brought to party work; and a sense that the work they did for the Labour Party was useful to them in terms of their own career development. These hired guns may have been committed to a Labour victory, but their party work seamlessly connected to their broader professional lives.[19]

A new professionalism was also brought to the problem of finding new sources of political funding for the Labour Party. The trade unions had long bankrolled the party. During the 1980s and early 1990s, party funding from the trade unions declined as union membership fell. Labour also found that the costs of administrating the party fees from its dwindling individual membership were greater than the amounts received. In response, a new 'business plan' was put in place to find alternative sources of funding – in particular, tapping not just party members, but rich individual donors. Despite this, Labour was unable to break its dependency on the unions for funding. By Labour's third term in government, for every £4 donated to the party, £3 came from union sources. With the Brown government continuing to push through policies opposed by trade unions, not least private sector involvement in public sector reform, union leaders such as Dave Prentis of Unison expressed their unhappiness at 'feeding the hand that bites us'.[20] So, while union power

in Labour's political machine has declined since the 1980s, the unions continue to be the principal source of income for the party – and this does pose
problems for the leadership in government or opposition.

Where does all this leave party members? The view that Labour was a party
run by its membership was always a pipedream – a myth Robert McKenzie
demolished back in the 1950s. But we also know that party members do
matter at election time. Simply in terms of numbers, while membership of
the Labour Party revived under Tony Blair in the first years of his leadership,
it subsequently fell again, reaching a new low in 2008. The new members the
party did pick up under Blair were also not very active in a conventional
sense. Despite the shifts in political campaigning over the years with the rise
of a mass broadcast media, local party activism is important to winning
national elections. This need for members does limit any shift to 'electoral-
professional' politics. But Labour's attempts at reviving a certain kind of
grassroots politics in the 1990s required, as Patrick Seyd and Paul Whiteley
argue, a careful balancing act between local activism and central party management. Labour, like all other parties, needs members to take part in political campaigning. But it doesn't want these members to be so active as to
challenge the management of the party from the centre. Equally, however, if
party leaders exert too much management from the centre, this undermines
the local political activism the party needs to get elected in the first place.[21]
This tension between local parties and the national leadership surfaced in
the Conservative Party in the run-up to the 2010 election, as we saw in the
last chapter.

## Women and the Labour Party

The role of women in British politics is a source of much concern. Participation rates, certainly compared with the best-performing Scandinavian
countries, are low. Before 1983, the number of female MPs in the House of
Commons was never more than 29 (in 1964). Since then the number
of women in parliament has increased, doubling in 1997 to 120 and reaching
128 in 2005, around 19 per cent of the chamber. Of these women MPs, 98 sat
on the Labour benches (28 per cent of all Labour MPs). At the 2010 election,
the number of female MPs went up again to 142. Is this increase in Labour
women MPs indicative of the 'feminization' of party politics?

As we saw in chapter 2, the feminization of party politics has two main
aspects: first, the number of women becoming involved in politics – in particular, in more formal roles involving policy- and decision-making; second,
political and policy debates increasingly addressing women's concerns and
perspectives. A feminist party is one in which there is parity in the gender of
elected representatives; women have a realistic chance of becoming party
leader; and feminist perspectives are embedded in the party's policies and
commitments.

During the bitter battles that divided the Labour Party in the late 1970s and early 1980s, feminists in the party demanded greater collective representation inside the organization – for example, through the Labour Women's Action Committee.[22] After 1983, demands for greater individual representation of women in the party, in particular as parliamentary candidates, grew, as did pressure for women's issues to be placed on the party's policy agenda. In 1987, Labour established that at least one woman should be included on a shortlist of candidates where a woman had applied to a constituency; and the idea of a women's ministry was floated. During the 1990s, the feminization of the Labour Party gathered pace as modernizers acknowledged that New Labour had to shed its male-dominated image. Lots of men in suits did not help win support among key groups of female voters. Under John Smith, the party adopted all-women shortlists for parliamentary candidates in 1993. Despite the successful legal challenge by two male Labour Party members against the policy in 1996, all-women shortlists had done enough to make a significant difference to the number of women MPs in 1997 – helped too by the scale of Labour's victory. With the growth in the individual representation of women across the party, so the push for more collective representation stalled. However, there remain in the party a range of women's organizations operating at a national and local level, including the National Women's Forum and the Women's Conference.

The position of women in Labour politics, then, has changed. But there are concerns that these changes have not gone far enough. There is no doubt that women in New Labour were better represented than ever, but questions remain whether Labour women are equally represented at all levels of the party, particularly in policy-making. While Labour's commitments on a host of policy questions, including equal pay, maternity leave, equal opportunities, childcare and domestic violence, show how far the party has moved to incorporate feminist perspectives in its politics, there is a concern that these lack legal bite, casting doubt on whether Labour, like other political parties, can really be described as a fully feminized party.[23]

## Let's stick together?

The political in-fighting that marked Labour politics in the 1970s and 1980s by and large dissipated in the 1990s. The 'realignment of the left' examined earlier in the chapter marginalized the hard left in the party. The soft left was behind reform. Moreover, the trade union movement was fighting for survival in a fast-changing world. Any Labour government would do. Defeat in the 1992 election led to a belief in all sections of the party that almost anything had to be done to beat the Conservatives. While there was considerable opposition on the left to Blair's reforms to Labour's constitution, the leadership won the day. But, having stuck together before the election in 1997, would New Labour stick together after?

Labour's first two years in power were notable for their caution – in particular, on public spending commitments. While significant policies were unveiled – on monetary policy (giving the Bank of England independence), constitutional reform and welfare to work – the government largely stuck to the spending commitments set out by the out-going Conservative government. This was New Labour putting 'safety first'. Some on the left were unimpressed. Tony Blair had promised a government of the centre left and all it appeared they were getting was a continuation of Thatcherism. When the government presented proposals to cut social security payments to single parents, Labour backbenchers revolted, with little effect. The size of Labour's majority in the House of Commons insulated the government against such action.

From 2000 onwards, however, the caution engendered by the government's desire to prove its economic competency was cast off. The first two years of Labour in government was marked by prudence – and by Chancellor Gordon Brown's insistence that this Labour government wouldn't go the same way as previous ones. The next two years showed more clearly the government's purpose: significant increases in public spending on collective public services, in particular the National Health Service, as well as modest redistributions to the working poor, especially those with younger families.

During this first term, the party did, by and large, stick together. Backbench rebellions were limited.[24] Between 1997 and 2001, there were 1,421 votes against the party whip in the House of Commons, comfortably below the trend rate of rebellion under the Conservatives. There were a number of rebellions, including the 47 MPs who voted against the cut to lone parent benefits and the 67 against reform of incapacity benefit. But the government learnt its lesson; and its first parliament was notable for its brotherly and sisterly love.

However, Labour's second term in power after 2001 was more problematic. The state of Britain's public services was a key election issue. Labour's message that only it could deliver reform in the NHS and the nation's schools won the day. But this reform programme was contentious for the Labour Party and the trade unions, in particular where it involved the private sector, market forces and welfare to work. The Labour government during this parliament poured huge sums of money into hospitals, schools and tax credits to poorer working families. Labour's critics on the left, however, were not convinced.

But it was the decision in 2001 to support the US-led invasion of Iraq that had a major impact on the Blair government, not least in terms of relations with Labour MPs and the wider party. The self-discipline of the first term in office gave way increasingly to backbench dissension, including a number of 'mega rebellions', most notably on the war in Iraq when 139 Labour MPs voted against the party whip. But the list of rebellions also covered the contentious areas of New Labour's public sector reforms: over student funding, NHS reform, welfare reform and law and order. In all, there were 3,579 votes against the government whip between 2001 and 2005. This made Labour's second term in office just as rebellious as its final term in government in the late 1970s – and more rebellious than John Major's ill-starred time in government. New Labour in power had, by the second term, produced a small but determined band of rebels more than happy to vote against the party whip. After 2005, rebellions continued – and with Labour's majority now much thinner, the government was forced into a number of concessions on its legislative programme, including education and welfare reform. Despite this, however, research shows that 'cohesion was the norm'. But with Labour's majority down to around 60 after 2005, it was only a matter of time before the government would lose a vote. On 9 November 2005, six months into the third term, it did, on its Terrorism Bill. With 49 Labour MPs – including 11 former ministers – voting against the government, and a margin of defeat of 31 votes, newspaper headlines the following day asked: was this the beginning of the end of the Blair premiership?

It wasn't quite. In the end a reasonably orderly succession from Blair to Brown took place in the summer of 2007. Whatever deal the two had struck back in 1994 was paid off. Despite the problems Brown faced in his years as prime minister over the question of his leadership, what is perhaps remarkable about the Labour Party's time in government was that the factionalism that had so nearly destroyed the party in the 1970s and 1980s was largely absent. Those forces on the left that were mounted against New Labour largely massed outside the Labour Party, as we shall see in chapter 7, although the hard electoral impact was limited. The one battle that did matter in this period, between Tony Blair and Gordon Brown and their supporters, was a split within New Labour: in large part about who should be prime minister and control the levers of power. There were differences of view between Blairites and Brownites on policy – in particular, reform of the public services – but not fundamental differences of ideology about the future of Labour politics and British social democracy. During the Blair/Brown years, the hard left was rebellious but small in number. And those on the softer left, such as Jon Cruddas and the Compass group of MPs and activists, were critical of but largely loyal to the Labour government.

The Labour Party under Tony Blair and Gordon Brown did, then, stick together – and went down together in 2010. But where did New Labour take social democratic politics in Britain?

## New Labour, new social democracy?

There are essentially three views on where New Labour took the Labour Party and British social democracy.

The first view sees considerable continuities between New Labour politics and past Labour politics. New Labour had 'old roots', as one former Blair advisor put it.[25] The shifts in ideology and policy under Blair and Brown are seen as being within the Labour tradition and, in many cases, as being remarkably similar to those pursued by past Labour governments. New Labour is part of revisionist social democratic politics that, in Britain, stretches back to the 1950s with Hugh Gaitskell and Tony Crosland, and even further back to the founding of Labour as a parliamentary party to advance the interests of trade unions and the poor. Just as Gaitskell wanted to make Labour 'relevant and realistic', so New Labour has sought to make Labour a progressive party attractive to voters from across the political spectrum. Similar traditions are found right across European social democratic politics – and New Labour can be seen as part of a broader continental 'neo-revisionism'.

In one sense the modernization camp does not think New Labour was very new at all. Certainly it sees Labour under Blair and Brown confronting the age-old dilemma for progressive politics from the turn of the twentieth century: how governments balance economic efficiency and social justice. The difference today is simply that times have changed – and New Labour offered a reinterpretation of these ideas to suit current circumstances. On this reading, New Labour's 'third way' was part of this attempt to re-think social democratic politics for 'new times'.[26]

A second view challenges head-on the perspective that New Labour was an up-dating of traditional Labour and social democratic politics. Simply put, this view sees the Labour Party from the mid 1980s onwards as moving to the right. To get elected, Labour sold out to Thatcherism and the New Right. New Labour abandoned socialist values and the critique of markets and private ownership. Colin Hay, for example, argues that after 1987 Labour played the politics of 'catch-up' not catch-all. Reflecting on the 1997 election, Hay suggested there was 'bi-partisan convergence': the post-war 'Keynesian-welfarist paradigm' was displaced by a new 'neo-liberal paradigm'. From this perspective, the pursuit of free market economics, work-orientated welfare reform and private sector investment in the public services, as well as the failure to create a more equal society through progressive taxation, consolidated the New Right consensus in British politics and policy-making. Talk of a 'third way' simply served to mask this fundamental accommodation to globalization and neo-liberal political economy.[27]

Some long-time critics of the Labour Party, notably David Coates, argued that this accommodation should come as little surprise: 'New Labour is . . . merely our contemporary moment in a longer story with its own internal logic – the story of British Labourism and its limited capacity for effecting social change'. Coates suggested the Labour Party is stuck, as ever, believing that the British state can be used for radical ends, when in reality the room for such a politics is constrained by powerful business interests that Labour, given its internal politics, always accommodates. And because New Labour did not wait until it got into government before changing political tack, it 'got its surrender in early'.[28]

A third view of New Labour suggests that the reform of the party in the 1990s was nowhere near as clear as either of the first two perspectives would suggest. Any audit of New Labour will uncover neo-liberal policies and social democratic ones (and ones that are harder to stick political labels to). The pressure is to define New Labour from this ideological balance sheet. The problems with such an audit, however, are manifold. The legacy of the eighteen years of Conservative government endured through the legislation, institutions, cultures and individual political actors that were shaped in these years. Even if a new government had a mind to start again, it would be difficult to found a year zero. Moreover, political values and public policies are not fixed in time. There is no simple ideological political benchmark for any party.

From this third perspective, then, New Labour was neither a single 'project' nor a clear ideological entity but a political composite. It was more an accumulation of different positions that do not always sit easily with one another. New Labour, in theory and practice, had both radical and conservative elements reflecting the views of individual modernizers, party traditions, intellectual influences, departmental cultures and political audiences. New Labour was a 'hydra'. It was neither straightforwardly Thatcherite, nor traditionally social democratic. Significant government interventionism was balanced with a critique of the post-war social democratic state. New Labour sought power by appealing to a broad slice of the electorate while, at the same time, seeking to address some of the fundamental problems facing British society in the 1990s.[29]

## New Labour post-Thatcherism

Political parties, as the political scientist Mark Bevir has observed, are always remaking themselves in the novel situations that confront them.[30] Faced with something new, political actors, like anyone else, will draw on the traditions they know, but in the process these traditions are invariably modified. In the 1980s, the Labour Party faced a Conservative government that was transforming politics and policy-making in Britain. To start with, as we have seen in this chapter, Labour turned in on itself. But then, slowly, the party started to change. A new reforming leadership under Neil Kinnock was supported by a loose coalition of the Labour right and the realigned left of the party, the trade union leadership weakened by legal reforms and economic change and, later, by individual members under rule changes to Labour's constitution that empowered the party leadership. Events, as they always do, played into the reformers' hands, not least when John Major's Conservative government lost its reputation for economic competency and imploded in the mid 1990s. But by 1997, Labour not only had undertaken a serious and wide-ranging review of its policies, but also had established a coherent and popular ideological narrative that brought together concerns about economic growth and social justice. In government, this narrative helped to shift British policy-making post-Thatcherism.

This post-Thatcherite settlement drew on many traditional Labour themes, in particular that social democratic politics was about finding a balance between the demands of private-sector-led growth and the need to find collective solutions to a range of social problems. New Labour's critics argue that this balance tipped too far in favour of business and the market; its supporters that, in the contemporary world, the centre left must acknowledge not just the limits of the market, but those of government as well. In either case, the Labour Party in the 1990s not only succeeded in becoming an effective catch-all party winning three straight elections and ending the Conservative Party's apparent dominance of the British party system, but also stuck together. The factionalism that tore the party apart in the 1970s and early 1980s was largely absent from Labour's years in government.

Labour's defeat in the 2010 election saw the electoral coalition the party had built since the mid 1990s crumble. David Cameron's Conservatives, as we saw in the last chapter, proved more adept at winning round enough of the undecided voters than the Labour Party. Gordon Brown resigned as party leader, sparking a contest that appeared to turn not just on Labour's past record in government (including the Iraq war) but also on how 'New Labour' the party should be in the future. Despite a field of five, the leadership contest turned into a two-horse race between the brothers Miliband: David and Ed. Both had been key backroom New Labour staff, David for Blair and Ed for Brown, before becoming MPs (David in 2001, Ed in 2005) and joining the cabinet (David rising to foreign secretary, Ed to the climate change and energy portfolio).

David Miliband had been widely tipped to succeed Brown (and Harriet Harman who acted as caretaker after the general election). David had the support of senior party figures – and was, if anything, the 'heir to Blair'. But, crucially, his younger brother Ed won the support of the leaders of the large trade unions in the party (the GMB, Unison and Unite) who were able to mobilize the votes of individual union members in the leadership ballot. Despite two decades or more of party reform, the Byzantine world of Labour politics gave some members not one vote but multiple votes: Labour MPs, for example, could vote in the MP and MEP section, the constituency section as individual members, and possibly even in the affiliates section as members of trade unions or other organizations linked to the party. The parliamentary party and individual members backed David by clear majorities. But the votes in the third affiliates section gave Ed Miliband enough support to cross the finishing line by the narrowest of margins.

Would the new Labour leader pay a price for all this trade union backing? Out on the hustings, Ed Miliband had positioned himself a little to the left of his brother by promising not just to make the party more a 'movement' and to reconnect with party members and trade unions, but also to keep the 50p top rate of tax and campaign for a 'living wage' (though, to be fair, the policy differences with David were paper-thin). New Labour was over – the party had to move on. All this was sweet music to the trade union barons tired of being cast as the 'forces of conservatism' by the Blairites. The danger for Labour in all this, however, is that the party turns in on itself just as it did in the 1980s (and the Conservatives did after 1997). Ed Miliband was quick to boast of 35,000 new members joining the party since the general election (time will tell how many Labour keeps). But with the economy struggling out of the deepest recession since the 1930s, the pressure to return to the party's labour roots will be intense. Opposition to cuts in public spending (and public sector jobs) will make Labour feel good about itself.

But such oppositional politics does come with a price. New Labour was politically successful because it appealed to a broad coalition of voters across the country. The party broke out of its heartlands and took the Conservatives on where it mattered, in the marginal seats of Britain. New Labour may have taken this strategy just a little too far. There are, as the 2010 election exposed (and the 2009 European elections before), a good many traditional Labour voters alienated from the party – and some are willing to switch their votes or not vote at all. But if Labour is to remain a serious player in British party politics, it must resist the pressure to turn away from the New Labour strategy of seeking a broad base of support in the electorate. Labour lost the vote in 2010 but not by as much as the party feared. The Conservative/Liberal Democrat coalition government combines a tough-minded approach to the economy with public service reforms and measures to boost social mobility – all very New Labour. There may be much here for Labour to oppose, but there may also be much here for Ed Miliband and his team to engage with and to support. This will be a test of leadership.

## Further reading and research resources

A good starting point for the history of the Labour Party is Shaw's *The Labour Party since 1945*. This history can be viewed in a wider European context in Donald Sassoon's encyclopaedic *One Hundred Years of Socialism*. For contrasting views of New Labour, see Hay's *The Political Economy of New Labour*, Bevir's *New Labour: A Critique*, Coates's *Prolonged Labour*, and Driver and Martell's *New Labour*. The Labour Party is online at www2.labour.org.uk/. The Fabian Society, a source of ideas for the party for over a century, is at www.fabians.org.uk/.

CHAPTER FIVE

# The Liberal Democrats: From Protest to Power

## The Liberal dilemma

The 2010 general election exposed the dilemma at the heart of Liberal Democrat politics. Should the party go it alone, prizing its independence and the purity of its liberal thinking, not least its commitment to electoral reform? Or should the Liberal Democrats seek power by entering into closer relations with one or other of the two main parties (and if so, which one?), potentially giving up its independence and compromising its political principles? After six days of negotiations with both the Conservative and Labour parties following the 6 May poll, the Liberal Democrats chose power.

The revival of the Liberal Democrats (and before that, the Liberal Party) since the early 1970s has been one of the important features of the new British politics. The year 2010 marked the end of two-party politics as party leader Nick Clegg got equal billing with Gordon Brown and David Cameron on Britain's first televised 'prime ministerial' debates. Voters were seeing the Liberal Democrats in a new light. While the result of the election turned Clegg and his party into king-makers, the result also brought out the very real tensions in liberal politics. What kind of party are the Liberal Democrats and what role should or could they play in a changing British party system? And if the party did seize the moment and join the business of national government, just as it had done in local and devolved administrations, could it stick together?

These questions were far from new for the Liberal Democrats. Back in 2005, despite a credible result in the general election, cracks were appearing in the party. The fact that then party leader Charles Kennedy had a drink problem didn't help. Kennedy had proved popular with voters and Liberal Democrats out in the country. Like Tony Blair, he had that rare ability to reach out beyond the narrow confines of party politics to the electorate at large. 'Chat show Charlie' could guest on the current affairs satire *Have I Got News For You?* – and he could also host it. Kennedy was also on the right side of the political issue dogging British politics: Iraq. The Lib Dem leader had opposed the invasion in 2003. But if Kennedy appealed to voters, by the end of 2005 he was starting to lose support inside his party, especially among the growing number of MPs who, as we shall see later, were seeking to exert greater power and influence over Lib Dem affairs. While Kennedy remained popular with

112

local activists, including the party's solid base of local councillors, at Westminster his support among fellow Lib Dem MPs was ebbing away.

By 2006, the leadership of Charles Kennedy was exhausted. The parliamentary party staged a coup. As one national newspaper put it, the 'defenestration' of Kennedy took place: Liberal Democrat MPs, to the dismay of the other sections of the party, threw him out of the political window (metaphorically speaking). But where should Liberal Democrat politics go next? On the choice of leaders, the party went for experience over youth in the shape of Sir Menzies (Ming) Campbell, a former Olympic sprinter who had impressed all sides as a commentator on foreign affairs. But in little more than eighteen months, experience had turned to age and Campbell was dumped by MPs for a rather younger man – the forty-year-old Nick Clegg, who narrowly beat Chris Huhne in a ballot of Lib Dem members.

The problem facing the Liberal Democrats, however, went rather beyond who led them. Since 1997, the Liberal Democrats had done well. Benefiting from the continued unpopularity of the Conservative Party, the Liberal

## Box 5.1 The Strange Death of Liberal England

In 1935 George Dangerfield's classic study of the downfall of the old Liberal Party, *The Strange Death of Liberal England*, was published. Up until the First World War, the Liberals had been a major force in British party politics. Dating back to the 1830s in Whig, radical and liberal conservative politics, the Liberal Party had first been a champion of free trade, limited government and political reform under William Gladstone. By the end of the nineteenth century, these classical liberal ideas were combined with a broader social agenda that saw a significant role for government in dealing with poverty and a range of other social problems. These 'New Liberals' shaped the early British welfare state in government after 1906 and would have a lasting influence on British public policy for the whole of the twentieth century.

By the 1920s, however, support for the Liberal Party had fallen off a cliff. Why? Dangerfield argued that four things destroyed the party: Conservative opposition to the Liberal government's constitutional reforms in 1910–11; the threat of civil war in Ireland; the suffragette movement; and the increasing power of the trade unions in British politics. But the Liberal Party was also divided over the First World War: in particular, between supporters of Herbert Asquith and David Lloyd George. In 1916, Conservatives switched their support for Asquith's wartime coalition government to one led by Lloyd George. The Liberal Party was split. Lloyd George, in effect, led a Conservative-dominated coalition government up until the end of the war; and, following the 1918 election, to 1922, when the Tories withdrew their support. In the 1922 election – and in all subsequent elections – Labour overtook the Liberals as the main party of the centre left. The Liberal Party was losing not only votes to Labour and the Conservatives, but politicians and activists as well. Tony Benn's father, later Lord Stansgate, defected to Labour; and Winston Churchill returned to the Tory benches.

*Further reading and resources*: for the origins of the Liberal Party, see John Vincent, *The Formation of the Liberal Party 1857–1868* (London: Constable, 1966); see also the Liberal Democrat History Group, www.liberalhistory.org.uk/.

Democrats were attracting a solid base of around 20 per cent of votes. Even with first-past-the-post voting penalizing the party's national but largely thinly spread vote, the Lib Dems had 10 per cent of the seats in the House of Commons. For a party that had not had an overall majority in the House of Commons since 1906, it was at least moving in the right direction. Moreover, the Liberal Democrats were becoming a national party, with MPs from across Britain. It had also staked out some distinctive policy ground on home affairs and foreign policy that many voters were finding attractive. Having come so far, however, there was a sense that the party should be doing better – but how much better? Could the Liberal Democrats really turn themselves into an alternative party of government?

## A Liberal revival

Back in the 1950s, with just six MPs in the House of Commons, the Liberal Party was enduring a good old-fashioned two-party squeeze. Duverger's law (see chapter 1), which states that third parties are penalized under a voting system that promotes two-party politics, was unrelenting. Labour and the Conservatives between them were hoovering up well over 90 per cent of votes in general elections. Tory voters, always the most important source of Liberal (and Liberal Democrat) votes, were loyally supporting the Conservatives. Labour voters, never very minded to support the Liberals, were staying put. Moreover, the Liberal base was shrinking to an alarming extent. The party could barely find enough candidates to stand in elections, national or local. And in the midst of factional ideological battles, Liberals were leaving for Labour and the Conservatives. The party's days appeared numbered.

But under new leader Jo Grimond, the fortunes of the Liberals started to revive in the late 1950s. Grimond took the party to the 'radical left' as a non-socialist opposition to the Conservative Party in government, and as an alternative to the trade-union-dominated Labour Party. This meant support for membership of the European Economic Community, as well as opposition to Britain's nuclear weapons. Clear opposition to a foreign war, Suez, also helped to draw support to Grimond's new model Liberal Party. There was an increasing emphasis too on a more localized form of politics that drew on decentralist and participatory traditions in liberal thinking. This new 'community politics' sought to make government more responsive to the needs of local people. It was enthusiastically supported by the party's radical and socially libertarian 'young Liberals'. During the 1960s and 1970s this new localism became bound up with political strategies to build bases of grassroots activism campaigning on local issues.[1] Such an approach went against the accepted political wisdom of the time that only national campaigns directed though the national broadcast media won elections. Later, as we shall see, it would form the basis for the revival of the Liberal Democrats under Paddy Ashdown in the 1990s.

Certainly, from the mid 1950s, the party leadership put more and more resources into winning by-elections – and the strategy paid off. The Liberal Party started to do what it would continue to do over the coming decades: win these one-off political contests. Generally speaking, Liberal by-election victories were at the expense of the Conservatives; and this exposes the dangers for the Liberals of tacking too far to the left (and getting close to Labour) when most of their potential supporters are disgruntled Tory voters. Despite these early successes, however, the Liberals failed to make political in-roads at the 1964 and 1966 general elections and Grimond resigned, replaced by Jeremy Thorpe.

Under Thorpe, the Liberals did well in the 1970 general election – and again at the two polls in 1974. Indeed, British politics, as we saw in chapter 1, was changing. Cracks were appearing in Britain's two-party system. The Liberal Party was once again becoming a force at Westminster, and its 'pavement politics' was helping to increase its base of representation in local councils. Following the tight result in the first election in 1974, Thorpe was invited by the incumbent Conservative Prime Minister Edward Heath to form a coalition government. The Liberal leader declined, offering instead a voting pact in the House of Commons, which Heath turned down.

There was an important element of the Liberal dilemma at work in the mid 1970s: should the party enter power in cooperation with one of the main parties (and risk its independence) or seek its own path to power (and risk never achieving it)? Both strategies also run the risk of splitting the party; and it is perhaps not surprising that successive Liberal and Liberal Democratic leaders have ended up waiting for something to happen, taking the decision out of their hands.[2]

Following Thorpe's resignation in 1976, the new Liberal leader David Steel joined the struggling Labour government led by James Callaghan in a parliamentary pact to keep the government going. By 1978, however, this Lib–Lab pact fell apart as the government floundered. None the less, it is clear that, by the end of the 1970s, the position of the Liberals, and the conditions of centre-ground third-party politics, had changed. British politics was taking on some of the characteristics of a multi-party system. Events after 1979, for a while at least, gave the impression that the mould of two-party politics would be broken and that a new era of party competition would emerge.

## Liberals and Social Democrats

One of the catalysts for the revival of third-party politics was the growing ideological polarization of Britain, as the last two chapters have shown. Under Margaret Thatcher, the Conservatives shifted to the right and the Labour Party to the left. A political space was opening up on the centre ground – a space soon to be occupied by a new political party. Labour's lurch to the left caused dismay among the party's pro-European social democrats.

In January 1981, four leading Labour figures, Roy Jenkins, David Owen, Bill Rodgers and Shirley Williams, launched the Council for Social Democracy. Nearly twenty Labour MPs and one Conservative came out in support of it. The Gang of Four took the plunge and formed the Social Democratic Party (SDP).

The SDP was more pro-European, more pro-NATO and more pro-market than Labour was quickly becoming. The SDP offered an alternative to a left-wing Labour Party and a right-wing Conservative Party (and would, in many ways, prove a first stab at New Labour). As opinion polls were showing, this was the kind of politics that many voters found attractive. By October 1981, the SDP were riding high on a wave of public support: a quarter of voters said they would vote for the party in a general election.[3] Shirley Williams took Crosby for the SDP from the Tories at a by-election in November 1981; Roy Jenkins did the same in Glasgow Hillhead in March 1982. But the SDP's brand of politics was much the same as on offer from the Liberals. Both parties were in effect chasing the same voters. Some kind of political alliance was necessary ready for the next election to ensure the two parties did not stand candidates against each other. There was real anticipation about political change. David Steel at his party's 1981 conference dared to suggest that Liberal members go back to their constituencies and prepare for government. Words that would come back haunt him. But the sense of confidence was real enough.

The 1983 election result was a blow to the two-party system in British politics. At the poll, the Liberal/SDP Alliance won nearly 8 million votes – just 700,000 fewer than Labour – making up 26 per cent of votes cast, but won just 23 seats in parliament (compared to the 209 for Labour). Even the most die-hard supporters of first-past-the post voting found this difficult to justify. One of the new in-take of Alliance candidates was Charles Kennedy, then only twenty-three, and a member of the SDP. Despite the poor return on votes in the House of Commons, it really did look for a while that the promise to 'break the mould of British politics' might be realized. Opinion polls still looked encouraging for the Alliance; and both parties scored important by-election victories between 1984 and 1987. The Liberals and the SDP, firmly camped on the centre ground of British politics, looked like breaking the hegemony of Labour and the Conservatives.

But (and there is always a 'but' in politics) by 1986, the alliance between the two parties was showing signs of strain. The political machine was still working: at by-elections in Truro (a Liberal hold) and Greenwich (an SDP gain from Labour). And opinion polls suggested that a fifth to nearly a third of voters supported one or other of the Alliance partners. However, tensions between the Liberals and the SDP surfaced over defence policy in the autumn of 1986 (the SDP wanted a tough stance). In the election campaign the following year, despite the dual leadership of the 'two Davids' (Steel and Owen), the Alliance's time was clearly up. Despite a reasonable showing – the Alliance won nearly a quarter of votes cast – it was obvious to most that the parties would have to merge or go their separate ways. In the end, they did both; and for the next two years – as the newly elected member for Truro, Matthew Taylor, subsequently wrote – 'we all but died'.[4]

Real tensions of tradition and substance existed between the Liberals and the SDP. To be sure, both parties shared an overarching social liberalism dating back to the New Liberals in the late nineteenth and early twentieth centuries. This brand of liberalism was committed to governments playing an active role in society to promote freedom, especially for the poor. Through figures such as the economist John Maynard Keynes and the social reformer William Beveridge, social liberalism did much to shape politics and policy in the first half of the twentieth century. The British welfare state was as much a product of liberal minds (and Liberal action) as it was social democratic thinking (and Labour action). Having said this, the Liberal Party and the SDP also came from different political traditions: one rooted in the Labour Party, the trade unions and collectivist social democratic politics; the other in the old nineteenth-century Liberal Party and in an individualist political philosophy that was suspicious of the state in general and central government in particular.

Such tensions over what the Alliance stood for became more relevant as the possibility (some argued necessity) of merger between the two parties came closer. To cut a long story short, both parties were split internally following a proposal from the Liberal Party leadership in June 1987 to form one party. The Liberal grassroots, hostile to other parties at the best of times, feared an SDP take-over. One former MP, Michael Meadowcroft, a long-time sceptic of the Alliance, having resisted the merger, re-formed the Liberal Party in 1989.

On the SDP side, a gang of three (Jenkins, Rodgers and Williams) all supported merger, but Owen and the majority of the party's five MPs opposed it (the young Charles Kennedy was a supporter). Following a close vote at a special conference, the SDP agreed to a merger. Talks began, led on the SDP side by MP Robert Maclennan, who became a caretaker party leader following Owen's resignation. The talks were never likely to be easy, especially as Dr Owen went off with the remaining MPs and the party's financial backers (including a member of the supermarket dynasty, David Sainsbury), insisting that the SDP would live on. As the merger talks dragged on, public support for the two parties drained away. By January 1988, a redrafted constitution had been agreed. The memberships of the two parties were canvassed and, on 3 March, the Social and Liberal Democratic Party came into being.

But the early signs for the Social and Liberal Democratic Party did not look promising. Still the polling looked dire (positive voting intentions did not get back above 10 per cent for the new party until the summer of 1990, shortly after the 'continuing' SDP finally gave up the ghost). To make matters worse, the party was broke and could not even agree on a manifesto. The 'annus horribilis' (Matthew Taylor's words) continued as the election took place for a leader in July 1988. The scene was set for the arrival of the former Royal Marine Paddy Ashdown.

## Leading from the front

When Paddy Ashdown took over, the Social and Liberal Democrats were at a low ebb – and stuck with a preposterously long name (following a ballot of members in October 1989, the party became more simply the Liberal Democrats). The formal merger between the Liberal Party and the SDP had been an electoral necessity. There is little enough space for one party, let alone two, on the centre ground of British politics under existing voting arrangements. But there was also real common ground between the Liberals and the SDP. European integration, constitutional reform, progressive social policy and liberal home affairs drew together politicians and activists from both sides. But was the new party doomed to remain the third man of British party politics? Ashdown didn't think so.

Ashdown was far from being a conventional Westminster politician. His days in the armed forces – and his brief stint at the foreign office – had left its mark. Ashdown's hyperactivity as party leader is the stuff of legend. And before he left his party exhausted and needing something more restful ('a pint and a chat with Charles Kennedy'), Ashdown turned the fortunes of his party around. After the political nadir of 1989, he took the Liberal Democrats to a position in British politics that gave them real presence at Westminster; and to a share in power in the new devolved governments created after Labour took office in 1997.

Much has been made of Ashdown's personal qualities as leader. He was certainly energetic, hard-working, had a real passion for his party (he had been an activist against US cruise missiles in Britain) and a desire to get things done.[5] Ashdown brought a professional quality to a party that had done all it could to create an organizational structure that gave little formal power to the party's politicians at Westminster. But Ashdown also had a plan. This was to end the party's traditional 'equidistance' between the two main parties and seek support from unhappy Tory voters by distancing the party from the Conservatives. This is (and always has been) a dangerous strategy for Liberals: will Tory-inclined voters like a party that defines itself as on the centre left? After all, in all general elections but 1979 between the early 1970s and 1992, Liberal voters had identified their party as being closer to the Conservatives than to Labour.[6]

As we have already seen, the old Liberal Party drew much of its electoral support from disgruntled Conservative voters. This enabled the party to pull off stupendous by-election victories in suburban Tory strongholds like Orpington on the edge of London. During the 1980s, the Liberal/SDP Alliance flourished with a 'plague on both your houses' politics, although its by-election triumphs were usually over the Conservatives. Ashdown's plan was to exploit the growing unpopularity of John Major's Conservative government after the 1992 election. It goes without saying that the Tories were unpopular with Labour voters. But Major's government was also losing support from those parts of the electorate that either always voted Tory or had supported the Conservatives through much of the 1980s. Some of these votes were heading in New Labour's direction. But some of them were available to the Liberal Democrats. It was Ashdown's intention that his party should grab this opportunity with both hands by stating clearly where it stood.

To do this, Ashdown set the ambition of creating a 'non-socialist' alternative to the Conservative Party (and there are obvious echoes of Jo Grimond here). In 1995, Ashdown announced that it would be inconceivable for his party to work with the Conservatives in government. Instead, the Liberal Democrats were part of a new 'progressive coalition'. They were on the centre left of British politics. Ashdown's 'project' was to build common cause on a range of policies with Labour. In certain respects, this was not difficult. Ashdown had steered the Liberal Democrats down a more pro-market economic path, just as Blair was doing with Labour. There was also considerable support for the European Union within both sets of party modernizers. While the Liberal Democrats were more cautious (or radical, depending on your point of view) on welfare and public sector reform, both parties were putting the provision of services by the state at the centre of an agenda for social justice post-Thatcherism. However, it was in the area of constitutional reform that the joint discussions between the two parties really got somewhere and led to the publication, before the 1997 general election, of a joint policy document on reform. Overall, there was support in both parties for some kind of anti-conservative 'progressive' alliance founded on a reconfiguration of centre left politics through a combination of market economics and progressive social policy. This had taken both parties to the right – but then, post-Thatcherism, the whole terrain of British party politics had shifted in this direction.[7]

Ashdown's answer, then, to the traditional Liberal dilemma of how the party should seek power was clear: get closer to Labour. As a vote-winning strategy, this would prove a great success; but it was never likely to go down well with local party activists and some MPs who feared the 'project' would sacrifice the party's independence and lead it into a dangerous alliance with a Labour Party that was moving further to the right than the Lib Dems were themselves. Certainly, the more conservative (or anti-liberal aspects) of New Labour, especially on law and order issues, caused considerable disquiet in the party. Eventually, this would form the basis for Liberal Democrat opposition to key areas of Labour's home affairs policies in government.

As the 1997 election approached, Ashdown's gamble on a new progressive project appeared to be paying off. The Liberal Democrats were doing well in the opinion polls. The election result, however, was a success, but not a triumph. Unfortunately for the Lib Dems, the real winner of the backlash against John Major's government was the Labour Party. The scale of Labour's victory put paid to any coalition with the Liberal Democrats. Instead, Ashdown and the party leadership were offered the crumbs of government: seats on a joint cabinet committee on constitutional reform. This was unlikely to endear Paddy to the party faithful; and, eventually, it would cost Ashdown the leadership.

Within a year Ashdown's love-in with Labour was fading. Discontent with their leader was growing inside the party. A series of conference votes in 1998, blocking closer links with the Blair government, marked the end of Ashdown's attempts to build an anti-Conservative alliance with Labour. In January 1999 he resigned, his 'project' seemingly a failure. But Ashdown left his party in a far stronger political position than the one it found itself in ten years before. Indeed, the enduring legacy of Ashdown's strategy to forge closer ties with Labour was a programme of constitutional reform that opened up new political opportunities for the Liberal Democrats in the devolved administrations in Scotland and Wales. For a party that had championed home rule for well over a century, this was not bad going.

## Kennedy turns away from Labour

Charles Kennedy became leader of the Liberal Democrats at a point when the party's fortunes were running high, but also when discontent with the Labour government was growing. Kennedy, who had beaten Simon Hughes, darling of the activist left in the party, for the leadership, had the support of his parliamentary colleagues and the less active members of the party in the country.

Kennedy's main action as leader was to distance his party from Labour – just as most Lib Dems wanted. Involvement in the joint cabinet committee on constitutional affairs stopped after the 2001 election, an election that suggested that the forward march of the Liberal Democrats would continue under Kennedy. With 18 per cent of the votes, the party saw a gain of six seats in parliament. In the House of Commons there was evidence of the turn away from Labour. Initially, Lib Dem MPs had been largely supportive of the legislative programme of the new Labour government. Indeed, Lib Dems were so supportive of Labour that it led to accusations they were 'in bed with the government' (Liberal Democrats argued that Labour was pursuing policies in tune with their party, so why shouldn't they vote with the government?). This pattern of voting among Labour and Liberal Democrat MPs stretched back to 1992 and shows that Ashdown's policy of moving closer to Labour really meant something in the division lobbies of the Palace of Westminster.[8]

But as Labour's first term wore on, Liberal Democrat MPs voted with increasing regularity against the government. Indeed, during Labour's second term after 2001, Liberal Democrat MPs were voting with the government only 25 per cent of the time. Increasingly, Lib Dems were siding with Her Majesty's Loyal Opposition in votes in the House of Commons. Similar patterns of support could be found in the House of Lords, where Liberal Democrat peers had in effect the casting votes on government legislation. Over the course of fifteen years, then, the Liberal Democrats went from equidistance, to a progressive project with Labour and all the way over to being part of the opposition to the government with the Tories.

## 'Where we work we win'

The political advance of the Liberal Democrats, first under Ashdown and then under Kennedy, was, in part, the result of the party's clear focus on building local political machines. This 'where we work we win' strategy had its roots in local radical liberalism in the 1960s. While this community politics was based on the idea that 'active citizenship' and popular participation could help government to meet the needs of local people, it also became the Liberals' favoured political strategy for winning elections.[9] At the time, political science had written off local campaigning in an era when national campaigns run in the glare of nationwide television were seen to be decisive. By the 1990s, as we saw in chapter 2, a revisionist view was questioning this argument. Local party campaigning, it was suggested, did make a difference to national elections – and the Liberal Democrats, under Paddy Ashdown, then Charles Kennedy, were leading the way.

What does this 'where we work we win' strategy amount to? Research shows the Liberal Democrats do better where they pick a local candidate and where the party campaigns on local issues.[10] What for the Lib Dems are scarce resources are targeted on these areas, supporting the candidate in intensive and continuous communication campaigns using leaflets and local media. When combined with success in local elections, this creates an impression of competency for the party in government; allows the party to deflect criticism that it has no experience of running anything; and attracts members, funding and voters to the party. The strategy paid off for the Liberal Democrats. Targeting resources on winnable seats and those where the sitting Lib Dem MP faced a serious threat from another party, combined with this 'where we work we win' local strategy, meant that under Ashdown, then Kennedy, the party won more seats even as its share of votes across the country fell. Indeed, for the Liberal Democrats, success in local government elections (between 2002 and 2004, the number of Lib Dem councillors increased by 345, many in Labour urban strongholds) had become 'integral to their long-term goal of obtaining greater parliamentary representation'.[11]

## Chasing Labour voters

Intensive local activism was necessary if the Liberal Democrats were ever going to break out of their electoral heartlands and really get stuck into the Labour vote. 'Where we work we win' had taken the party forward at a

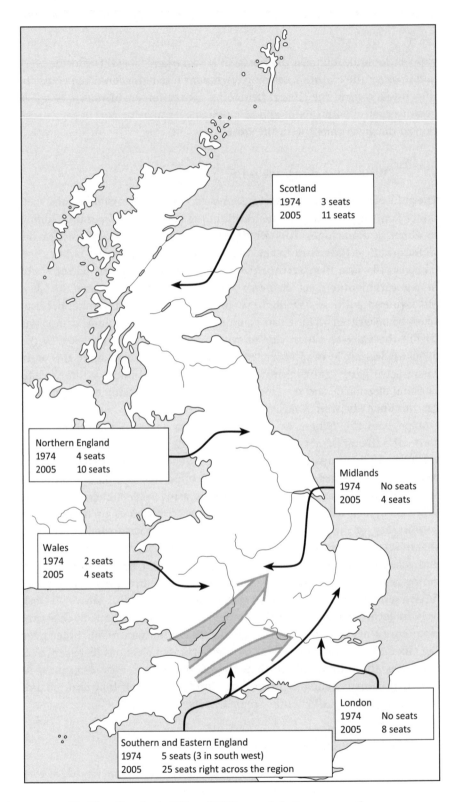

Scotland
1974    3 seats
2005    11 seats

Northern England
1974    4 seats
2005    10 seats

Midlands
1974    No seats
2005    4 seats

Wales
1974    2 seats
2005    4 seats

London
1974    No seats
2005    8 seats

Southern and Eastern England
1974    5 seats (3 in south west)
2005    25 seats right across the region

*The Liberal breakout: 1974 and 2005 general elections compared*

national level in 2001 beyond those areas of the country where Liberals had traditionally done well, for example in south-west England. Here, as Andrew Russell and Edward Fieldhouse point out, there was no 'credibility gap' for the party that had to be filled by local activism. The Lib Dem ambition in the 2005 election was not just to win key Conservative seats (the so-called 'decapitation strategy' of defeating senior Tory MPs), but to make serious headway into what was traditional Labour territory in urban Britain, particularly in the growing number of seats where the Lib Dems not the Tories trailed Labour in second place.

At first glance, the result of the 2005 general election suggests the Liberal Democrats did well. The party's vote was up 4 per cent to 22.7 per cent of the vote; and the party won sixty-two seats (the highest number of Liberal MPs since 1924). Following a by-election in 2006, sixty-two became sixty-three. The Liberal Democrats in parliament had developed an oppositional profile largely to the liberal left of the Labour government through opposition to a host of domestic policies including ID cards, anti-terrorism legislation and student top-up fees. Kennedy's opposition to the critical foreign policy question of the Blair government, the invasion of Iraq, also marked the party out. But behind the headline results from the 2005 election, the dangers of chasing Labour voters were apparent. The Liberal Democrats were certainly winning over voters, but who was switching and how loyal might they be in subsequent elections?

As we have seen, Liberal politics in Britain's two-party system relied on disenchanted Conservative voters deserting the Tories. But the switch to chasing Labour votes had the potential to create a 'dangerous asymmetry' for the party.[12] The danger of this strategy is not just that the scarce resources of the party are stretched as it tries to attack sitting Labour MPs while defending its own MPs against any Tory revival, but that the party will alienate its most consistent source of votes: Conservative supporters.

The 2005 result exposes the risk of creating a gap between the party's political strategy and its traditional sources of support at the polls.[13] The election result showed the Liberal Democrats making in-roads into the Labour vote in urban Britain. Indeed, the party's vote increased more where it was chasing Labour in second place (up by 8 per cent) than where it was second to the Conservatives (up just 0.5 per cent) or defending a seat against the Tories (where its vote fell). As a result, the Lib Dems took eleven seats from Labour, but only three from the Conservatives – and a further five were lost to the Tories. So, despite advancing in traditional Labour-held seats, the party did not advance as it thought it would in Tory areas. In fact, the ambition to defeat key Tory MPs in vulnerable seats was a clear failure.

So, if the Liberal Democrats were attracting votes away from Labour, was something rather important happening to the party's base of political support? While often written off as a party propped up by (Conservative) protest votes, the Liberal Democrats (and the Liberals before them) do have something of a core vote – or, at least, a social base of support. The typical Liberal voter is middle-class, well educated (to degree level), works in the public sector and lives in a rural or suburban area. The old Liberal vote was also high among non-conformist religious groups, such as the Methodists (though this link disappeared in 2005); and in parts of the country, notably south-west England, where Labour did not take over as the main alternative to the Conservatives in the twentieth century. Where Liberals have always struggled to win support is among urban, working-class and less educated parts of the electorate – typical Labour territory. But did this change in 2005?

Labour voters did switch to the Liberal Democrats in 2005 – and Iraq was a big reason for this switch. But what is interesting is that the typical Liberal Democrat voter didn't change very much. To be sure, the Lib Dems did attract more votes among students and Muslim voters: not surprising given the party's stance on student fees and Iraq. This helped the Lib Dems to advance in places where there were significant numbers of students, teachers and lecturers, as well as Muslim communities. But otherwise, the people voting Liberal Democrat in 2005 were the same old middle-class, well-educated social groups that had always voted Liberal. What was important was the shift in the political geography of Lib Dem support. The party was successful in attracting these educated middle-class voters in places where traditionally they had struggled: in particular, in urban Britain – though largely in university towns. These were the same old Liberal voters, just living in different (Labour) places. This accounted for the advances the party made outside its traditional strongholds.

So, while the Liberal Democrats did well in 2005, their position was fragile. The result showed the party capable of winning Labour votes and Labour seats, but not urban working-class voters. These remained, in the most part, solidly Labour. The Labour voters who did switch were not the tactical switchers to the Lib Dems who had helped to defeat the Conservatives in 1997, but protest votes against the policies, notably tuition fees and the war in Iraq, of the Labour government. By chasing these protest votes, the Liberal Democrats made themselves vulnerable to the cause of the protest disappearing – and 'normal' patterns of voting resuming. And by chasing these Labour protest votes, the party risked alienating its traditional source of support among middle-class Conservative voters, not least in places where it was defending a seat against the Conservatives.

The Liberal Democrats' advance in 2005 had taken the party to second place in 189 constituencies – 106 of these held by Labour, 83 by the Conservatives. But in most of these Labour-held seats, the Lib Dems were well behind. The result of the 2010 general election, after a campaign in which Nick Clegg transformed the normal pattern of two-party politics, further illustrates the problems the party faces in winning more seats, certainly under the existing electoral rules of simple plurality. More than half a million extra votes, and a share of the poll up 1 per cent, saw the Liberal Democrats drop 5 seats overall. And this was after a mid-campaign surge of support that saw the party barge past Labour into second place in the opinion polls. The Liberal Democrats gained 8 new seats, but lost 13 – and the gains and losses were from both Labour and the Conservatives. The Liberal Democrats, in electoral terms, are no longer a party that, with Labour, are looking to knock over sitting Conservative MPs. They are a party facing both ways at the ballot box – and must campaign against both other parties in different places and, perhaps inevitably, in different ways. The geography of contemporary British party politics, as the 2010 general election showed all too clearly, has become a complex thing indeed.

### Struggling for power in the party

With the merger of the Liberals and the SDP in 1989, there was a clear ambition to create a different, far more democratic, political party. In particular, the new party was conceived as an organization that would fully involve its members in the policy-making process, and as an organization not dominated by its elites at Westminster and in the leader's office. In fact, at the time of merger, the Liberals were the party with the grassroots: in the ballot on the new party, over 58,000 Liberal Party members had a vote, compared with 28,651 SDP members – and this imbalance in Liberals and Social Democrats continued in the membership of the Liberal Democrats.[14] Membership of the merged party grew substantially in the first half of the 1990s, up from around 80,000 in 1988 to over 100,000 in 1994. Since the mid 1990s, however, membership has fallen, down to nearly 83,000 in 1999, falling further to around 60,000 in 2008.[15] Whatever the ups and downs of party membership, it is widely agreed that these grassroots members have played a key role in the electoral revival of the party since the early 1990s; and, in the longer term, in keeping the flame of Liberal politics burning when seats in parliament were few. It almost goes without saying that the vast majority of Lib Dem members are middle-class; and in this, they are no different – other than in degree – from the individual memberships of the Labour and Conservative parties.

But how successfully has the ambition of creating a more grassroots-based party been realized, and what problems does it pose for the leadership of the party?

In keeping with a party committed to a federal constitution for the United Kingdom, one of the most striking features of the organization of the Liberal Democrats is the federal structure of the party. This means that the party is divided between three 'national' parties (England, Scotland and Wales) and a UK-wide federal party. There is a branch of the Liberal Democrats in Northern Ireland and the party is aligned with the cross-community Alliance Party in the province. Each of the national (or sub-national) parties is responsible for the running of Liberal Democrat affairs in its territory. This includes:

selecting parliamentary candidates, party membership and 'policy matters relating specifically to their state'. In the case of the English party, these policy matters have been given over to the federal party.

This federal party takes overall responsibility for UK-wide policy, parliamentary and European elections, fundraising and public relations. In addition, there are 'specified associated organizations' (such as Ethnic Minority Liberal Democrats and Youth and Students) that are officially recognized and part-funded by the party, as well as other 'associated organizations' (e.g. the Liberal Democrat Christian Forum) that also have party recognition and rights within the policy consultation processes.

The founding constitution of the Liberal Democrats left the parliamentary party in a rather odd position, certainly by comparison with the Labour and Conservative parties.[16] Liberal Democrat MPs have no obvious formal role within the party's federal structure. By 2006, the number of Liberal Democrat MPs had hit sixty-three – a significant presence in the House of Commons. The party also had nearly eighty peers in the House of Lords. What was the impact of this parliamentary pressure, especially on a party that, as we have seen, was set up with few MPs?

As the size of the parliamentary party has grown since 1989, so the power of MPs, in practice, has increased. This is not simply about the MP body count. With the growth in the parliamentary party has come the full panoply of political armour at Westminster: the researchers and advisors in well-resourced offices with their connections and access to the party leadership, which itself has become increasingly professional in its operations. At the same time, the activism of Liberal Democrat members has declined, contributing to a weakening of the relationship between the party and its members.[17]

Taken together, the decline in activism and the professionalization of the national political machine based around Westminster has, as with political parties in general, shifted the balance of power inside the party away from the grassroots to the parliamentary leadership. So have Liberal Democrat MPs established a 'de facto veto' over the party decision-making, in particular regarding policy and the leadership?

According to Russell, Fieldhouse and Cutts, there can be little doubt that the power of the parliamentary party has increased in two significant areas. The first is on the question of who leads the party. In theory, the leader is chosen by the membership as a whole. There is nothing in the party's constitution that gives MPs the power to change leaders. But the 'coup' against Charles Kennedy was instigated by the party's MPs, against the views of local party activists, among whom Kennedy remained popular. The second coup against Ming Campbell was also led by the parliamentary party.

The second area that indicates the growing power of MPs is over policy-making in the party. This is, as we have seen, divided between the national and the federal parties. The supreme policy-making body is the annual conference of the federal party; and this was in the past the scene of many a ritual humiliation of the party leadership on issues such as privatization, the minimum wage and the legalization of drugs. The conference, as with other party events, was traditionally dominated by party activists rooted in local parties and local government. But the professionalization of the party machine under Paddy Ashdown and subsequent leaders has brought a more top-down approach to policy-making. Not only has the annual conference become friendlier to the leadership and the parliamentary party, but also the leadership has become the main originator of policy at the conference.

Increasingly, then, the Liberal Democrats have become a party run from Westminster, not the country. Since the 1990s, what MPs say and do matters more and more in terms of the direction the party takes. The moves Nick Clegg made when he became leader, to centralize power over the committee structure, will only take this further.[18] As the party has become more success-ful at winning elections, so it has changed. In many ways, the Liberal Demo-crats are becoming just like the Labour and Conservative parties, far more in the mould of the electoral-professional parties that have come to dominate contemporary catch-all politics. Indeed, Liberal Democrat parliamentarians, who were once overwhelmingly drawn from the activist base in local politics, are now, like MPs from other parties, increasingly born and bred seemingly in the corridors of the Palace of Westminster (and the European parliament in Strasbourg). The lawyers who in the past have made up the largest group of Lib Dem MPs have been overtaken by a mix of teachers, business executives, political activists and miscellaneous white-collar professionals.

As we saw earlier in the book, political parties in general have become more professional and less dependent on an active base of grassroots members. But there are limits to this process. Political parties still need local foot soldiers; and the Liberal Democrats, with their need to fight for every inch of political space, perhaps need them more than most. Indeed, as we have seen, one way through the electoral roadblock of Duverger's law (the electoral system forcing voters into the arms of one of the two 'main' parties) for the Liberal Democrats is community-based political strategies. Local success has built political reputation and bridged the credibility gap; and the targeting of seats during national campaigns has allowed the party to make the most of this local success. None the less, power in the party has shifted to the leadership and to the party in parliament.

## From protest to power

Liberals have spent the best part of seventy years waiting for something to happen – and in 2010 it did. Liberal Democrat MPs were on the government benches in the House of Commons, and Lib Dem ministers were sitting around the cabinet table of a coalition administration led by the Conserva-tives. Nick Clegg was deputy prime minister. The party had their hands on the levers of national power.

As we have seen in this chapter, this transition from protest to power has been a while coming. By 2005, the position of the Liberal Democrats was as good as it had been for a very long time. The party had a firm base of political support in the country and in local government, and it had shared power in the devolved assemblies in Scotland and Wales. At Westminster, its sixty-two MPs in the House of Commons took the party back to 1922 levels; and it was an often-decisive influence in the upper chamber. There was also a sense the party could do better – as Clegg said as he battled to replace Ming Campbell in 2007, being forever the third party in British politics 'wasn't good enough'.

For decades, Liberals held on to the hope that electoral reform would deliver a step change in its political fortunes. It was certainly part of Ashdown's 'project' that getting closer to Labour would lead to a serious review of the voting system once Labour got into power. Proportional representation would be the Lib Dems' chance of power. In the party's mind, electoral reform would solve the age-old dilemma for liberal politics between fighting for its independence (and possible irrelevance), on the one hand, and influence (and possible loss of autonomy), on the other. Some form of PR would increase the chances of people voting for the party by removing the sense that a Lib Dem vote was a wasted vote, and it would also deliver to the Lib Dems a greater number of seats in parliament. Any participation in a coalition government would be from a position of strength, not weakness. Paddy Ashdown got the review – an elegant study by Roy Jenkins – but no action. Nick Clegg got voting reform written into the coalition deal with the Conservatives – but not PR, only the alternative vote.

Whether voting reform would on its own deliver more votes for the Liberal Democrats is an open question. Do the Liberal Democrats suffer because of Duverger's law or because voters are confused about what the party stands for? When the single transferable vote was introduced into local elections in Scotland, the party did not see any great change in its support. While considerable numbers of voters did use their second preferences to support a party different from their first preference, voters in general were still 'guided by party loyalty'.[19]

But beyond the tactical advantages of proportional representation over simple plurality for the Liberal Democrats, there are other, more fundamental questions facing the party, questions that came to the fore before and after the 2010 poll. What do the Lib Dems stand for today? Are they a party of the centre left or the centre right – or even one that straddles this political divide in some kind of 'radical centre'? Are they a party that is more likely to side, even form a government, with Labour (as part of a 'progressive alliance'), or are the Lib Dems just as likely to find common cause with the Conservatives?

One way of looking at these questions is to acknowledge that the Liberal Democrats are not one party but two: the old Liberal and Social Democratic parties. These two former parties shared much in common. The intellectual heritage of social liberalism, dating back to the turn of the twentieth century and stretching through Keynes and Beveridge into the post-war welfare state, was one that liberals and social democrats drew from. Both agreed that individual freedom was nothing without the material resources to realize such freedom. But the formation of the Liberal Democrats also arose out of the merger of the Liberal Party and the SDP, with quite different traditions and ideologies. There remain significant differences of view on the future direction of the party.

Such ideological divisions as do exist inside the Liberal Democrats surfaced with the publication in 2004 of *The Orange Book: Reclaiming Liberalism* (the title refers back to the jacket colour of the influential policy documents produced by the party in the 1920s and 1930s). The 'reclaiming' in the title reflected a concern among some in the party, such as David Laws, that the Liberal Democrats had drifted too far to the left; that the party had become too social democratic (given in to 'soggy socialism', as Laws put it) in looking to the state too often to solve problems; and that the party had lost its traditional commitment to economic freedom. *The Orange Book* was widely interpreted as a statement of politics by the party's 'economic liberals', intent on wresting the political initiative from the 'social liberals' who had had the ear of former member of the SDP Charles Kennedy; and who were anxious to reclaim the centre ground of British politics. This meant pushing for a greater emphasis on free trade and open markets, competition and choice in economic and social policy. In a follow-up volume, *Britain after Blair: A Liberal Agenda*, much the same message of economic liberalism was advanced, though in this book the party's social liberals, led by Simon Hughes and Sarah Teather, were also able to state their position in an attempt by the then leader Ming Campbell to unite both wings of the party.[20]

But these ideological divisions within the party, as significant as they might (or could) be, are more often than not overlaid with other divisions within the party, in particular, the growing divide between the parliamentary party and the party in the country. Indeed, as Andrew Russell and his co-authors have pointed out, most of the *Orange Book* economic liberals ended up with front bench jobs under Ming Campbell. Moreover, the subsequent leadership battle between Nick Clegg and Chris Huhne – both contributors to the *Orange Book* – was essentially between two liberals who had very similar views on most issues. The contest was really about leadership and who could do it better. The main stalwart of the social activist wing of the party, Simon Hughes, ruled himself out of the contest (he had stood twice before for the leadership). Following his election as leader, Clegg did take the Liberal Democrats to the right with policies to cut taxes and reform public services. The political space between New Labour, the Cameron Conservatives and Clegg's Lib Dems narrowed.

The result of the 2010 general election gave the Liberal Democrats little option but to join the Conservatives in some kind of political deal. Despite the attempts by Labour to form a rainbow coalition including the Lib Dems, the SNP and Plaid, the SDLP in Northern Ireland and the new Green Party MP, the only deal that would have any legitimacy with the electorate, and any chance of staying in power, was one involving the Conservatives and the Liberal Democrats. Ideologically, this was a difficult step for the Lib Dems. During the 1990s and 2000s, the party had staked out a position in British politics on the liberal left: liberal on issues of civil liberties, and left on the economy and the provision of welfare. To many in the party – from grassroots activists to leading party figures such as Paddy Ashdown and Simon Hughes – the Liberal Democrats were a party of the 'progressive centre left', and an alliance with Labour was a more natural home.

Having said this, the danger Nick Clegg and his colleagues faced in the aftermath of the 2010 poll was one of credibility. For more than a decade, the Liberal Democrats had clawed their way out of their heartlands in south-west England by working hard at a community level to build local political machines and get people elected in local government. 'Where we work we win' bridged the credibility gap the party faced in areas where it had no historic bedrock of support. This meant the party had to be ideologically, as well as politically, pragmatic: fighting the Conservatives in ways that would attract votes away from the Tories in rural and suburban Britain; and engaging with Labour in ways that would attract votes in urban Britain. The party, if it is to be a national party, must play to its different strengths in different situations. The Liberal Democrat option is not, as Russell and Fieldhouse argue, between moving left or right, but 'neither left nor right'. In other words, the party has to be pragmatic in fighting a middle way between the two parties, attacking both Labour and the Conservatives where appropriate. The ever-present danger in this strategy is that, at a national level, the party's message gets muddled. Indeed, after the initial excitement of Clegg's performance in the first TV debate during the 2010 campaign subsided, the ideological mix the party presented looked less like a radical centre and more a confused mess.

But not to have entered power in 2010 would have been a disaster for the Liberal Democrats. The party had already pragmatically gone into government with both Labour and the Conservatives in the devolved administrations and in local town halls. Not to have done so at a national level would have brought accusations that the Lib Dems were not serious about holding national office. Indeed, the pragmatism of the party was clearly in evidence as both the parliamentary party and the party in the country moved swiftly to ratify the coalition deal with the Conservatives, despite the cumbersome rules put in place during the 1990s to ensure the leadership did not get into bed with one of the main parties without the agreement of members – and despite the obvious unease many in the party felt with sustaining the Conservatives in power.

Having said this, the deal that was struck between the Liberal Democrats and the Conservatives after the 2010 poll was made possible by the changes that had taken place to the party. In particular, the emergence of a leading group of politicians in the party with a more economically liberal view of policy allowed the Lib Dems to find sufficient overlap with a party that, as we saw in chapter 3, had itself changed to become more socially liberal. There was real common ground around economic policy, welfare reform and the public services between Clegg's Liberal Democrats and Cameron's Conservatives. Whether this 'liberal conservative' government – or 'radical centre' that Roy Jenkins argued for in 1979 – will hold, only time will tell.

## Further reading and research resources

For the origins of the Liberal Party, see Vincent, *The Formation of the Liberal Party 1857–1868*. The Liberal Democrat History Group is also a good source: www.liberalhistory.org.uk/. Some of the challenges facing the Liberal democrats today are put in context by Bogdanor in 'The Liberal Democrat dilemma in historical perspective'. Ivor Crewe and Anthony King's *SDP: The Birth, Life and Death of the Social Democratic Party* (Oxford: Oxford University Press, 1995) is the definitive book on the SDP. Research by Andrew Russell, Edward Fieldhouse and David Cutts is a must for any contemporary understanding of Lib Dem politics: see Russell and Fieldhouse, *Neither Left nor Right*, and further references in the bibliography. The Liberal Democrats are online at www.libdems.org.uk/home.aspx; and blogging at www.libdemvoice.org/.

CHAPTER SIX

# Putting the Boots Away?
# The Far Right
# in British Politics

## Going mainstream?

Since the late 1960s, far right parties have survived on the fringes of British political life. Few regarded them as a serious threat to mainstream party politics. The National Front, the most prominent far right group during the 1970s and 1980s, just occasionally grabbed a by-election headline. But its neo-fascist ideological baggage – and its frequently thuggish and violent actions – made the party unelectable in Britain. The far right might make it in other parts of Europe, most commentators agreed, but British party politics was different. The United Kingdom was an exception to the European political rule.

This theory of 'exceptionalism' suggested that far right politics would never work in a liberal, tolerant and constitutionally robust country like Britain. Parties such as the National Front would always be starved of political support. There were not enough votes in this sort of fascist-inspired jackboot politics. Moreover, the checks and balances of British parliamentary government and first-past-the-post voting gave far right parties little opportunity to prosper. Factionalism didn't help the credibility of the far right either. And what votes were available on the back of issues such as immigration were taken by the dominant force on the centre right, the Conservative Party.[1]

By 2004, however, question marks were being raised about how different British politics really was. The British National Party (BNP), which had taken over from the National Front as Britain's leading far right party, was winning votes in local, national and European elections. Under its leader Nick Griffin, the BNP appeared to have turned its back on old-style neo-fascist politics. One commentator suggested that the BNP had 'unquestionably become the most successful far-right party in British history'; another that: 'For the first time in its history, the British National Party stands on the brink of entering the political mainstream.'[2]

So, did Griffin's strategy to make the BNP politically credible work? By putting the jackboots away, has far right politics entered the political mainstream in Britain as it is has done in other parts of Europe? And is the rise of new Euro-sceptic nationalist parties such as the United Kingdom Independence Party part of the emergence of a new block of right-wing parties and right-wing voters in British politics?

## Oswald Mosley and the British Union of Fascists

Any study of far right politics in Britain is inevitably drawn back to Oswald Mosley, who fled mainstream politics to found the British Union of Fascists in 1932. Mosley was from a privileged English family – he was Sir Oswald, a baronet. He first entered parliament as a Conservative MP after the First World War, but then joined the Labour Party, becoming a junior minister in 1929.

These were hard times. As the Great Depression swept the world economy, unemployment and poverty created misery in communities across Britain. The restless Mosley resigned from government and formed the New Party in 1931. He campaigned for economic protectionism and state intervention to tackle lengthening dole queues – policies that had supporters in both main parties, as well as the mainstream press. After touring Mussolini's fascist Italy, he returned to establish the British Union of Fascists (BUF). The party was increasingly influenced by the far right politics on the continent. It supported a corporate state and an end to the party system. The BUF was stridently nationalistic and anti-communist. Mosley established his own military-style party stewards, the infamous Blackshirts, as the BUF took to the streets in provocative and often violent demonstrations. The party stood candidates in local elections in London, winning a few thousand votes in Bethnal Green and Shoreditch. But that was about as far as the BUF got. The Second World War more or less finished Mosley off as a political figure. He had opposed Britain's declaration of war (Britain, he said, should 'mind its own business') and was interned by the government because of his close links with Hitler and Mussolini.

## The end of empire, immigration and Enoch Powell

Far right politics in the post-war years, in organizations such as the League of Empire Loyalists, looked backwards to an age when the British Empire spanned the world. The 'winds of change' that Conservative Prime Minister Harold Macmillan recognized in a speech in South Africa in 1960 were not ones that these right-wing Colonel Blimps acknowledged. By the sixties, however, British society was changing in ways that would provide new opportunities for far right politics in Britain. Mass immigration from many former British colonies made race a hot political issue. In the 1964 general election, Labour lost the safe seat of Birmingham Smethwick to the Conservatives. The Tory candidate Peter Griffiths's message was: 'If you want a nigger for a neighbour vote Labour' – and local voters, it appeared, didn't.

Four years later, the leading Conservative politician Enoch Powell, MP for Wolverhampton South West, brought race and politics centre-stage in Britain in his 'Rivers of blood' speech to West Midlands Conservatives on 20 April 1968. It also led to his own dismissal from the Tory opposition frontbench by leader Edward Heath. Powell did not actually use these exact words, but, as a former professor of Greek, he had a habit of quoting classical scholars. Using the words of the Roman writer Virgil, Powell said: 'As I look ahead I am filled with foreboding. Like the Roman, I seem to see "the River Tiber foaming with much blood".' The speech was about what Powell believed were the consequences of mass immigration for British society. Such immigration, Powell thought, would cause social conflict by undermining the common bonds of national identity. He was also against European integration and British devolution for much the same reason.

Was Powell being racist? It is certainly true that he quoted the racism of his constituents in his speech ('the black man will have the whip hand over the white man', was one such quote). Powell claimed he was only highlighting the dangers of mass immigration. Immigration on a modest scale, if new-comers to Britain integrated into society, was possible, he believed, but large-scale immigration was a different matter. Powell also argued that multiculturalism (he then called it 'communalism') would lead to significant tensions within communities, especially as white British families felt like 'strangers in their own country'.

Powell's opponents argued – and continue to argue – that, at the very least, in making such an inflammatory speech he gave credence to racism and stoked the fire of far right politics. Indeed, on the back of Powell's brand of nationalist conservatism came a revival of such politics not seen since the 1930s. In white working-class Britain, under pressure in more unstable economic times, 'Enoch is right' was a slogan many supported. Disillusioned Conservatives also looked to the new political movements emerging on the far right to further their nationalist views. But, as we shall see, the lack of mainstream political support made this new far right politics, at best, marginal. It did not, however, stop parties like the National Front from causing trouble on the streets of Britain.

## Jackboot politics: the National Front

The fracturing of British society in the 1970s saw a proliferation of political movements on the extremes of the ideological spectrum facing each other, often in pitched battles in urban Britain. The most significant group on the far right was the National Front (NF). The party had its roots in a mix of post-war neo-fascist politics – notably the British National Party and the Greater Britain Movement – and right-wing conservative bodies – in particular, the League of Empire Loyalists. John Tyndall, along with Martin Webster, was a key figure in the founding of the NF in 1967. Tyndall did much to set the tone for the British far right and its neo-Nazi-style politics. On a trip to Germany to attend a meeting of right-wing nationalists in the 1960s, Tyndall is reported to have spent an hour buying his first pair of 'genuine German jackboots'.[3] But the NF from the start had its internal divisions, in particular between those like Tyndall anxious to maintain the party's lineage with earlier national socialist movements and more traditional – and to a certain extent, more moderate – right-wing conservatives who bemoaned the decline of Britain and believed, however misguidedly, that it was their patriotic duty to take action to stop the rot, whatever that was.

Accurate figures on the membership of political parties are difficult to obtain at the best of times – and those for minor parties, especially ones that refuse to publish membership figures, can be even more unreliable. Estimates of the NF's membership suggest that numbers grew to around 20,000 in 1975, although this included something like 6–8,000 individuals who had not paid their fees. By the end of the decade, the number of members was down to about 5,500.[4] These relatively small numbers did not stop a hard core of NF activists, in as many as 130 branches across the country in 1976, engaging in provocative street politics. NF meetings and demonstrations, often in communities at the heart of multicultural Britain, were always aggressive and frequently ended in violence. The NF wrapped itself in the union flag. Its message was simple: 'Britain for the British'. NF ideology combined traditional national socialist themes of ultra-nationalism, anti-Semitism, white biological supremacy and opposition to liberal democracy. The party advocated the ending of 'coloured immigration' and the repatriation of 'immigrant peoples'; withdrawal from the (then) European Economic Community; opposition to free trade; and the creation of a corporate state. There were always those in the party who opposed some of the more hard-core Nazi aspects to the party's ideological strategy, and who favoured an approach that might distance the NF from the legacy of Hitler and German fascism. But those voices were marginalized in the party and damaging factional splits resulted.[5]

The electoral record of the NF was modest in this period. In 1970, the party put forward 10 candidates, who won on average 1,145 votes apiece. At the two elections in 1974, the number of candidates rose to 54 (February) and 90 (October). And while all NF candidates lost their deposits, as they always did at general elections, the party's national share of the vote reached 0.4 per cent in the autumn election. By 1979, the NF was fielding candidates in half of the seats in Britain and its national share of the vote was reaching 0.6 per cent, although individual candidates on average performed worse than in 1974. Where the NF succeeded in grabbing headlines was at by-elections. In 1972, the NF candidate in Uxbridge won 8.2 per cent of the vote; at West Bromwich in 1973, 16 per cent; in Newham South in 1974, 11.5 per cent; at Thurrock in 1976, 6.6 per cent; and in Birmingham Stechford in 1977, 8.2 per cent.[6]

## Far right splits

As with much fringe politics, party in-fighting led to the break-up of the NF. Following what was a poor result in the 1979 general election – an election that brought into government a party that had shown itself more than willing to play the immigration card – the NF tore itself part. The two men who had dominated NF politics in the 1970s, Tyndall and Webster, were at logger-heads. In the early 1980s, the party split and Tyndall left to form the New National Front and then, in 1982, the British National Party. Indeed, the Tyndall wing of the old NF provided the bulk of the members, branches and candidates for the new BNP. Another faction of the old NF left to form the Constitutional Movement, later the Nationalist Party. The NF itself continued until 1995 when it split again, with one grouping renamed as the National Democrats, and another continuing as the National Front. Such factionalism did little for the far right's electoral credibility, meagre as it was. For much of the 1980s and 1990s, the NF, the BNP and the New Democrats could muster few votes between them. Only at the Dagenham by-election in 1994 when Tyndall stood for the BNP did the far right perform well, capturing 7 per cent of the vote – and holding on to the party's deposit.

By the end of the 1990s, the far right was where it had always been – on the very fringes of British politics. As Matthew Goodwin argues: 'Adherence to political violence and street-based marches, blunt racist discourse, anti-Semitism and general nostalgia for fascism have combined to ensure that, historically, the far right in Britain has starved itself of any sense of political legitimacy.'[7] Indeed, the setting-up of Combat 18 (the name was a numeric version of Hitler's initials) to steward BNP events simply attracted right-wing thugs who were more than happy to target the party's opponents with physical attacks. The later split between Combat 18 and the BNP led to an often violent struggle between the two groups and did little to dispel the image that this was extremist politics at its very worst.

The influence of the old NF on the BNP, in terms not just of its ideology but also of its membership, recruitment and organization, was also significant in keeping the BNP on the fringes. The party saw itself as a paramilitary-type body; and recruitment was largely among disaffected working-class young men (the 'young skinhead') and from other right-wing parties and the more extreme sections of the Conservative Party. For much of the 1990s, membership of the party was never more than around 2,000 – and few of these were very active and turnover was high.[8] It was, then, not very surprising that the BNP was going nowhere fast.

## Far right politics across Europe

As far right politics in Britain imploded in the 1990s, the idea that British party politics was different from that in the rest of Europe appeared to be confirmed. This theory of British exceptionalism was boosted by the success of the far right across the English Channel. During the 1990s, right-wing parties in continental Europe attracted support at the polls, and by the end of the decade were even taking seats in government.

The National Front (FN) in France, and its leader Jean-Marie Le Pen, led the way. Founded in 1972, the FN prospered in places like Marseilles in the south of the country by playing on fears of immigration from North Africa, and in traditional working-class districts decimated by de-industrialization. In the 1974 presidential election, Le Pen barely registered on the political radar. By 1988, he won 14 per cent of the vote, and 15 per cent in 1995. In the 2002 presidential race, Le Pen shocked France and the rest of Europe by coming second in the first ballot, winning 17 per cent of the votes. He was soundly beaten in the second round, 82 per cent to 18 per cent, by the conservative candidate Jacques Chirac. But still a marker had gone down for far right politics in the rest of Europe.

Other far right parties in Europe in the late 1990s also prospered. In Austria, the Freedom Party (FPO) led by Jörg Haider attracted votes on the back of a populist right-wing message of opposition to immigration and to the EU. In the 1999 general election, the FPO won 27 per cent of the vote and fifty-two seats in parliament, making it the second-largest party. Despite the hostility from other EU member states, the FPO joined a coalition government with the conservative People's Party. This taste of power did not prove easy for the FPO – and in the 2002 elections, with Haider having retreated to his regional power base in Carinthia, the party's share of the vote fell back to 10 per cent: enough, however, to retain a share in government.

In Italy right-wing politics also got a taste of power. Following the collapse of a centre left government in 2001, the conservative Silvio Berlusconi led a new right-wing coalition administration that included members of two far right parties, the Northern League led by Umberto Bossi and the 'post-fascist' National Alliance, whose leader Gianfranco Fini joined Berlusconi's government. Like Haider in Austria, Fini and his National Alliance sought to move nationalist politics on from its associations with fascist far right politics in their respective countries by pushing a populist message tapping into resentments about immigration, European integration and mainstream domestic politics.

These anti-immigration/anti-EU messages were resonating with voters elsewhere – enough for far right parties in Norway and Denmark to shape the governments of these traditional bastions of social democratic politics. In Norway, Carl Hagen's Progress Party won nearly 15 per cent of votes in the 2001 election and supported the formation of a right-wing coalition government. In Denmark, the Danish People's Party led by Pia Kjaersgaard became the country's third-largest party with 12 per cent of the vote, and, as in Norway, propped up a right-wing coalition administration. Again, far right politics was moving from the fringe to the mainstream; and far right parties were joining with more traditional conservative parties to form governing coalitions.

In Switzerland, the right-wing Swiss People's Party (SVP) led by the billionaire industrialist Christoph Blocher became the joint second-largest party with 22.5 per cent of the vote following elections in 1999. In 2003, the SVP did even better, winning 27 per cent of the vote and taking more than a quarter of the 200 seats in the lower house of the Swiss federal parliament. Elsewhere across Europe, the Popular Party in Portugal led by Paulo Portas won fourteen seats in the national parliament in 2002, with nearly 9 per cent of the vote, and joined another right-wing coalition government. In Belgium, the Flemish Block and its leader Frank Vanhecke won nearly 10 per cent of the vote in national elections in 1999, as well as making considerable advances in the Flemish city of Antwerp.

Perhaps the most striking advance of the far right was in the Netherlands – a country with a deeply engrained liberal culture. The right-wing Liveable Netherlands party sacked its charismatic leader Pim Fortuyn in 2002 after he called for Holland's anti-discrimination law to be cut from the constitution. Fortuyn's uncompromising message on immigration ('this is a full country') and his anti-Islamic views (he branded the religion 'backward' and said it threatened the Netherlands' liberal culture) quickly won him support. Following success in local elections in Rotterdam, his new party looked set to be a significant force in national elections in 2002. His murder nine days before the election did not stop the party, Pim Fortuyn's List, from winning twenty-six parliamentary seats, coming second to the conservative Christian Democrat Party.

### Why far right politics advanced in continental Europe – and didn't in the UK

The study of the far right raises methodological issues concerning how researchers go about studying these kinds of parties. Traditionally, research has focused on the social and economic conditions that might generate far right or extreme right-wing politics. We might think of this as the demand for far right politics among voters. This approach has tended to treat far right political activists as 'extremists': 'as individuals helplessly susceptible to irrational outbursts of aberrant extremism'.[9] By contrast, more recent research has sought to get inside the parties themselves to study the strategies of political activists. Such an approach attempts to balance structural accounts of far right politics with explanations that focus on political agency and the supply of far right politics by parties.

Orthodox accounts of European far right politics, then, have tended to focus on how factors such as immigration, de-industrialization, unemployment and the economic insecurity brought about by globalization have weakened traditional social and political identities and driven demand among voters for the far right. For example, the French National Front, far from being a protest vote party, had by the 2002 presidential election established significant support from two groups of voters: first, among more traditional, older, middle-class Catholics fearful of crime, hostile to migrants and anxious about cultural change; and second, in the insecure working-class communities that once lined up *en masse* behind socialist and communist parties.[10] These voters in southern and north-eastern France were drawn to Le Pen's populist appeals to national identity, economic nationalism and the strong state.

But why did far right parties in many parts of continental Europe prosper while they did not in the UK? After all, Britain faced many of the same economic and social problems as her continental neighbours. One reason was that parties in other parts of Europe were able to exploit these new political opportunities because mainstream political parties did not. The degree of consensus between the established parties on issues such as immigration and European integration provided political spaces for right-wing parties to tap into these concerns, as well as broader feelings of political disillusionment. Parties on the right across Europe were able to position themselves as popular champions of ordinary people in the face of out-of-touch mainstream politicians.[11] In Britain, by contrast, the 'authoritarian populism' of the Conservative Party during the 1980s and 1990s led to stricter controls on immigration; and its broader narrative of national renewal limited the space in British politics for far right parties to exploit nationalist issues, in both the political system and the media.

There are also institutional factors in play that help to account for the success of the far right on the continent and its failure in the United Kingdom, in particular the role of electoral systems in providing opportunities for (or conversely, putting up barriers against) the advance of far right parties in mainstream politics. In Britain, the electoral system for national elections to Westminster, as we have seen, works against small parties, except those with regionally concentrated bases of political support (such as nationalist parties in Scotland and Wales). In other parts of Europe, a variety of more proportional electoral systems allow smaller parties to get their feet in the political door – and, importantly, the opportunity to establish some credibility with voters and legitimacy within the political system.

The success of far right parties in other parts of Europe in the 1990s was also, to an important extent, down to the parties themselves: to the ideologies they adopted and the political strategies they engaged in. Far from distancing themselves from mainstream electoral politics, right-wing parties in continental Europe were able to engage with the electorate in a way that was just not happening in the UK. The political scientist Matthew Goodwin suggests it was the National Front in France in the mid 1980s that established a new political template for far right political activism. This template not only gave the FN political leverage within French politics, it also helped to prevent the party being stigmatized and marginalized by other parties and the media.

This template had two important features. First, biological arguments against immigration were replaced by cultural ones ('differentialist racism'). Le Pen and the far right in Europe tended to use cultural and ethnically nationalist, rather than biological, arguments against immigration: their parties were defending 'France' (or 'Austria', 'the Netherlands', and so on) rather than (biologically 'superior') white people. To a certain extent, this allowed far right parties on the continent to deflect accusations of racism – though it did not, of course, stop such accusations being made.

Second, the FN (and far right parties across Europe that followed in Le Pen's wake) insisted they were on the side of ordinary people. This populism in large part focused on established political processes and institutions, claiming that they were out of touch and elitist. This anti-establishment politics allowed far right parties to present themselves as defenders of national sovereignty and national identity in the name of 'real people', against the incursions of the political elite through European integration. It also allowed them to address the anxieties of many voters in a period of significant economic and social change brought about by globalization.

Rather than embrace the past, then, the far right on the continent wore suits and acted like politicians who understood, and wanted to do something about, the concerns of ordinary people. Whether this image is false or not is not the point. Such a strategy gave far right parties in Europe credibility with sizeable parts of the electorate and helped them avoid being written off by the media and other political actors as beyond the pale. As Goodwin argues, many of these parties did not have fascist baggage but drew on the populist and even liberal backgrounds of their parties. But even in Italy, for example, where there was such baggage, the National Alliance worked hard to ditch it and establish a more mainstream image ('post-fascism'), even if this led to factional splits, as happened in 2003 when Alessandra Mussolini, the granddaughter of the Italian dictator, left the party after its leader Gianfranco Fini described fascism as an 'absolute evil' on a visit to Israel.

## Classifying the new European far right

The right-wing political parties that emerged as significant players in European politics in the 1990s are a mixed bunch. This begs the question whether they are all part of the same ideological family of parties.

Some of the European right parties, notably the National Alliance in Italy, have links back to fascist politics in the 1930s and 1940s (the National Alliance was formed out of the break-up of the neo-fascist Italian Socialism Movement (MSI) in 1995). Other parties have arisen out of the post-industrial transformation of Western Europe – and are better thought of as a conservative response to the post-materialism that has cut across traditional class-based political cleavages and broken up established patterns of political support. Further still, some of these parties are rooted in regionalist political cleavages – such as the Northern League in Italy. Others are anti-tax parties that combine neo-liberalism with traditional conservatism (as we see later, the United Kingdom Independence Party fits this description).

Cutting across these divisions is, according to a number of academics working in the field, a populism led by charismatic leaders aimed at mobilizing resentment among voters towards established parties and political elites. This populism operates, by and large, within established political structures: while this new European right challenge liberal democracy, they play on the sense of political alienation of many voters and what is often seen as the corruption of national and European political elites and the exclusion of ordinary people and their communities. This leads Cas Mudde to label the European right as 'populist radical right' parties: parties that blend a xenophobic nationalism with an authoritarianism that places great store by law and order and traditional social structures such as the family. This populist radical right is more concerned with cultural questions – social diversity, national identity – than economic ones, though clearly the sweeping changes to Western European economies are an important backdrop to any understanding of this new European right. By contrast with twentieth-century fascism, the European far right today is, by and large, pro-capitalism; and the main focus of its politics is immigration, national (western) values and reform of political systems.[12]

## Suited not booted

The far right in Britain had spent the best part of three decades parading around in steel toecap boots. By the end of the 1990s, they were just as much on the political fringes as they had ever been. But were there lessons the BNP could learn from across the Channel? Its new leader Nick Griffin thought there were. But in swapping its boots for suits, and by tapping into what some think is a significant level of potential political support, has the BNP challenged the long-held view that the far right would never make it in mainstream British party politics?

Nick Griffin joined the NF as a teenager in the mid 1970s when his father, a right-wing Conservative, took his family to an NF meeting. Later graduating in law from Cambridge University, he worked for the party until it imploded in the late 1980s; and again for the BNP from the mid 1990s. He became party leader in 1999 in a coup against John Tyndall. The fact that Griffin has sought to 'modernize' the BNP may be surprising. His background in the NF; his hard-line position in the party, opposing change for most of the 1990s; the denial of the Holocaust; and the conviction for inciting racial hatred against Jews in 1999 (and the acquittal on similar charges, against Muslims, in 2006) – none of these speak of a man who might want to turn, as one writer put it, 'a bunch of neo-Nazi skinheads into an electable party'.[13] But since the late 1990s, under Griffin's leadership, the BNP has developed a clearer vote-seeking strategy. There are two key elements to this strategy – elements that draw explicitly on the experience of the far right on the continent in general, and the National Front in France in particular.[14]

The first element seeks to create an anti-establishment, community-based politics in an attempt to make the party more credible with a wider electorate. This has seen the BNP's political agenda shift from one that focuses almost exclusively on race and immigration (though this remains a big part of the BNP's appeal) to one that engages more broadly with the concerns of local people, in particular, over issues of housing, public services and civic amenities. This localist politics sought to win recruits and support at the ballot box by presenting the party as being in touch with voters, in comparison to the established parties who are presented as self-serving, corrupt and out of touch. Griffin, for example, has talked about the BNP as a 'peasants' revolt' against elitist Westminster politics.[15] The party's list of policies around crime (civilian patrols, hanging), schooling (Christian worship and corporal punishment), foreign workers in the NHS and leaving the European Union are all part of a broad populist message aimed at disillusioned voters turned off by established Westminster politics.

The second element of the BNP's political strategy under Griffin has been to embrace 'differentialist' arguments against immigration. The question of race obviously looms large in any debate about the BNP. Critics insist that if you scratch the surface, nothing has changed: it is still the same old racist party that until 2009, when it was declared illegal, had a whites-only membership rule. In interviews, Griffin argues that nationalist politics in Britain mistakenly based its politics on white supremacist views. Following the 'differentialist' arguments of the far right on the continent, Griffin shifted, in public at least, to a position that races are different, and that any attempt to create a multicultural society was doomed to failure[16] – echoes here of Enoch Powell back in the 1960s. So while BNP policy remains the deportation of asylum seekers and foreign nationals who are a threat to national security, compulsory repatriation was dropped in 2001 for a voluntary scheme under which existing 'non-ethnically British' people would be paid to leave the country. Post 9/11, the BNP also played the culture card, claiming that Britain's Christian way of life was being undermined by immigration, multiculturalism, globalization and 'Islamification'.

### The BNP at the polls

Have any of these changes made an impact on the electoral record of the far right? This record, we saw earlier, is poor in the UK. But did the 'modernization' strategy of the BNP work in attracting more votes at the polls?

By the late 1990s, there were indications that the size of the far right vote was increasing. In 1997, 2001 and 2005, the BNP received less than 1 per cent of votes cast (0.1 per cent in 1997; 0.18 in 2001; and 0.7 in 2005). At the 1997 general election, the BNP stood 57 candidates, up from just 13 in 1992, with each candidate gaining on average 1.3 per cent of votes cast. In four seats (West Bromwich West, Bethnal Green and Bow, Dewsbury, and Poplar and

Canning Town), the candidates held their deposits with more than 5 per cent of votes cast. In 2001, 33 BNP candidates stood, with an average of 3.9 per cent of the vote each. In 2005, the BNP was represented in 130 seats, with its candidates gaining on average 3.5 per cent of the vote. In Barking, the BNP gained nearly 17 per cent of the vote (pushing the Liberal Democrats into fourth place); and in West Yorkshire, the BNP candidate won just over 13 per cent in Dewsbury; and Nick Griffin won 9.2 per cent in Keighley.[17]

Results in elections for the European parliament also suggested the political fortunes of the BNP were changing. In 1999, the BNP polled nearly 1 per cent of the national vote (just over 100,000 votes), which, despite the low turnout, was its best result for some time. Five years later, in elections held at the same time as polls for the London mayor and the London Assembly, the BNP increased its share of the national vote to 5 per cent, with over 800,000 votes cast for BNP candidates. In Burnley the party was placed third with 16.7 per cent of votes; in Stoke-on-Trent, it won 15.3 per cent; and in Barking and Dagenham in East London, 14.9 per cent.

In the elections for the Greater London Assembly, where voters have two votes – one for a constituency member and another for a London-wide member – the BNP secured 2.9 per cent of the vote for the London-wide members in 2000; and 4.8 per cent in 2004. While the party failed to win any seats in the assembly, it was clear its strategy to focus on local issues was paying some dividends. In the London mayoral election itself, the BNP candidate in 2000 won 2 per cent of first-preference votes and 3.2 per cent of second-preference votes. In 2004, the BNP candidate, beating the Green candidate into sixth position, won 3.1 per cent of first-preference and 4.4 of second-preference votes. In 2008, the BNP passed the 5 per cent threshold necessary to win a seat in the assembly and Richard Barnbook was elected as a London-wide member (he came fifth in the mayoral race with 69,000 votes). In other mayoral elections, the BNP also showed it could win support in particular political locations. In the London borough of Newham in May 2002, the BNP candidate gained just over 7 per cent of the vote; and in Stoke-on-Trent City, the BNP were third with 18.7 per cent in October 2002.

The BNP were also making some ground in local council elections. In 1993, the party's candidate in the Millwall ward of Tower Hamlets in East London won a seat on the council in a by-election, only to lose it at the full election the following year. In the 2002 local elections in England, while only contesting a small number of wards, the BNP won 3 seats and came close in a number of others. The following year, the party won 2 further seats in by-elections in Blackburn and Calderdale, and in further local elections in May 2003, the BNP stood candidates in 215 wards, winning 13 seats. In local elections held in England in 2006, the BNP fielded over 350 candidates and more than doubled its total of councillors to 46. Indeed, in Barking and Dagenham in East London, the party won 11 seats, making it the second-largest party on the council. The BNP won 3 seats on each of the councils in Epping Forest,

Stoke-on-Trent and Sandwell in the Black Country. It also picked up seats in Burnley, Leeds, Pendle, Redbridge, Redditch and Solihull, though it lost one in Bradford.

At the 2008 local elections in England and Wales, the BNP had mixed fortunes, doing well in new areas – winning seats on Nuneaton council in Warwickshire, Amber Valley in Derbyshire, Thurrock in Essex and Three Rivers, Hertfordshire – but not building on previous success. While it gained 2 seats on Rotherham Council (and had an average of nearly 29 per cent of the vote in the 5 seats it contested), it failed to win a seat on next-door Barnsley council, despite coming second in 6 out of 20 wards where the party stood. Over in West Yorkshire, the BNP made no progress in an area where it had previously done well. While in Stoke-on-Trent the party increased its number of councillors to 9 on the Labour- controlled council, it lost 2 out of 3 councillors in Epping Forest on the edge of London.

From the late 1990s, then, the BNP's performance in local and European elections suggested the party was having some success in mainstream politics. But who was voting for the BNP – and what did the size and demographics of BNP support say about the potential pool of nationalist votes in Britain?

## Voting for and joining the BNP

During the campaign for the 2006 local government elections, Margaret Hodge, Labour minister and MP for Barking, caused controversy when she suggested that 80 per cent of white voters in the area were 'tempted' to vote for the BNP.[18] This rather put paid to the idea that there was something different about British politics when it came to support for the far right. Mrs Hodge's comments were made in the light of a report from researchers at the University of Essex.[19] According to this work, the underlying potential support for the far right is higher than is generally thought – and contemporary social attitudes, especially towards immigration, are increasing this pool of potential voters for the far right. This pool, the research suggests, is something like 18–25 per cent of the electorate.

While it is clear that a large majority of the electorate are hostile to far right parties – and would never vote for them – nearly 20 per cent of the public said they might vote for the BNP in the future. And in a study of the London electorate, over 25 per cent of them had voted for the BNP in European or regional elections or said they identified with or might vote for the BNP at some time. As we shall see shortly, while there is little love lost between the BNP and the United Kingdom Independence Party (UKIP), according to this research the two parties appeal to the same pool of voters. The combined support for the BNP and UKIP at the European elections was just over 21 per cent.

Who is voting for the BNP? Across Europe, evidence on far right voting points to patterns of lower-middle-class support, though these parties also draw support from important sections of the skilled and unskilled working class. Significantly, voting for the far right on the continent is not simply associated with economic insecurity; support for the far right is found in affluent regions and among the well-heeled middle classes. As we saw earlier, culture – and questions of national and ethnic identity – is as important as the state of the economy.[20]

In Britain, evidence suggests that support for the far right is linked to social class, age and education. Traditionally, it is not the manual working class that turns to far right parties. Support for the NF in the 1970s tended to be concentrated among skilled workers and the self-employed. It was also greatest in areas with relatively high numbers of migrants from the Caribbean and the Indian sub-continent.[21] Equally, highest support for the BNP has come from semi-skilled and self-employed male workers, not unskilled manual workers. While the publication on the internet of around 11,000 alleged members of the BNP in 2008 showed that the party was attracting some support from middle-class teachers, doctors, lawyers, clergy, police and military officers and those working in government, the reality is that electoral support for the BNP is lowest among middle-class and skilled workers. Older people are also more likely to vote BNP, as are those with few or no qualifications.

The concerns of Mrs Hodge were in part about the challenge BNP support poses for the Labour Party. The BNP under Griffin has made no bones about its bid for 'Old Labour' voters: the BNP is 'the Labour Party your granddad voted for'. It is, in particular, the very issue of immigration that plays into the hands of the BNP in traditional Labour-voting areas, where, as one political scientist puts it, 'senses of vulnerability and insecurity in relation to changes such as those induced by immigration may be high'.[22] Though, interestingly, a study by the Institute for Public Policy Research based on the 2009 European election results suggested that BNP support was lower where there had been higher rates of immigration. Only in Barking and Dagenham in East London were higher levels of migration and support for the BNP found together. The incidence of the BNP support was, according to the study, linked more with patterns of 'social exclusion'.[23] Certainly the BNP has made some in-roads into Labour's electoral base in the white working class, especially in those parts of the country that gained little from the boom years under the Blair government after 1997 – and which suffered as that boom turned to bust in 2008. In these parts of the electorate, insecurity is allied with a sense of pessimism not just about their own lives but, perhaps more importantly, about the chances of the established parties doing anything about it. Indeed, the success of the BNP with these groups of voters is in part because, on a range of economic and social policies, the party is now well to the left of Labour.[24]

If the BNP has had some success at turning latent support at the polls into votes, it has also turned some of this support into members. During the 2000s, membership of the party increased significantly, from under 2,000 at the end of the 1990s to somewhere between 10,000 and 12,000 in 2009 (the party claims around 14,000, but a lower figure is more widely accepted[25]). Particular concentrations of members are found in the East Midlands, the old Lancashire mill towns, West Yorkshire and Essex. The retention of members, such a problem in the 1990s, remains one, but under Griffin there have been clear attempts to recruit and retain members through better communication, a shift away from the NF-influenced paramilitary culture and the establishment of a range of supporting organizations, including Great White Records, youth and student wings and an annual party festival to boost the socialization of members into the party. While most early activists for the BNP were ex-NF members (or members of other far right groups such as the British Movement), an increasing number of activists in the 2000s have no links with far right groups. Some are disillusioned Conservative, UKIP or Referendum Party (see below) members; others are entirely new to politics. There has also been a very limited attempt to promote internal democracy in the party through an advisory council. But still the BNP, true to its roots, has a highly centralized party structure with an authoritarian style of leadership.[26]

## The forward march of British nationalism?

Populist radical right parties across Europe, as we saw earlier in this chapter, were able to exploit the weakness of mainstream conservative parties, in particular on issues such as membership of the European Union. Christian democracy, the main force on the centre right in Europe, is, by and large, wedded to the European project. In Britain, by contrast, the Conservative Party tapped into right-wing political sentiment during the 1980s with its flag-waving project of national renewal. Government policy led to tighter immigration restrictions and tougher stances on law and order. This helped to block the advance of other nationalist forces in Britain such as the NF – though many of the NF's political wounds were self-inflicted, as we have seen. The implosion of the Conservative Party in the 1990s brought fresh opportunities for right-wing politics to flourish in Britain. Europe fractured the country and the Tory party – and as a result, new nationalist forces emerged on the political right.

UKIP was set up by the academic historian Alan Sked in 1993. Sked, a former member of the Liberal Party, was part of the Anti-Federalist League, a group established to campaign against what they saw as the drift towards a European federal state in the Treaty on European Union signed at Maastricht in 1991. The treaty split the governing Conservative Party of John Major and the ratification of the treaty in parliament was bitter. UKIP drew considerable support from both Conservative members and voters in its opposition to the treaty and its policy of supporting withdrawal from the EU.

At the 1997 general election, UKIP found itself in competition for the eurosceptic vote with the Referendum Party, set up by the billionaire financier

James Goldsmith in October 1995. Goldsmith's party had one policy – to force the government of the day to call a referendum on Britain's membership of the EU. With £20 million of Goldsmith's fortune, the Referendum Party was able to attract much publicity (it sent an anti-EU video to 5 million homes). With 547 candidates, it won 2.3 per cent of the UK vote (3.1 per cent per candidate). Goldsmith himself stood in Putney against the former Conservative minister David Mellor. As the returning officer called the result late in the evening, Goldsmith taunted the defeated Mellor in a rancorous series of exchanges between the two men. In truth, the votes that Goldsmith won were not the difference between winning and losing for the Tory candidate. A month later, Goldsmith was dead from cancer – and the Referendum Party folded. The more immediate political impact of Goldsmith's intervention was on UKIP. At the 1997 election, following a credible showing at the 1994 European elections (the party won 3.3 per cent of the vote in twenty-four contests), UKIP won 0.3 per cent of the vote (1.2 per cent per candidate).

So what kind of party is UKIP? Ideologically, the party combines a mix of old-style liberal commitments to free markets, limited government and individual freedom with conservative appeals to national sovereignty and traditional social values appealing to normally Conservative-supporting middle-class voters. The party has been shaped by, and attractive to, disillusioned Thatcherites such as leader, and leading UKIP figure in the European parliament, Nigel Farage. In 2002, the party had around 10,000 members, increasing to 26,000 in 2004 before falling back to around 15,000 in 2008.[27]

UKIP has not been without its own power struggles. Following Sked's resignation from the party after the 1997 election, UKIP went through three leaders in relatively quick succession: Roger Knapman, Jeffrey Titford and Michael Holmes. This did not stop the party making electoral advances on the back of its anti-Europeanism in elections for the European parliament. In the 1999 elections, UKIP won 7 per cent of the vote, winning two seats at Strasbourg. In the 2004 European elections, its vote more than doubled to 16.2 per cent. Robert Kilroy-Silk, former Labour MP and day-time television host, was one of the twelve UKIP MEPs elected. Following an acrimonious split, however, he left the party, setting up Veritas (it means 'truth'), as an alternative to UKIP.

Beyond elections for the European parliament, the success of UKIP has been far more mixed. In the local election results for the London Assembly, UKIP won two seats in 2004 in the London-wide vote (10 per cent in constituency; 8.4 per cent London-wide); and the UKIP candidate in the London mayoral election, Frank Maloney, came in fourth, winning over 100,000 first-preference votes. In the 2008 contest for London mayor, UKIP came in seventh on first-preference votes, with only around 22,000 votes, and lost votes and its two seats in the assembly.

One problem UKIP faces is that of credibility: a problem of establishing itself as anything more than a one-policy ('get out of Europe') party. While it prides itself on a host of policy positions on domestic and foreign affairs, it remains known only for its Euro-scepticism. UKIP has also been dogged with accusations of extremist infiltration (infiltration the party says it has put measures in place to counter). Conservative leader David Cameron accused UKIP of being full of 'fruitcakes, loonies and closet racists'. The party could probably survive with fruitcakes and loonies – most parties are full of them. But it is the racism the party has difficulty shaking off: the taunt of being the 'BNP in blazers'.

Part of the problem is that UKIP and the BNP are in certain respects competing in the same political marketplace. According to the Essex research introduced earlier, the BNP and UKIP are 'part of the same phenomenon': a sort of anti-politics populism that melds concerns about the decline in the British way of life with anxiety over mass immigration and the elitism of mainstream political parties. While there has in the past been little love lost between the BNP and UKIP, the two parties appeal to the same pool of votes: voters who generally put immigration at the top of their political concerns; who vote for the rival party where there are second preferences (e.g. for London mayor); and who vote for the other party in different elections (e.g. European and local).

## The future for far right nationalist politics in Britain

One of the central themes of this book is that British politics is becoming more fragmented. This fragmentation has two aspects. The first is about voters turning to parties beyond the usual suspects; the second is about the development of a more complex multi-tier party system that gives more parties an opportunity to compete in elections. These two aspects are, obviously, connected: voters are turning to non-mainstream parties, in part, because they have more opportunity to; and these opportunities are giving smaller 'niche' parties a greater presence and legitimacy in British party politics.

The results from the elections to the European parliament in June 2009 were, on the face of it, further confirmation that the BNP and UKIP were now heading for the mainstream of British party politics. The BNP won two seats in the election: Nick Griffin was elected in the North-West region, and Andrew Brons in Yorkshire and Humberside. But while the party came sixth overall nationally with nearly a million people voting BNP (just over 6 per cent of the vote), both Griffin and Brons were elected despite a fall in their vote in both regions. The BNP's success was built on the public not voting Labour. The performance of UKIP was, again on the face of it, a triumph. With 17.4 per cent of the national vote, the party beat Labour into second place and increased its number of MEPs by one to thirteen. However, UKIP's share of the vote increased by only just over 1 per cent; and in some areas, such as the East Midlands, the UKIP vote fell away.

So, is the support for the two parties on the nationalist and far right side of British politics just a temporary blip, or are we likely to see the kind of transformation of party politics that has happened in other parts of Europe?

The advance of populist radical right parties in Europe in the late 1990s and early 2000s has continued, if not uniformly. Indeed, their success, and the accession of Bulgaria and Romania into the EU, led to a new voting bloc (Identity, Tradition and Sovereignty) in the European parliament, though it then disbanded in 2007 after a dispute between Italian and Romanian members. But the 2009 European elections were further evidence that, while populist radical right politics was winning votes in some countries, it wasn't in others. In Austria, Denmark and the Netherlands, far right parties did well. In Italy, the new Berlusconi-led governing centre right coalition, the People of Freedom party, including far right nationalists, polled 35 per cent, with the anti-immigration Northern League also doing well. In Hungary, the far right Jobbik party won three seats. Elsewhere, however, the far right vote fell. In France, with the centre right ruling party led by President Sarkozy in the ascendancy, the National Front won just 6.3 per cent of the vote. In Belgium, the vote of the far right Flemish Interest party also dropped.

In many respects, the continuing success of populist radical right parties in continental Europe put the results of the BNP and UKIP into perspective. While the BNP in particular has to a certain degree been successful in turning itself into a democratic, non-violent political party, there remain question marks about how much further nationalist and far right politics are likely to advance in Britain. Certainly, the conditions that support the development of far right parties and give them opportunities to attract support among voters persist. Issues of immigration, employment, law and order, terrorism and access to public services remain high on voters' political agendas – and, given the right conditions, play into the hands of the far right. Post-recession, the BNP's message on 'British jobs for British workers' struck home, even if it didn't always win it votes. A credibility gap remains.

The results from the European elections in 2009 certainly raised the profile of the BNP. To date, the party has relied on the digital media to bypass broad-casters and newspapers traditionally hostile to it to get its message across to voters. Success in October 2009 gave the BNP the financial and administrative support that comes with representation at Strasbourg – and also considerable coverage across the mainstream media.

Having said this, and despite the 2009 European elections, the political advance of both the BNP and UKIP has been limited; and both parties are vulnerable to any revival of the mainstream parties. Local election results in 2007 and 2008 were mixed for the BNP. And while the BNP has, like similar parties on the continent, attempted to broaden its appeal, it finds it difficult to shed its extremist tag. This turns voters off, even if they agree with the policies.[28] The BNP may play down its neo-fascist, anti-Semitic, racist and authoritarian past, but still the ghost of John Tyndall haunts far right politics in Britain. Behind the public suits and family-friendly politics – and hand-books advising activists how to smarten up their acts – lurks a private politics that remains as hate-filled as ever. At an official level, the BNP proscribes links with the extremist and extra-parliamentary English Defence League, but political activism on the far right at a local level has long been fluid, cutting across organizations, in large part because the ends of these groups are so similar.[29] Moreover, the BNP has struggled to be anything more than a local threat. The party is a real presence in local government in only a handful of Midland and northern towns and London boroughs. Otherwise, it remains still very much a minor party. This localism also makes the party vulnerable to concerted campaigns against it, as was proved in Barking in East London during the 2010 general election.

UKIP has had greater success in attracting a more mainstream national image, despite the continuing problems the party has in shaking the 'BNP in blazers' tag. Its hard line on immigration, however, is why that tag sticks. Despite UKIP's performance at the polls, most recently in the 2009 European elections, significant obstacles remain in the way of a further advance in the British party system. The electoral system for Westminster works against small nation-based parties; and the hegemony of the Conservative Party on the centre right of British party politics casts doubt on how far (and how often) Tory voters will be willing to break ranks when it really matters. Despite the fact that UKIP is on the right side of the European issue for many voters, it is also an issue that generally is low in any order of importance for the electorate.

There are also organizational challenges for UKIP as it shifts from being a populist, anti-political movement to one that puts far greater emphasis on winning votes and, potentially, places in government. In its early days, UKIP was driven by forceful personalities (Sked) and attracted others with equally forceful personalities (Kilroy-Silk). The organization of the party was open and democratic to fit its populist and anti-establishment message ('we're differ-ent'). But this unorthodox structure became problematic when the party decided to get serious about winning votes (as Kilroy-Silk was). This required better organization, not least a more centralized party structure that rather went against the grassroots-type movement (and grassroots-type people) fight-ing against mainstream politics. To win votes, in other words, and to be taken seriously as a political player in government, a party like UKIP (or the Greens, as we see in the next chapter) has to become like all the other parties it was meant to be different from in the first place. This creates internal dissent and splits (Kilroy-Silk left to form Veritas). But unless it does get organized, it remains, as one piece of research argues, 'doomed to failure'.[30]

Looking back over the past two decades, political support for nationalist and far right parties has been fragile. Good results are invariably followed by bad ones. And a good result in European elections can be deceptive. The election is a 'second order' poll the British electorate struggles to understand and ends up using as an opportunity to cast a protest vote, especially in periods of antipathy towards mainstream parties that work to the advantage of all smaller parties. It is all too easy for a group such as the BNP to publish posters promising to 'Punish the pigs' (poor old Westminster MPs in the wake of the expenses scandal) and to present itself as a 'liberating army'.[31]

But success in these second-order elections is no guarantee of success in the poll that really matters, the general election. Whatever differences there are between the BNP and UKIP, both are heavily reliant on a 'plague on both your houses' sentiment from voters. This makes their votes more fragile, as the main parties win back support as the mood changes. To date, UKIP has proved an outlet for Conservative protest votes – and for the Tories themselves, it may be no bad thing for traditional Conservative voters to have the opportunity to blow off steam when it doesn't really matter. The result of the 2010 general election showed, perhaps, the limits of far right politics in Britain. Both the BNP and UKIP increased their share of the national vote by 1.2 per cent and 0.9 per cent respectively, but both parties singularly failed to win their target seats: Griffin came in a distant third in Barking, with Farage also coming third in his attempt to unseat the speaker of the House of Commons, John Bercow. The two parties believe the anti-political current is in their direction – and nearly 1.5 million votes would suggest some base of far right nationalist support in Britain. But when set against the advances made by the populist radical right in many other parts of Europe, UKIP and the BNP remain minor parties in British politics.

## Further reading and research resources

The question of the BNP heading for the political mainstream is addressed head-on by Copsey in *Contemporary British Fascism*, and Goodwin in 'The extreme right in Britain'. Goodwin's research more generally is vital for understanding the BNP as a political party (see Eatwell and Goodwin (eds.), *The New Extremism in 21st Century Britain*, and the bibliography). Where the BNP fits in European right-wing politics is examined in Mudde's *The Populist Radical Right in Europe*. On the challenges facing the United Kingdom Independence Party, the article by Abedi and Lundberg, 'Doomed to failture?', is the place to start. The BNP website is at www.bnp.org.uk/; UKIP's at www.ukip.org/.

# CHAPTER SEVEN

# Reds and Greens

## Behind the banners

On 15 February 2003, an estimated 1 million people marched through central London in opposition to the threat of war in Iraq. Smaller demonstrations took place in Glasgow and Belfast, as well as in other cities across the world. The invasion of Iraq the following month by British and American forces provoked further civil action. In London, students marched on the US Embassy in Grosvenor Square – an echo of similar demonstrations against the Vietnam War in the 1960s. British foreign policy handed the left a common cause it could take to the streets against Tony Blair's Labour government.

Such direct civil action has long been an important feature of left-wing politics. Since the 1950s, the Campaign for Nuclear Disarmament and other groups (including thousands of women at the Greenham Common airbase in Berkshire) opposed the proliferation of nuclear arms. In the 1970s and 1980s, alliances of political activists on the left campaigned against racism, in support of the striking National Union of Mineworkers, and in opposition to virtually anything the Conservative government of Margaret Thatcher had a mind to do (including the 'poll tax' that led to rioting in Trafalgar Square in March 1990). By the 1990s, anti-globalization groups, largely made up of socialist, green and anarchist activists, were laying siege to the annual G8 summit, bringing together leaders from the US, Canada, France, Germany, Italy, Japan, the United Kingdom and Russia, wherever it was held.

Such activism breathes life into politics. Indeed, the decline in membership of the three main political parties has been mirrored by a growth in support for pressure groups, as well as an increase in the membership of smaller parties such as the Greens. This chapter will explore the development of political activism beyond the mainstream on the left of the political spectrum in Britain. What organizations were behind the banners against globalization, climate change and the war in Iraq? How significant were former Labour MP George Galloway and the Respect Party as an alliance of left-wing parties? And is this political activism among reds and greens translating into votes at the ballot box as part of Britain's new multi-party politics? Does the election of the first Green MP to Westminster in 2010 mark a new chapter in British party politics?

## A new socialist alliance?

Labour's election victory in 1997 was hardly greeted with universal joy by the left in Britain. During the 1990s, as Neil Kinnock, John Smith and then Tony Blair reformed the Labour Party, broad sections of the left vented their criticisms that New Labour was little more than Thatcherism Mark II. Labour's modernizers promised that 'things could only get better' after eighteen years of Conservative rule. Many political activists on the left held their noses and voted for a Labour government, but feared it would, like previous ones, turn out to be a bitter disappointment. After all, Labour was mired in a trade union 'labourist' political culture that inoculated the party against anything more dangerous and radical. To the far left, Labour was a 'right-wing bourgeois workers' party' that did nothing to challenge the capitalist system or advance a socialist alternative. During the first term of the Blair government, the tight fiscal settlement did little to appease this critical view. Things could only get worse . . .

But what was the left to do? Split between usually hostile camps of communists, Trotskyites and left-wing social democrats, there was little opportunity, or political will, for any kind of joint political movement. Electoral support for the far left was meagre; simple plurality voting at the best of times provides few electoral opportunities for small national parties; and these parties were themselves unstable and fractious. Moreover, the 'hard' left inside the Labour Party was marginalized and had little influence on the shape of the party – as it had done in the 1970s – as chapter 4 showed. Elsewhere in Europe, as we shall see, the left had been more able – and had more opportunities – to carve out political niches. Not so in the UK.

During the 1970s and 1980s, unstable alliances of political activists cutting across party lines did exist, in particular, in campaigns against racism and nuclear weapons. During the 1990s, a further attempt was made at bringing the left together under one banner, although the prospects of such an alliance did not look good given the popularity of the Labour Party. The Socialist Alliance formed in 1999 pulled together most of the main players on the British left, including: the Socialist Workers Party, the Alliance for Workers' Liberty, the International Socialist Group, the Socialist Party, the Communist Party of Great Britain, and Workers' Power. The new alliance did not include the former leader of the National Union of Mineworkers, Arthur Scargill who, after leaving the Labour Party, ploughed a lonely and somewhat fractious furrow with his Socialist Labour Party set up in 1996.

Who, then, was behind this socialist alliance? Broadly speaking, the far left is split between Communist and Trotskyite parties.

## Communists and Trotskyites

The Communist Party of Great Britain (CPGB) was established in the wake of the Russian Revolution as part of the new Soviet Union's international network of communist parties for promoting world revolution (the Comintern or third international).[1] After the Second World War, like other European communist parties, British communists struggled with their relationship with the Soviet Union – and what road they should take to socialism: revolution or reform? In 1951, the party chose reform, but its continued attempts to join the Labour Party as an affiliate were rebuffed. The Soviet Union's invasion of Hungary in 1956 to put down an uprising against the Soviet-puppet government (and the repeat performance in Czechoslovakia in 1968) was a hammer blow for the credibility of the CPGB. While some in the party continued to pay homage to the mother party in Russia (so-called 'tankies', after the tanks sent into Budapest and Prague), others took a more 'eurocommunist' line that advocated a democratic socialist politics independent of the Soviet Union. By the 1980s, the party's magazine, *Marxism Today*, edited by Martin Jacques, was at the forefront of the critique of Thatcherism. But with the collapse of the Soviet Union in 1989, the Communist Party's days were numbered and it finally wound up in 1991, becoming the pressure group Democratic Left.

### Box 7.1 Communist parties today

There are a number of communist parties in existence today (and this is quite complicated): the Communist Party of Britain, led by Anita Halpin (the main CPGB off-shoot and still publishing the old party's daily *Morning Star*); the Communist Party of Great Britain (more ex-CPGB, publishing the *Weekly Worker*); the Communist Party of Britain Marxist-Leninist (originally a party siding with Mao's China against the Soviet Union, publishing *Workers*); the Communist Party of Great Britain (Marxist-Leninist) (set up in 2004 by activists expelled from Scargill's Socialist Labour Party, publishing *Proletarian*); the Revolutionary Communist Party of Britain (Marxist-Leninist) (another party owing its origins to the split between China and the USSR, publishing *Workers' Weekly*); and the New Communist Party of Britain (actually not that new, set up in the 1970s by those opposing the eurocommunist drift of the party, publishing *New Worker*).

A second stream of far left politics has its roots in the fourth international, a body established by the Russian revolutionary Leon Trotsky in 1938 after his expulsion from the Soviet Union for leading opposition to Stalin's rule. Like the third international, the objective of the fourth international was to support and promote Marxist-Leninist politics across the world – except that Trotsky's organization opposed Stalinist Russia, not just western capitalism. Trotsky's legacy, and that of the fourth international, came to dominate the usually fractious revolutionary politics of the far left in Britain as elsewhere.

The Revolutionary Socialist League (Militant or the Militant Tendency) was one such Trotskyite party. The League was set up in the mid 1950s as a Marxist-Leninist party. In theory, this meant that members of Militant couldn't join the Labour Party. Marxism-Leninism is committed to the revolutionary overthrow of the state and the abolition of capitalism. The Labour Party was committed to a parliamentary road to socialism – and to a mixed economy (that's what made it a social democratic or democratic socialist party). Militant activists, however, were 'entryists'. Rather than work independently to further its ambitions, Militant chose to 'enter' – infiltrate really – the Labour Party. Members of Militant would turn up at a local Labour Party branch and join. Their objective was to gain power and influence and to sell copies of their newspaper *Militant*. This strategy certainly had some success. The political journalist Michael Crick estimated that, by the mid 1980s, Militant had some 8,000 members.[2] A group led by Militant member Derek Hatton also controlled Liverpool City Council until their actions in resisting spending controls were declared illegal. Militant also had some success getting its members into parliament as Labour MPs. Dave Nellist and Terry Fields were elected in 1983; Pat Wall in 1987.

By this time, however, the Labour Party was moving to expel members of Militant. The party established a register of groups not officially affiliated to the party but which would be allowed to exist inside it. Militant, being a party within a party, applied to register, but the 1982 Labour conference voted against its application. In 1983, two Militant leaders, Peter Taaffe and Ted Grant, were expelled, followed by around 200 activists over the next ten years (including the two remaining MPs in 1991). Militant lives on today as the Socialist Party set up in 1997, and went on to join the Socialist Alliance.

Militant shared its political roots with a second significant Trotskyist party, the Socialist Workers Party (SWP). The SWP began as a small group of left-wing

### Box 7.2 Trotskyite parties

Aside from Militant and the SWP, Trotskyite parties proliferated in the 1960s and 1970s. They included: the International Marxist Group, founded in 1964, which published the *Black Dwarf* edited by Tariq Ali, and folded in a blaze of factions in the 1980s; the International Socialist Group, the 'British section of the fourth international', founded in 1987, but dating back to the 1960s, which still publishes *Socialist Outlook*; the Workers Revolutionary Party (WRP), another group embedded in the complicated web of post-1960s far left politics, famous for having the actors Vanessa and Corin Redgrave as members, which again went to pieces in the 1980s, but still the WRP and its publication *News Line* continue the struggle; the Alliance for Workers' Liberty, formerly Socialist Organiser, with a complicated past in Trotskyite politics and, like Militant, engaged in entryist strategies until Labour banned the group in 1990, helped to set up the Socialist Alliance in 1998, and publishes *Solidarity*; and the Revolutionary Communist Party (RCP), in part a 1970s off-shoot of the International Social Group (the forerunner of the Socialist Workers Party), with Frank Furedi (now professor of sociology at Kent University) prominent in the leadership, published the *Next Step* and the monthly *Living Marxism* (later *LM*), shifted away from Marxist-Leninism to a more radical libertarianism and, when it all folded in 1997, leading RCP activist Claire Fox set up the Institute of Ideas and ex-*LM* editor Mick Hume wrote columns for *The Times*.

activists running the Socialist Review Group led by Tony Cliff – so small in fact that they agreed that their only chance to influence politics on the left was to work inside the Labour Party. The group's distinctive argument was that the USSR was an example of 'state capitalism', and so had nothing to do with what real socialism would look like. In 1962, Socialist Review became the International Socialist Group. By the 1960s, disillusionment with the lack of any progress at all towards socialism, as they saw it, by the Labour government of Harold Wilson led in the 1970s to the group planning an electoral campaign of its own against Labour. It didn't prove a success. And in 1977 the group became the SWP and its political activism switched to working on campaigns often in collaboration with other groups. These included the Anti-Nazi League and Rock Against Racism in the late 1970s and 1980s – both aimed at the far right NF; and, later, the Stop the War Coalition.

## The far left at the polls

These far left parties, communist or Trotskyite, have generally poured scorn on the Labour Party for its parliamentary-based politics, although groups from both sides of this oddest of political cleavages have from time to time tried to use Labour as a vehicle for their own brand of socialist politics. More-over, far left parties have themselves over the years stood candidates in elections. Their record, unsurprisingly, is very poor. Back in 1945, the Communist Party stood 21 candidates and won two seats with an average of around 15 per cent per candidate. By 1979, the party's 35 candidates won only 1 per cent of the vote on average. The best result for the Workers Revolutionary Party came in the October 1974 election when its ten candidates had an average of 0.9 per cent of the vote – but no saved deposits.[3]

But did this change? Was there, as a result of the foreign and domestic record of the Labour government after 1997, new support for the left in British party politics? In the 2001 election, the Socialist Alliance fielded candidates in 98 constituencies, with 1.1 per cent of the vote across all seats and 2 saved deposits.[4] In the 2005 election, the alliance stood 199 candidates – with 199 lost deposits. North of the border, the Scottish Socialist Alliance was set up in 1996, bringing together Militant in Scotland, the Scottish Republican Socialist Party, the Communist Party of Scotland and later the SWP in Scotland. Following the 1997 election, in which this alliance stood 16 candidates, with an average vote of 1.8 per cent, a single party, the Scottish Socialist Party, was formed. Its national convener, Tommy Sheridan, was elected to the new devolved parliament in Edinburgh for Glasgow in 1998 (and the party won five more seats in 2003). In 2001, the Scottish Socialist Party put forward 72 candidates, with an average vote of 3.3 per cent, with 10 saved deposits. After this relatively impressive showing, the party fielded 58 candidates in 2005, with 2 per cent of the vote and just 2 saved deposits.[5]

It is clear from this that the electoral record of the far left remained poor in 1997 and 2001. Only the Scottish Socialist Party made any kind of showing in 2001. But, like many experiments in socialist 'non-sectarian' coalitions, both the Scottish Socialist Party and the Socialist Alliance suffered damaging splits. In 2006 Tommy Sheridan left the Scottish Socialist Party and a damaging court case followed. The Scottish Socialist Party continued and fought the devolved and local elections in Scotland in 2007, but performed badly, losing all their seats in the devolved parliament, as well as most of their council seats (see also chapter 8). The Socialist Alliance also fell apart, but was partly put back together through opposition to the war in Iraq and the formation of the Respect Party.

## War and politics

While opposition to the invasion of Afghanistan was somewhat muted, the war in Iraq gave the socialist alliance its biggest boost since Tony Blair was elected in 1997. The Stop the War coalition was set up in September 2001 at a rally in London and drew support from individuals and groups across the spectrum of left-wing politics, including the Labour left (e.g. Jeremy Corbyn), the Socialist Workers Party, CND and other smaller far left parties and groups, as well as prominent individuals such as the playwright Harold Pinter and the former activist and writer Tariq Ali. The coalition also drew support from trade unions, the Muslim Association of Britain, and Charles Kennedy from the Liberal Democrats. In 2003, the coalition organized a mass demonstration in London against the war in Iraq. Behind the banners, the Stop the War coalition was run by a national council that included the SWP and the Labour left. The president was the veteran Labour left-winger Tony Benn. The war in Iraq also handed the Labour left in parliament their greatest opportunity to turn against the Blair government. In March 2003, 139 Labour MPs – way beyond the usual suspects of left-wing critics – voted against the Iraq war, the largest parliamentary rebellion since the Corn Laws.

The war in Iraq also led to a reworking of left-wing coalition politics. By 2005, the Socialist Alliance had more or less fallen apart. But its place had already been taken by Respect, a party formed in 2004 by environmentalist George Monbiot and Stop the War activist Salma Yaqoob (Monbiot left soon afterwards). But the most prominent figure in Respect, despite the absence of any formal leader, was former Labour MP George Galloway.

The life and times of George Galloway are fairly colourful. In 2006, he appeared as a contestant on Celebrity Big Brother. Galloway said he was reaching out to a new generation of voters – aged fifty-two, dressed in a leotard, pretending to be a cat. Galloway is often called a political maverick. He isn't one for toeing the party line. Supporters say this shows his independence of mind; critics, simply the size of his ego. Before entering parliament, he was general secretary of the international development charity War on Want. Galloway became Labour MP for Glasgow Hillhead in 1987 (a seat won by Roy Jenkins for the SDP and before that solidly Tory), and a constant thorn in his party's side. He was an outspoken left-wing critic of the Labour leadership – in particular, its Middle East foreign policy. In October 2003, Galloway was expelled from the party. The Labour leadership accused him of inciting foreign powers to take up arms against troops in his opposition to the government's invasion of Iraq. Galloway accused Labour of putting on a show trial.

Following his expulsion, Galloway became active in the Respect Party. Respect stands for: 'Respect, Equality, Socialism, Peace, Environmentalism, Community and Trade Unionism'. Its aim was to provide a 'left-wing alternative' to the three main parties and to oppose 'war, privatization and unemployment'. The party's policies are traditionally leftist and anti-capitalist (Labour *circa* 1983): public ownership, public spending, redistributive fiscal policies (including high taxes on the rich), the repeal of 'anti-trade union laws' and the end to what are seen as imperialist wars in countries such as Iraq.

Respect was also another attempt at building a coalition on the left of British politics by bringing together, among others, dissident elements on the Labour left, the SWP, what was left of the Socialist Alliance, the International Socialist Group, trade unionists such as Mark Serwotka of the Civil Service Union and the Fire Fighters Union, various rebel celebrities (such as film-maker Ken Loach) and the Muslim Association of Britain. What they agreed on was how awful the Blair government was generally – and its foreign policies in particular. Respect certainly had some success as part of the broader anti-war movement. But was it part of a broader revival in the political fortunes of the left – and part of the shift to a more multi-party political system?

Respect stood candidates in the European parliament and the London Assembly and mayoral elections in 2004, winning 1.7 per cent of the vote in the European poll, and nearly 5 per cent of the vote in London. At the 2005 general election, the party were represented in twenty-six seats across England and Wales, winning 0.3 per cent of the vote nationally, with an average of 6.9 per cent per candidate. The big story for Respect was Galloway's result in Bethnal Green and Bow in East London where he beat the sitting Labour MP Oona King in what Paul Webb described as a 'notably vituperative' campaign (King didn't fit the usual political stereotype being a Blairite, a black Jew and a supporter of the Iraq war – and the war of words between Galloway and King was bitter).[6] At the same election, in the Birmingham Sparkbrook seat, the Respect candidate won more than 25 per cent of the vote, falling just short of the winning Labour candidate's vote. In the East London seats of East Ham, Poplar and Canning Town, and West Ham, Respect polled between 17 and 21 per cent of the vote.

The key to these results lay with the concentration of Muslim voters in East London and Birmingham who, according to Webb, supported Respect largely because of Iraq, not because they shared the party's ideological views. This strong link between support for Respect and Muslim voters suggests that the electoral base the party may have built in this period was fragile. As with all protest votes, once the source of the protest disappears, so do the protest votes.

## Lacking respect

The fragility of Respect's electoral base was not helped by the perennial problem of small-party politics: factionalism. Where larger parties are able to withstand internal divisions and exert greater authority, for smaller parties faction fighting can rip them apart. Key to the formation of Respect was a coalition of dissident ex-Labour activists around George Galloway, the SWP and Muslim political activists. What united them was opposition to the war in Iraq. But there was also much that could divide them, including the every-day spoils of a party, such as the selection of candidates to stand in elections. The relationship between Galloway and the SWP had never been easy – and so it would continue. In August 2007, Galloway sent a letter to Respect members calling for more leadership and greater party unity. By November, the tensions between Galloway and the SWP had reached the point where each faction held their own conference on the same day. Both sides fought over the Respect name, with the SWP campaigning under the Left List banner in the 2008 elections for the London Assembly (they attracted just under 1 per cent of the vote; Galloway's Respect won 2.5 per cent).

These sorts of problems are familiar to politics beyond the mainstream. Anti-establishment parties such as UKIP and Respect are formed on the basis that they are different from the main parties. This includes not only their policies, but also how they are organized and whom they attract as activists. In their early stages of development, parties such as Respect spend an awful lot of time establishing their ideological identity; and they attract activists who are themselves highly ideological and uncompromising in their approach to politics. The structure of the party sets great store by internal democracy and holding the leadership accountable to the membership. Inevitably, this makes parties such as Respect and UKIP vulnerable to ideological divisions and highly damaging splits that, to the rest of the world, appear like nothing more than debating how many angels can dance on the head of a pin. As parties move on and focus more on attracting votes and even seeking office, they not only must become more professional in their approach to campaigning, they also have to establish clearly defined mechanisms for dealing with internal disagreements and be more willing to accommodate different points of view, not least with potential partners in government. This, as we shall see later in the chapter, was the same challenge as that faced by the Green Party as it sought to become a more effective vote- and office-seeking party. Respect never left the blocks.

Beyond the sound and fury, there remains a question mark over the sustainability of left-wing parties in the mainstream arenas of British party politics. No doubt the electoral system in national elections acts as a block on parties such as Respect gaining representation at Westminster. In other parts of Europe, left parties have been much more successful in gaining a foothold in mainstream electoral politics, in part because votes have been turned into seats by systems of proportional representation. But these left parties in Europe have also been more successful in developing an alternative to reformist social democrat parties through a combination of a defence of welfare and labour rights with 'new left' policies on the environment, globalization, international development and social equality. In Sweden, for example, the former communists rebadged themselves as the Left Party and attracted 12 per cent of the vote in the late 1990s (though this has since fallen back). The left in Norway and Denmark has also built support and won seats with a red–green message. In Germany, the former East German Communist Party joined forces with left-wingers from the Social Democratic Party in 2007 to form Die Linke (The Left). In the 2009 national elections, the party increased its share of the vote by 3 per cent to over 11 per cent.

By contrast, the left in Britain did little to help its own cause. While Respect sought to build a wider political platform, it struggled to be anything more than a one-trick pony, whose support was overly reliant on opposition – in particular among Muslim voters – to the war in Iraq. So, when this issue moved off the political agenda, as it did with withdrawal of British and American troops, Respect returned to the margins of British party politics. The party did not stand candidates in the 2009 European elections (the party supported the Greens); and the leading party of the left was Arthur Scargill's Socialist Labour Party, winning 173,115 votes nationally or 1.1 per cent of the vote. The 2010 general election witnessed what were perhaps the final death throes of Respect. Galloway chose to fight the Poplar and Limehouse constituency adjacent to Bethnal Green and Bow. He went down heavily to Labour. Galloway's old seat was also taken easily by Labour, and not only did its candidate Rushanara Ali become the first Bangladeshi MP in parliament, but she was also the former aide to Oona King. Revenge, as they say, is a dish best served cold.

## Green politics

In March 2009, the G20 bandwagon came to London – and a grand coalition of protestors was ready waiting for them. Essentially, the G20 brought together the G8 group of leading industrialized countries with other states including China, India, Brazil, Australia and South Korea. The presidents, prime ministers, finance ministers and bank governors (and their entourages) had come to the British capital to talk about the global recession and climate change. The coalition of some 100 organizations lying in wait for them had been assembled by Put People First and included a huge range of views and ideologies. Taking up what the anti-globalization movement had started back in the 1990s, there were development organizations such as ActionAid and War on Want; green groups like the G20 Climate Camp, People and Planet and Friends of the Earth; faith groups such as Tear Fund and Cafod; the Trade Union Congress; the Social Workers Party; and the anarchist group Rampart. Reds, greens, Christians, aid workers, anarchists and trade unionists – and probably many more besides – they were all there not just to denounce capitalism (or some version of the global free market system), but to meld together concerns about the environment with those of poverty, insecurity and democracy across the world.

In certain respects, there is nothing very new about green politics. Venerable institutions such as the Royal Botanic Gardens at Kew, the Royal Society for the Prevention of Cruelty to Animals and the National Trust in Victorian Britain campaign on, among other things, the environment. But green politics as we understand it today is something more recent, bound up with interest in environmental issues, and in membership of and support for a wide range of green groups (not least the Green Party in the UK); and the rise of governmental and non-governmental agencies that have sprung up around environmental concerns.[7]

Politics in industrial societies like Britain was dominated by the question of economic growth (how could we have more of it?) and how the proceeds of that growth should be distributed across society. These classic left–right questions prompted quite different responses across what was the dominant political cleavage, social class. Parties on the left wanted more state intervention: by themselves, markets weren't very good at delivering economic growth; and markets also favoured property owners over the working class and the poor in handing out the spoils of growth. Parties on the right disagreed: only free enterprise could deliver growth and higher (if unequal) incomes for all. Parties trying to occupy the centre ground favoured some combination of the two arguments in a mixed economy. But in all three cases, politics was organized around how to generate growth and distribute wealth and income.

The de-alignment of politics in the 1960s and 1970s, as we explored in chapter 1, saw the erosion of the link between politics and social class. Some political scientists suggested that an important shift was taking place in the values held by the public away from materialist concerns with economic growth, public safety and national defence towards post-materialist concerns with individual rights, the environment and social equality.[8] This was reconfiguring political cleavages. While the majority of voters remained materialists, a significant minority of post-materialists were being drawn to, among other arenas, green politics because of their concerns with the state of the environment, an issue that cut across traditional left–right politics.

This new green politics was bound up with the founding of pressure groups and new social movement organizations in the 1960s and 1970s and the formation of explicitly green parties across Europe and elsewhere. The World Wildlife Fund was set up in 1961, Friends of the Earth in 1969 and Greenpeace in 1972. There is some debate in political science about how we should categorize these groups (see box 7.3 below and chapter 9 for further discussion). But these organizations helped to bring a different set of issues onto the political agenda: not just issues about the environment, but broader values about what life should be like in advanced industrial societies. At the heart of this politics was a challenge to established industrial politics: rather than thinking about the possibility of economic growth being limitless (human societies could simply become richer and richer and richer), there were real limits to growth imposed by the natural environment.

At the same time, political activists on the left (and to a lesser degree on the right) were being drawn to green politics. This was partly about political economy. Traditionally the left opposed capitalism not because it delivered too much growth, but because it was not good enough at promoting it, especially to the benefit of everyone in society. Some socialists, forerunners in many respects of the anti-globalization movement a few decades later, were attracted to green politics because they saw in it a way of challenging the industrial societies, whether in the capitalist west or the communist east, that they believed were destroying the natural environment. One leading red–green, the German Rudolf Bahro, suggested that the public should be given 'the practical opportunity to completely drop out of the industrial system that produces for the world market and construct an alternative way of life in the direction of a self-reliant society'.[9] Some on the left were also drawn to green politics because they saw in the developing green movements (as well as feminist, anti-racist and anti-nuclear movements) a possibility of a new form of politics and a new agent for social change. For this new left, the problem with traditional socialist politics was the failure of the working class and trade unions to be the agent of social change: they had become part of the system and were in decline. Their place would be taken by these new social movements, green ones included, blending socialist and environmentalist concerns in an anti-capitalism movement. Reds were becoming more green (and pro-feminist and anti-racist) – and in some cases, simply green.

## Green divides

From the start, there were a number of questions dividing those involved in green politics. The first concerned whether green politics was about caring for the environment because of nature's intrinsic value or because it better served human society to do so. This question divided ecologists (or 'dark greens') from environmentalists ('light greens'). Green politics was also divided about how to go about its politics: should green activism be channelled through established political processes, that is, by setting up a green party to campaign in elections on a pro-environment platform, or was it better to find alternative channels for political activism, such as pressure groups, new social movement organizations or much more informal network-based forms of activism (or even withdrawing from mainstream society, which, in the conventional sense, means not being very active at all)? This question divided those willing to work through mainstream political and policy-making channels from those who weren't and who saw green politics as offering quite radical alternatives to the governance of modern society (for example, the 'off grid' movement).

Green politics was also divided on how red it should be, if at all. Since the 1960s, there has been a divide between those green activists who link their politics to a broader socialist critique of capitalist economics and those for whom green politics is a rejection of all growth-based politics, whether from the left or right. There are also pro-capitalist greens who see the free market as offering solutions to issues such as climate change through, for example, carbon trading.

### Creating green parties

The first green party was set up in New Zealand in 1972: the New Zealand Values Party. In Europe, British environmentalists led the way into politics. In 1973, a group of activists with links to the *Ecologist* magazine, first published in 1970, set up People, fielding five candidates in the February 1974 election. The following year People became the Ecology Party. Many of the ideas for this new green politics had been aired in a *Blueprint for Survival*, a special edition of the *Ecologist*. The themes of this manifesto soon became familiar ones. What a leading party member and green activist Jonathon Porritt called 'the politics of the industrial age' was rejected. Instead, politics should concern itself with sustainability, not growth. The way forward was through the creation of local, decentralized communities. These were better for people – and for the planet.

*Blueprint for Survival* put the new green movement and the Ecology Party on the political map. But where to place it on that map was not straightforward. Some of the arguments of this new green politics shared common ground with left critiques of the market economy, while others echoed traditionally conservative views on the sustainability of population growth. The rejection of materialist concerns with economic growth, and the ultimate impossibility of controlling nature (as the ecologists argued), led many like Porritt to argue that green politics broke with the established politics of left and right. Having said this, the green ethos that human beings should work with rather than against nature, and that to do this requires creating communities that are not only sustainable but also democratic, egalitarian and socially just and respecting of human rights, clearly draws on established political traditions, including liberal, socialist, feminist and anarchist ideas. In Britain, the Ecology Party, in part because it had so few opportunities to move forward in the established political system, leant heavily towards the ecologist view of green politics that rejected the red–green blend of politics that was emerging in places such as West Germany.[10] This would change in the 1990s, as what became the Green Party shifted to a more environmentalist position on the centre left of British politics.

In electoral terms, the success of green politics was slow in coming. At the 1979 general election, the Ecology Party fielded 53 candidates, winning 0.1 per cent of the vote, 1.5 per cent per candidate. In 1983, the party stood 108 candidates, winning over 50,000 votes. In 1985, the Ecology Party was renamed the Green Party; and in 1989, the party in Scotland broke away to form the Scottish Greens. In European elections, green candidates averaged 2.6 per cent in 1984.[11] These electoral returns were very modest by comparison with the political advances made by green parties in other parts of Europe – and even more disappointing given the clear growth in interest in the environ-ment in public opinion. One factor behind this was the difficulty for a dark green party such as the Ecology/Green Party in operating in a party political system dominated by materialist concerns with economic growth. This led to green activists throwing themselves into pressure group politics, not electoral politics. The relative openness of the civil service in the UK also meant that such activism brought greater returns than trying to win votes in elections – though it also contributed to a co-option of green policy by mainstream parties.[12]

Another factor that has clearly worked to the advantage of green parties in other, but not all, parts of Europe is systems of proportional representation. These provide the opportunities for small parties with national support to gain seats in national parliaments. In 1979, the first green candidate was elected to a national parliament in Switzerland. In the former West Germany, Die Grünen, formed in 1980 but with roots deep in radical red/green German politics since the 1960s, was winning votes and securing seats in parliament: in 1983, twenty-eight party candidates were elected under the country's system of proportional representation. By the end of the 1980s, Die Grünen was winning 8 per cent of the vote in national elections. During the 1990s, the electoral advance of green politics would see green parties sharing power across a number of European states, including Finland (which saw the first green party enter government in Europe in 1995), Germany, Belgium, France and Italy. But green politics had less success in southern European states such as Spain and Greece, in part because the less developed state of these econo-mies limited the development of green political awareness. Outside of Finland, Scandinavian states saw a mixed record from green parties: from the late 1980s, the Greens in Sweden averaged around 4 to 5 per cent of the vote; but the Greens in Norway and Denmark struggled, although red–green parties had more success.

On the back of a continued growth in interest in the environment (even Mrs Thatcher made a speech on the environment in 1988 to the Royal Society) and a buoyant economy that pushed worries about growth to one side, the Green Party made its first real mark on British party politics at the 1989 European elections when nearly 2.3 million people voted for Green Party candidates: 15 per cent of those who voted. In all but one constituency, the party pushed the Liberal Democrats into fourth place. But, under simple plurality, the Green Party won no seats. It should be added that all three main parties were in difficult waters at the time, as we saw earlier in this book: the Conservatives were getting in a mess over Europe; Labour was in the middle of reform; and the Liberal Democrats were struggling to create a new party out of the old SDP/Liberal Alliance. The Greens won votes from all three.

## Green politics in the doldrums

The results of the elections to the European parliament in 1989 suggested the future for the Green Party in Britain over the next decade might be bright. Membership of it was rising (peaking at nearly 20,000 in 1989/90); leading party activists such as Porritt and Sara Parkin brought the Greens into the public eye; and the tensions within green politics between those who wanted to engage more professionally in electoral politics and those who wanted to stick to the party's decentralist traditions were, more or less, under control. The Green Party had set out its stall combining messages about environmental issues with broader ones about governance (decentralization and participation), social justice and human rights. In this, they appeared to be riding a green wave of interest and activism that saw support for environmental politics in organizations such as Friends of the Earth and Greenpeace growing dramatically. Membership of these green groups was increasing rapidly just as membership of mainstream political parties declined. Between 1981 and 1991, for example, membership of Friends of the Earth in the UK increased by over 500 per cent from 18,000 members to 114,000. By 1992, estimates of total membership of green groups stood at 5 million.[13] This new wave of 'environmentalism' was capturing public attention, not least with high-profile direct action by campaigners keeping green issues such as road building on the news agenda. Green arguments were also entering the political mainstream as the Conservatives, Labour and the Liberal Democrats moved to react to voter concern with the environment. And with Prince Charles, a friend of Porritt, green politics found itself with friends in high places.

In the early 1990s, however, the Green Party saw its support ebb away. In the 1992 general election, in which the party might have expected to push on, the result was a disappointment. While the party stood nearly double the candidates compared with 1987 (254 against 133), and its share of the national vote went up from 0.2 per cent to 0.5 per cent, its share of the vote per candidate fell slightly from 1.4 per cent to 1.3 per cent (a level that would remain much the same in 1997, despite the party fielding only 95 candidates). In the 1994 European elections, the Green Party came fourth in votes cast, but its 2.3 million votes in 1989 had fallen back to just under half a million, a 3 per cent share of the national vote. Membership of the party also fell sharply – down to around 4,500 in 1993.

So what were the factors behind this decline? In part, the problem faced by the Greens in the early 1990s was one of expectations. The success of the party in 1989 was in a low-turnout poll – the kind that voters often use to

## Box 7.3 Green politics on the streets – and in the gardens . . .

If green politics in the electoral arena was suffering, green politics on the streets (and up trees and in all kinds of other places) was not. 'Guerrilla gardening', for example, saw green activists squat on a piece of unused land and live and grow food on it. This environmental action seemed a world away from mainstream politics. Such activism forces us to reconsider what we traditionally understand as politics. Green protest has certainly been very successful at grabbing headlines in the media. But do the campaigns against digging roads, genetically modified food, coal-fired power stations and airport runways, and the huge events in opposition to globalization and climate change, offer something new to politics?

There are, broadly speaking, two main perspectives on this. The first argues that the new green politics is part of the growth of 'new social movements' very different from the traditional forms of political mobilization rooted in interest group politics of parties, trade unions and other professional bodies. By contrast to the formal, centralized and hierarchical structure of traditional political parties and trade unions, these new social movements are more informal, decentralized and flatter in organization. And rather than campaigning in mainstream political arenas, new social movements are seen to employ a far wider range of political 'repertoires' aimed at broader social and cultural change. In this way, they not only widen what counts as politics but also offer a more participatory and inclusive model of democracy.

An alternative perspective suggests that, far from being very new, green politics – at least the big players such as a Greenpeace and Friends of the Earth – are little different from the interest groups that dominate the world of pressure group politics. While this perspective concedes that there is a type of green politics in which the concept new social movement might be appropriate, it sees the big campaigning organizations, which in membership terms dominate green politics, as more like 'protest businesses'. The so-called members have very little involvement in the group, paying what in effect is a donation to the organization, and high membership numbers belie the high turnover of members (and groups) in green politics. Moreover, these green groups are highly professionalized (in particular, in marketing), with members having little or no say in the running of the group or the campaigns they develop. Rather than offering new models of democracy, new social movements have become part of the political mainstream.

*Further reading*: Jordan and Maloney, *The Protest Business*; Jordan and Maloney, *Democracy and Interest Groups*; Luke Martell, *The Sociology of Globalization* (Cambridge: Polity, 2010), ch. 11; Norris, *Democratic Phoenix*.

express their frustrations with mainstream parties (it is, as such, a second-order rather than first-order election). The party also suffers under simple plurality voting for Westminster and lacks the sources of funding necessary for competing in nationwide elections. But, as Sarah Birch argues, there were also factors specific to the early 1990s that caused the Greens problems.[14] In particular, party divisions on strategy and organization re-emerged, between those who wanted a more clearly defined executive leadership (led by the Green 2000 group) and those who insisted that the Greens must remain committed to a decentralized and democratic structure. At the 1992 general election, the Greens just didn't have the professional electoral machine to mount a national campaign. Moreover, the mainstream parties were in a much better state in 1992 than in 1989 – and had also been busy adding the environment to their own policy manifestos. Indeed, the accessibility of British public administration also meant that green pressure groups could gain access to the civil service and local government, thereby sidelining the Green Party. It was also the case that green politics in other countries, such as Germany, suffered a dip in its fortunes.

## A revival in Green Party politics

Following the 1994 European elections, one study of the Green Party suggested it was, as an electoral force, 'virtually irrelevant'.[15] By 1999, however, the Green Party was staging something of a political revival. In the elections for the European parliament held that year, using for the first time a type of proportional representation (the party list system), the Greens polled just over 625,000 votes – 6.25 per cent of the vote – and elected 2 MEPs, Caroline Lucas (the current party leader) in South-East England and Jean Lambert in London. However, the party was beaten into fourth place in the national vote by the UK Independence Party. At the 2001 general election, the party stood 145 candidates, winning 0.6 per cent of the national vote, with an average vote per candidate of 2.7 per cent (and 10 saved their deposits). At the 2005 general election, 229 Green candidates won 1 per cent of the UK vote: 2.8 per cent each. While still not winning seats at Westminster, the Greens in 2005 had 64 local councillors, 2 members of the European parliament, 2 members of the Greater London Authority and 1 member of the House of Lords. The Scottish Greens had 7 MSPs. The Green Party did particularly well on the south coast of England in Brighton and Hove, winning 22 per cent of the vote in Brighton Pavilion, taking third place; 7.1 per cent in Brighton Kemptown; and 5.7 per cent in Hove. Green candidates in Lewisham and Deptford and in Norwich won 11.1 per cent and 7.1 per cent respectively.[16] In the 2009 European elections, the Greens came in fifth nationally. With just over 1.3 million votes, the party increased its share of the vote by 2.5 per cent to 8.6 per cent. It failed, however, to win any more seats, despite a strong showing in Norwich, Oxford, and Brighton and Hove.

**TABLE 7.1**  Green Party record in European elections 1979–2009

|  | % vote | seats |
|---|---|---|
| **1979** | 0 | 0 |
| **1984** | 1 | 0 |
| **1989** | 15 | 0 |
| **1994** | 3 | 0 |
| **1999** | 6 | 2 |
| **2004** | 6 | 2 |
| **2009** | 9 | 2 |

*Note*: 1979 and 1984, results for Ecology Party; 1999 first election held under proportional representation.

*Sources*: Tetteh, 'Election statistics 1918-2007'; BBC Online.

The Green Party also advanced in elections for the devolved assemblies, particularly in Scotland and the London Assembly. In 1999, the Scottish Greens won 1 seat, rising to 7 in 2003, but falling back to 2 in 2007. In London, the Green Party candidates won 3 seats in 2000 and 2 in 2004 and 2008. As Sarah Birch points out, the Green members of the London Assembly had considerable influence given Labour Mayor Ken Livingstone's reliance on the two votes to get his annual budget approved.

So, what were the factors that led to this revival of Green Party politics? Birch identifies a number of them. The first was the growing popularity and awareness of green issues coupled with a rise in the number of disillusioned Labour voters as a result – not least – of the Iraq war. The introduction of PR for European parliament elections also helped the party to turn votes into seats, thereby overcoming the perception that a vote for the party was 'wasted'. Representation in the European parliament, and in local government, also allowed the party to develop a record in the public arena, adding to the credibility of the Greens. The party also became better at campaigning, in particular through the targeting of wards in local elections. While the number of Green councillors has only increased to around 100, a very small slice of the total in local government, 'it demonstrates that by adopting an organized and focused electoral strategy, the Greens are capable of overcoming the barrier of the simple majority electoral system'.[17] Significantly, in 2008, the Greens, with 29 per cent, had the largest share of the vote in Norwich, coming in second in the council chamber with 13 seats. The party also did well in local government in Brighton and Hove, Oxford, Lancaster and Lewisham in London. In total, the Greens have seats on forty local councils across Britain. As we saw in chapter 5, the Liberal Democrats' 'where we work we win' strategy paid off in national elections. The Greens were following a similar path.

## Green voters

Who is supporting the Greens? And what lessons are there as the party moves further into the mainstream? Judging from the places where the Greens do well, the party performs best in traditionally Labour university towns – notably Brighton and Norwich – and areas with significant student populations, such as Lewisham and Hackney in London, and in parts of Leeds and Glasgow. Green voters are in general younger and better educated than the average voter. They are also likely to be on the centre left and also hold post-materialist values (they're green, after all). There is also evidence that there are more people who think well of the party than actually vote for them. There may, however, be a shift in the pattern of Green voting beyond the traditional pool of young, student, post-materialist types to a more mainstream group of voters, similar in demographic profile, but more likely to be or have been Liberal Democrat voters. As Birch points out, 'a liking for the Greens is no longer a quirky taste shared by a small "alternative" sub-culture, but rather a preference held by many people who appear to be relatively well-adjusted to the traditional political system and the values embodied in it . . . The main challenge to the party at the present juncture is to match the new-found respectability of its policy agenda with credibility as a party.'[18]

Looking to the future, voters may be increasingly inclined to support green issues, but the competition for this green vote from all parties is intense. As we saw in the last chapter with UKIP, as the Green Party edges away from the culture of a social movement to that of a serious electoral and governmental player, it needs to become more organized – and more professionalized. The party ditched its joint 'principal speakers' for a more traditional party leader in 2008 (although the Scottish Greens retained joint leaders). Caroline Lucas, leader of the party, embodies this shift from protest politics to the political mainstream. After her election to Westminster as the Greens' first MP in 2010, for Brighton Pavilion, Lucas said: 'We won because we've got a really good set of councillors here. People are used to voting Green here in Brighton.'[19] (The Greens are the joint second-biggest party on the council.) Lucas herself has had a career as Oxfam advisor, local councillor in Oxford and Member of the European parliament – a profile rather like that of many MPs today. The reforms to the Green Party are likely to go further, centralizing and institutionalizing the structure of the party. Paradoxically, perhaps, this is likely to find favour with those party members – and former members – who have voiced dissatisfaction with the running of the party.[20] Membership of the Green Party has grown since the late 1990s, up from 5,000 in 1998 to 8,000 in 2008. But such moves are also likely to create problems as the party strives to be both radical (in a political sense) and traditional (in an organizational sense), whereas previously it was radical both politically and organizationally. Serious politics comes at a price.

## Conclusion

So, how far is this political activity by reds and greens helping to break the mould of traditional party politics in Britain? Or does it remain just a colourful sideshow to the main action? The question of the balance between political parties and other agencies of political mobilization (whether new social movement or 'protest business') will be taken up further in chapter 9 – in particular, within the context of the debate over levels of political participation. The issue here is whether parties representing radical socialist and green politics have advanced to the extent that their presence is contributing to a more fluid, multi-party politics.

As we saw in chapter 1, contemporary political science uses an indicator of political fragmentation – the effective number of parties – as a means to answer this question. This can be measured either by using the shares of the vote won by competing parties or by shares of seats gained in parliament as a result of the election. Simple plurality voting will tend to limit the degree of political fragmentation because smaller national parties struggle under the system to turn votes into seats. None the less, as we saw earlier in the book, the effective number of parties for both votes and seats has risen. Between 1945 and 1970, the effective number of parties based on voting shares was 2.36; after 1970, the average rose to 3.21. Using party shares of seats in parliament, the effective number of parties still increased from 2.05 to 2.21. At the 2005 poll, the effective number of parties by share of votes rose further to 3.48; and by share of seats, to 2.44. Parliamentary representation may still be dominated by two and a half parties, but multi-party politics has taken hold at the polling station.[21] The result of the 2010 election has not changed this trend. Beyond Westminster, again as we saw in chapter 1, red and green parties have made advances in both votes and seats.

Greens (and red–green alliances), in particular, have thrived in the more contingent, less class-based political world seen since the 1960s. The traditional two-party dog fight between the class enemies of industrial capitalist society has given way to something more fragmented and complex. Indeed, the success, especially beyond mainstream political arenas, of reds and greens has depended in large part on escaping from class politics into other areas of political campaigning, drawing upon environmentalist, feminist, anti-racist and anti-imperialist critiques of modern society. This has generated new political alliances, witnessed in the anti-globalization movement and its offshoots. These new alliances haven't always proved very stable, particularly when they have attempted to form alliances to stand candidates for election. But this street politics has had some pay-off at the ballot box, with the Green Party in particular becoming a more established player in electoral politics. This has meant that we are seeing not only a fragmentation of the British party system in the electoral arena, but also more polarization as a wide range of ideological perspectives are reflected on ballot papers.

These trends are unlikely to be reversed. The social conditions that have slowly transformed British party politics are not about to change. And while some of the issues that have clearly worked to the advantage of alliances of left-wing activists, such as the war in Iraq, will move off the political agenda, there are others that clearly will not. Unless someone comes up with an overnight solution to climate change, green politics is here to stay. However, unless there is a change to a far more proportional system of voting, the opportunities for the Green Party to progress beyond its single MP at Westminster will be limited.

### Further reading and research resources

On the tortuous history of the left in Britain set in a wider European context, see Sassoon's *One Hundred Years of Socialism*. The position of the left in Britain's multi-party politics in the mid 2000s (a point when support for the Respect Party had hit a high) is clearly addressed in Webb's 'The continuing advance of the minor parties' – which is no less important on the decline in this support since. There have been a number of studies of green politics across Europe, including Richardson and Rootes, *The Green Challenge*, and Jon Burchell, *The Evolution of Green Politics: Development and Change within European Green Parties* (London: Earthscan, 2002). The contemporary challenges facing the Green Party are analysed in Birch's 'Real progress'. The party itself is at www.green-party.org.uk; and what is left of Respect at www.therespectparty.net.

# CHAPTER EIGHT

# Party Politics after Devolution

## All change?

The year 2007 was a big one for devolved party politics in Scotland, Wales and Northern Ireland. In elections to the parliament in Scotland, the Scottish National Party (SNP) sneaked past Labour to become the largest party in Edinburgh. Coalition talks between the SNP and the Liberal Democrats in Scotland came to nothing and SNP leader Alex Salmond formed a minority government. A party of nationalist protest had become a party of government. In elections in Wales, the Labour Party emerged as the largest party in the Welsh Assembly, but, with support for other parties increasing, the political dominance of Labour in Wales looked shaky, held up by a fragmented opposition.

But perhaps the biggest shock in 2007 was the sight of Ian Paisley, leader of the Democratic Unionist Party (DUP) and arch-loyalist to the British state, and Martin McGuinness, leader of Sinn Fein and arch-enemy of that state, agreeing to share power in the devolved administration in Belfast. Religion divides politics in Northern Ireland in a way quite different from in the rest of the United Kingdom. The DUP had by 2007 replaced the party of establishment unionism, the Ulster Unionist Party, as the main party representing the Protestant loyalist community. Likewise, Sinn Fein, the political wing of the Irish Republican Army (IRA), had displaced the moderate and non-violent Social Democratic and Labour Party (SDLP) as the party of Northern Irish Catholic nationalism. Paisley and McGuinness couldn't bring themselves to shake hands in public, but their increasingly frequent and jovial joint appearances as the devolved heads of government led the local media to call them the 'chuckle brothers'. Thousands had died in the troubles in the province since the late 1960s. Peace was bringing some normality back to life in Northern Ireland.

This chapter will explore the giant step taken by British party politics as a result of devolution. The Labour government's constitutional reforms after 1997 established a new level to British government and to party politics in the UK. Elections to the devolved bodies in Scotland, Wales and Northern Ireland created new political jurisdictions with different electoral systems for party competition across the country, jurisdictions where the so-called 'minor parties' at Westminster, as Paul Webb puts it, are 'not so minor'.[1] These new political jurisdictions exposed a territorial dimension to British party politics that had for many years, at least in Scotland and Wales, remained dormant under the 'normal' two-party unionist politics in Britain. Post-devolution, this territorial dynamic has kicked in hard, giving rise to a more complex multi-level, multi-party picture of politics across the UK.

## Territorial politics

As we saw in chapter 1, the established view in post-war political science was that class was the only political cleavage that really mattered in British party politics. It was, more or less, everything. This view underpinned the idea that Britain had a two-party system. It might be different in other countries. In places such as Germany and Belgium, religion as well as issues of state and regional power and identity mattered in forming political cleavages and political parties in ways that had long since died out across the British Isles. On Britain's party family tree, only two parties really mattered: the Conservative Party and the Labour Party. At best, the old Liberal Party added an 'and a half' to this equation. But regionally based parties competing for 'home rule' or even independence, and drawing support from minority populations, were largely absent from the UK party system. The story of British democracy involved national parties turning particular regional concerns into a common language that everyone in the UK could understand and work around.[2]

Such a view immediately runs into the question of politics in Northern Ireland. Here place and faith (and the two are very much entwined) matter enormously. The principal political divide in the province is religion, not class. If you are Catholic, you are almost certainly an Irish nationalist and vote for one of the nationalist or republican parties. Equally, if you are a Protestant, you are more than likely to be a unionist, a loyalist to the British state, and to vote for one of the unionist parties. There are class divides in Northern Irish politics, in particular within the Protestant community, that have important implications for the spread of political support between unionist parties, as we see later. But certainly, class is far from being everything in Northern Ireland politics. What does help in understanding party politics in the province is the sense of identity (who we think we are): how a bundle of place-specific cultural, social and religious loyalties shape politics and much else besides.

Northern Ireland has often been treated as the exception to the general rule of UK politics that class was 'everything'. Up until the 1960s, this wasn't far wrong. But in the second half of the twentieth century, the traditional alignments of British politics began to shift. A more powerful territorial dynamic kicked into life in British politics. Questions of national identity came to the fore in shaping politics in Scotland and Wales. A new political geography emerged.

## Building a British state

Inevitably history matters to all this. From the eighteenth century onwards, the British state was held together with a sense of (Protestant) national identity that transcended the historical cultures and identities of the nations and peoples that made up this new multinational polity.[3] This state-building over the course of many centuries was often bloody and repressive as the English state imposed its authority over the British Isles. The Act of Union in 1707 brought England and Scotland under the sovereignty of the Westminster parliament, although the crowns of England and Scotland had already fused with the accession of James VI of Scotland to the English throne in 1603. This Act of Union may have cost the Scots their parliament, but it preserved many of the country's distinctive institutions that helped to define its national identity – in particular, the law and established church. Wales and Ireland were more unions by force. Wales, in effect, became part of England from the thirteenth century onwards as a result of military conquest. Ireland too was more or less ruled by England from the late middle ages and was fully incorporated into the new United Kingdom by another Act of Union in 1801.

The status and governance arrangements of this multinational state had been an issue that divided British politics in the nineteenth century. Home rule for Ireland split Gladstone's Liberal Party and led to Chamberlain's unionist liberals leaving the party for the Conservatives. How Ireland was governed – and who should govern it – continued throughout the twentieth century to dominate politics in this part of the British Isles. But on the mainland, politics lacked a significant regional dimension. In the 1960s, this all started to change.

## Nationalism, unionism and the British state

When Britannia finally stopped ruling the waves in the decades after the Second World War, nationalist sentiments began to creep back into British politics. The attachments and allegiances to the British state were beginning to weaken just at the time that attachments and allegiances to social background were also weakening – and the two are connected. Questions of constitutional rights, in particular the organization and distribution of power across the United Kingdom, were re-emerging. In Ireland, of course, these questions had never gone away, and had led after the First World War to the creation of the Irish Free State, now the Republic of Ireland, in the south. By the 1960s, it was becoming apparent that Britons were not all the same politically; and the sense of being British was breaking up, with attachments to other national identities – being Scottish, Welsh and Irish – becoming more important. To some, this shifting sense of identity demanded devolving some power back to the nations of Britain (i.e. home rule); to others, it meant independence for Scotland and Wales – and a united Ireland ruled from Dublin, not London.

This was not easy for the established political parties in the UK. Both Labour and the Conservatives are unionist parties, committed to the unity of the United Kingdom and to the indivisibility of the sovereign authority of the British nation, the parliament at Westminster. As a result, both parties were traditionally hostile to arguments for devolved government. The Liberals, by contrast, were far more sympathetic to home rule through new devolved or federal institutions.

But the UK has never been a unitary state in any straightforward way. Britain has long been governed in different ways in different places. Not only was Northern Ireland governed by a devolved executive in Belfast between 1922 and 1972, but Scotland – with its own distinctive legal system, schools and established church – also had its own devolved administrative institutions: the Scottish Office, as well as arrangements in parliament to deal with legislative business that only concerned Scotland. Wales, always more integrated into the English state than Scotland, had less administrative autonomy, though it too had its own 'regional department', the Welsh Office. This complexity in British governance arrangements led the United Kingdom to be described as a 'union state' rather than a unitary state.[4]

## Nationalist political divides open up: the SNP and Plaid Cymru

The re-emergence of nationalist politics in Britain in the 1960s reflected a feeling that, while Britons were all legally citizens of the same state, the sense of belonging to that state was beginning to fray. This shifting sense of belonging saw allegiances transfer from Great Britain to the nations that historically made up the United Kingdom. This movement in allegiances was manifested in a revival of a politics rooted in what political science calls ethno-nationalist cleavages. By contrast to socio-economic cleavages concerned with the distribution of wealth and power between different social groups, ethno-nationalist cleavages are territorially bounded, rooted in questions of culture and identity and concerned with the spatial distribution of wealth and power (sometimes conceptualized as being between a dominant 'core' and subordinate 'periphery').

These new political cleavages opening up in British party politics were apparent in shifting patterns of voting from the late 1950s onwards for the two main nationalist parties on the British mainland, the SNP and Plaid Cymru. Both parties, like similar minority nationalist parties in Europe, sought to represent ethno-nationalist groups in particular parts of the British state: Scots in Scotland and the Welsh in Wales. Both parties articulated the interests, as well as the cultural identity, of these groups in opposition to what is viewed as the power of the dominant majority group in the UK, the English and the English state. To put it another way, the public in the peripheries of Scotland and Wales were attracted to political parties that sought to advance the interests of these territories in relation to the geographical core of the British state with London at its centre. While both the SNP and Plaid Cymru have, over time, become in ideological terms social democratic, historically membership of and support for both parties encompassed a wide range of nationalist views.

The SNP has its roots in the merger of the Scottish Party and the National Party of Scotland in 1932: parties on the right and left of the political spectrum respectively. Ideologically, this set up a tension in the party between a conservative nationalist politics primarily concerned with issues of cultural identity and a progressive nationalist politics blending the issue of Scottish independence with a social democratic state. During the 1960s and 1970s, the SNP campaigned for a series of left-wing causes, including supporting the striking ship-workers on the Clyde. With North Sea oil coming on stream, the party also insisted the wealth created should go to Scotland, not the British exchequer. During the 1980s, constitutional issues divided the SNP. The party was split on how best to create an independent Scotland: between those who wanted to stick to a clear independence for Scotland position; and those taking a more gradualist position that saw devolution as a stepping stone to Scottish independence – a position, as we shall see later, that eventually won the day. Early electoral victory came in April 1945 when the SNP won the Motherwell by-election. But it lost the seat at the general election three months later. The SNP did not win again until 1967, when it took Hamilton in another by-election, but lost the seat at the following general election in 1970.

In Wales, Plaid Cymru (meaning 'the party of Wales') was established in 1925 but didn't have its first parliamentary success until 1966 when it won the Carmarthen by-election (a seat it would keep winning and losing at the next three elections). Like the SNP, Plaid has long been divided both on traditional left/right lines and on the devolution/independence question. But while the SNP has traditionally campaigned on the distinctiveness and independence of Scotland's civic institutions, Plaid has built its support on the back of Welsh culture. For Plaid, independence was more than just about home rule; it was enmeshed in campaigns for the Welsh language and culture. Speaking Welsh had been in long decline since the nineteenth century. By the 1960s, an attempt was made to revive it. In 1967, the Welsh Language Act began a process that has, in effect, turned Wales into a bilingual society – at least in public life, in schools and on television, with the setting up of S4C in 1982. Welsh cultural nationalists saw Plaid as a vehicle for their ambitions. Indeed, Plaid's bedrock of support in the electorate lay in Welsh-speaking, rural and often middle-class Dyfed and Gwynedd in north-west Wales – where it has had its electoral success at general elections. But this cultural politics did not always sit easily with the 'community socialism' which social democrats in the party saw as their main weapon in their battle for votes with Labour's 'state socialism'. Like the SNP, Plaid by the 1990s was a progressive nationalist party sitting more or less on the centre left of the political spectrum, with clear social democratic policies within the context of support for independence within membership of the EU.

Up until the 1950s, support for the SNP and Plaid barely registered on the national political radar. The combined votes for the two parties totalled in the tens of thousands – 0.1 to 0.2 per cent of the vote nationally. Even on their own turf, where nationalist parties would hope to prosper, both were very much minor parties. But by the late 1950s, support for the two parties was beginning to change – and by the 1970s, it was clearly on an upward trend. In 1970, the SNP and Plaid captured nearly half a million votes (1.7 per cent of votes cast in Great Britain) at the general election. At this poll, the two parties stood 101 candidates, winning 1 seat in parliament (for the SNP in the Western Isles). By the two elections in 1974, nationalist politics in Britain was winning a million votes (3.4 per cent of the total) and returning 14 candidates to Westminster in the October election (11 for the SNP, 3 for Plaid). Given that home advantage is what really counts in nationalist politics (the SNP and Plaid are looking to win seats in Scotland and Wales, not England), the territorial distribution of votes is interesting as a key indicator of changing patterns of voting. In Wales, Plaid in 1970 and 1974 won over 10 per cent of the vote. In Scotland, the SNP won over 11 per cent in 1970; and 22 per cent and 30 per cent in the two elections in 1974.

The growth in support for the two mainland nationalist parties had a real impact on national politics at Westminster. The beleaguered Labour government after 1974 – a minority one after 1976 – looked to other parties to shore up its majority in the House of Commons. With the parliamentary pact between Labour and the Liberals looking shaky, the government of James

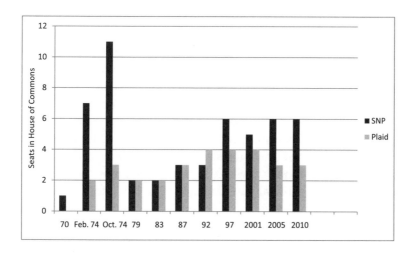

Source: Tetteh, 'Election Statistics 1918–2007'.

**Figure 8.1** *Seats won in general elections, SNP and Plaid Cymru, 1970–2010*

Callaghan saw the nationalists as a source of support. The nationalists wanted something in return: devolution. But the Labour government made a real hash of the proposed legislative process. The referendum in Wales was lost, not surprisingly perhaps given the limits of Plaid's brand of Welsh-speaking nationalism, which has always had less of a broad appeal in Wales than the SNP's more civic version has in Scotland. Here there was a majority for devolution, but not the necessary level of support to pass the threshold for the legislation to be enacted. Home rule failed and the Labour government was sunk, losing a vote of no confidence in the House of Commons without the support of nationalist MPs. A new political era was about to begin.

## Thatcherism and the English party

It might be expected that the 1980s would have provided some good times for nationalism in the UK. The dominance of a hard-line unionist party should have played into the nationalist parties' hands. But it didn't – or at least, not in any straightforward way. While support for the SNP and Plaid declined over the decade, the hegemony of Thatcherism in England led to a growing territorialization of British politics which contributed to Labour becoming more convincingly a party in support of devolution.

During these Conservative-dominated years, the SNP lost votes and seats, Plaid more votes than seats (but then it had fewer to start with). The nationalist vote fell back to the half-million mark. Many of the problems faced by nationalist politics in the 1980s were self-inflicted. The impact of the Conservative victory in 1979 was to intensify factional struggles within the SNP and Plaid between nationalist economic radicals and nationalist cultural conservatives. In Scotland, in particular, Gaelic cultural nationalists (Siol nan Gaidheal) pulled the SNP in one direction, while left-wing socialists (the 79 Group) pulled in the other. This did little for the party's electoral prospects – and the leadership at the time resorted to expelling dissidents. The SNP and Plaid were also divided about devolution and independence: should they campaign for a more limited constitutional settlement in the hope that this might lead to a Scottish state or hang on for full-blown independence?

These arguments preoccupied nationalist politicians in Scotland and Wales for much of the 1980s. By the early 1990s, both the SNP and Plaid were becoming more clearly defined pro-European social democratic parties. Indeed, by looking to Europe, nationalist parties in Britain sought out a political space to define and secure national independence, as well as create, as they saw it, a more modern, even progressive nationalism, combining constitutional demands with a strong social agenda and economic intervention to promote national economic renewal.

Away from Scotland and Wales, the other big story of the period was a wider territorialization of British politics. The Conservatives, *the* party of the union, were quickly becoming the party of England. It hadn't always been such. In Scotland in 1979, the Conservative Party won 22 out of 71 seats north of the border with 31 per cent of the vote. But after a decade of Thatcherism, the Tory vote in Scotland had slipped to 25 per cent in the 1992 election and thereafter kept falling. By 2005 it was down to 15.6 per cent. Conservative representation in parliament from seats in Scotland went the same way: down to 11 in 1992, ending up with zero in Labour's landslide year of 1997. In 2001, the Conservatives won back 1 seat and, with the reduction of Scottish seats in 2005, held on to it amidst significant boundary changes.[5] During the Thatcherite period, the Tories lost touch with their traditional voters in Scotland: in rural Scotland and among the Protestant and unionist working classes who were as British as they were Scottish. These became available to the other parties in Scotland, not least the resurgent SNP. And as the nationalists in Scotland grew in strength over the years, this tended to be at the expense of the weaker main party, the Conservatives. The opposite happened in southern England, where the revival of the Liberals was usually at the expense of Labour, the weaker main party in the south.[6]

The electoral numbers in Wales tell a very similar story to that in Scotland. Back in 1979, the Conservative Party won 32 per cent of the vote and 11 out of 36 seats. By 1992, the Tory vote had slipped to 28.6 per cent and 6 out of 38 seats; and by 1997, just under a fifth of voters in Wales voted Conservative, not enough to win a single seat west of Offa's Dyke. While the result of the 2010 general election confirmed that the Conservatives were going nowhere in Scotland (they held their only seat), in Wales, the Tories regained some of their lost ground, winning 5 seats and coming second in the share of votes.

The Englishness of the Conservatives was reinforced by their relative success in England itself. In 1979, the Tories won 47 per cent of the vote in England, and in 1992, 45.5 per cent. This translated into 306 out of 516 seats in the House of Commons in 1979, and 319 from 524 in 1992. For the Conservative Party, not only was it winning a majority of English seats, but, relatively speaking, the proportion of seats in England compared with seats in the rest of Britain was rising; and the majorities secured in parliament during the 1980s and 1990s were on the back of its success in England. As a result, the Tories not only looked like an English party, but an English government as well. The year 1997 saw much of what was solid blue territory turn red – or at least, turn to New Labour. Indeed, it was Tony Blair's great success as Labour leader in the 1990s that he was able to take on the Tories in England and win, not simply rely on Labour's heartland votes in the big cities and in Scotland and Wales.

The decline of the Conservative Party in Scotland and Wales reinforced Labour's growing dominance in these nations, in part because it contributed to the fragmentation of the political opposition to Labour in Scotland and Wales. But behind this headline, something else was happening. As we shall see in the next section, the creation of devolved constitutions was contributing to the growth of multi-party politics in the UK – even if, in national elections for Westminster, simple plurality meant that Labour still won the lion's share of the seats in parliament.

## The devolved constitutional settlement

During the 1960s and 1970s British party politics saw the emergence of nationalist parties promising a new political deal, usually outside the United Kingdom. Public support for some kind of new deal was growing, though support for outright independence remained relatively low. This tended to cap the level of voting for nationalist parties in Scotland and, in particular, Wales, where Plaid struggled to break out of its Welsh-speaking heartlands in the north-west of the country. But the growth in nationalist politics led to a broader reconsideration of the territorial governance of the UK. Some in the Labour Party, a party traditionally hostile to home rule, turned to devolution both out of commitment to more decentralized forms of government and as a matter of political expediency: if Labour couldn't beat the Tories in England, they might as well beat them in Scotland and Wales.

The election of a Labour government in 1997 marked the beginning of a short period of quite remarkable constitutional change. Legislation was passed to establish devolved institutions in Scotland, Wales and Northern Ireland, as well as a human rights act. The government's constitutional settlement established a parliament in Scotland and an assembly in Wales. These new representative bodies and their respective executives were responsible for those areas of public policy not 'reserved' by Westminster (reserved areas included economic policy and defence and foreign affairs). This meant, in effect, that the new devolved institutions had considerable powers over key areas of domestic policy including health, education, law and order, and social care (though this was 'asymmetrical devolution' with differences in these powers between the three nations).

Significantly for party politics in the new devolved political arenas, elections used different voting systems from that used for Westminster. Two systems were introduced. In Scotland and Wales, voters are faced with the additional member electoral system, a system that combines elections by simple plurality with proportional representation (PR). It is used, for example, in national elections in Germany. In Northern Ireland, explained in more detail later in this chapter, another system of proportional representation was introduced: the single transferable vote.

The additional voting system employed in Scotland and Wales introduced a greater element of proportionality into elections by giving voters a second (the additional) vote. The first vote uses the Westminster-type constituency list of candidates and voters cast their ballots in exactly the same way as in a general election. The second ballot has a list of candidates for the larger electoral region in which the constituency is found. In the constituency votes, the candidate with the highest number of votes takes the seat. The additional members in each region are elected to ensure that the number of seats in each region, including the constituency members, matches, as closely as is possible, the number of votes cast in that region for a particular party. This additional vote, then, brings greater proportionality to the representation of parties in the legislature.

The introduction of the additional member system to devolved elections in Scotland and Wales has had one clear and important impact. As we shall see shortly, the election results are far closer than is typical under simple plurality, and coalition or minority governments, rather than administrations with clear absolute majorities, have become the norm. Another impact is that parties that might otherwise have little or no representation – in particular, red and green parties – have been able to win seats in the Scottish parliament. Whether the introduction of this form of PR encourages voters to vote differently is another question examined shortly.

Even before the first elections to the devolved bodies were held in 1999, however, there were indications that a new political map was emerging.[7] While Labour won a crushing victory in the 1997 general election, and looked to be the predominant party in Scotland and Wales, certainly on seats won, there were already signs that elections in these two nations were becoming more competitive. In elections for the European parliament, the SNP increased its seats from 1 to 2 in 1994, holding on to these seats in 1999. Plaid won its first European seats in 1999.

## Devolved party politics in Scotland 1999–2007

The devolved election results in Scotland in 1999 and 2003 provided further evidence of political fragmentation and ideological polarization in Scottish politics post-devolution. While both Labour and the Liberal Democrats continued to prosper under first-past-the-post voting in the constituency ballot, the SNP and the Conservative Party did well in the top-up additional regional vote. Indeed, this measure of proportional representation offered the Scottish Tories a political lifeline. The voting system also provided opportunities for the smaller parties in Scotland. In 1999, the Scottish Socialist Party (SSP) won 1.5 per cent of the vote and 1 seat; in 2003, this jumped to 6.4 per cent of the vote and 6 seats. The Scottish Greens went from 1.8 per cent of the vote in 1999 and 1 seat, to 3.4 per cent of the vote and 7 seats in 2003. The relatively poor showing of the SNP in 2003 suggested a nationalist party struggling to present a clear message on independence in the world of devolved politics. Indeed, the SNP also performed poorly in the 2005 general election, beaten into second place by the Liberal Democrats. Still, at the 2005 poll, the effective number of parties north of the border was not far short of four.[8]

In the 2007 devolved elections, a resurgent SNP did battle with Labour and won – just. The SNP clawed its way past the Labour Party despite Labour's strength at the constituency vote level and its capacity to turn votes into seats.

**TABLE 8.1**  Devolved election results in Scotland 1999–2007: share of vote and number of seats

|  | 1999 % vote (seats) | 2003 % votes (seats) | 2007 % votes (seats) |
|---|---|---|---|
| **Labour** | 36.2 (56) | 32 (50) | 30.6 (46) |
| **Conservatives** | 15.5 (18) | 16.1 (50) | 15.2 (17) |
| **Lib Dems** | 13.3 (17) | 13.6 (17) | 13.7 (16) |
| **SNP** | 28 (35) | 22.3 (27) | 32 (47) |
| **SSP** | 1.5 (1) | 6.4 (6) | <1 (0) |
| **Scot Greens** | 1.8 (1) | 3.4 (7) | 4 (2) |
| **Others** | 3.7 (1) | 6.2 (4) | 4.4 (1) |

*Source*: Tetteh, 'Election Statistics 1918–2007', table 17.

The SNP won more votes in both ballots than it had done before – and, importantly, more seats. The result was, as the election expert John Curtis put it, 'truly historic'.[9] It could have been far worse for Labour, as some of the votes were very close and the Liberal Democrats and the Tories performed poorly. For the smaller parties, the success of 2003 was short-lived. With the improved performance by the SNP in 2007, and the Scottish Socialists shooting themselves in the foot, these minor parties were squeezed out: the SSP losing all its seats and the Greens down 5 to 2.

The 2007 result showed how far the SNP had regrouped under Alex Salmond's second spell as party leader after 2004. Back in the 1990s, Salmond revived the party's fortunes after the fractious and amateurish 1980s. He led the party down a moderate social democratic path and to a gradualist position on the question of independence. Under his leadership again, the SNP was vocal in its opposition to the Iraq war and to New Labour's stance on public sector reform. Membership of the party, which had dropped sharply in 2002, grew steadily, reaching 15,000 in 2008.[10] The growing professionalism of the party machine was rewarded. The 2007 election to the Scottish parliament was the breakthrough the SNP had long waited for. In Labour and its then leader Jack McConnell, the SNP faced an opponent weakened by internal arguments. On policy, aside from the constitutional question, there wasn't much between the two parties. The SNP went into the election promising much of the same as part of its 'progressive nationalist' politics that fused an upbeat message on a future independent Scottish economy with a commitment to social justice. On independence, Salmond was canny enough to realize this might be an easier sell having proved the party's competence in government. Salmond had in any case become a gradualist in party debates, opposing the fundamentalists in his party who opposed devolution as a compromise to their ideals of national independence. In the end, the 2007 devolved election was about which party would best run Scotland. This

## Box 8.1 Working together: competition and collaboration in devolved party politics

Back in the 1970s, the idea of parties working together in government as they did in many parts of Europe was seen by some as a stable alternative to the see-sawing of two-party politics. But it never caught on. British politics didn't do coalition government – and probably never would. Everything was wrong. Not just the first-past-the-post electoral system, but the whole competitive, adversarial and frankly tribal culture of British politics. Consensus and collaboration was impossible. But British political parties have cooperated with each other more often than is imagined. In the 1970s, cabinet posts were offered to members of third parties. Approaching the 1997 general election, Paddy Ashdown was close to getting a seat in government if Labour won. And during Labour's first term, Lib Dem MPs were given places on a cabinet sub-committee looking at constitutional reform. Parties have also cooperated in parliament – e.g. the Lib–Lab pact in the late 1970s that kept a minority Labour government in power. And they have also formed alliances to fight elections: the Liberals and the SDP did it in the mid 1980s. At a local level, while the majority of councils are under one-party rule, the rest are run by a striking variety of combinations between all the main parties, as well as independents.

Devolution has led to parties working together in a more sustained way. In Scotland, Wales and Northern Ireland, parties compete in elections, but may go on to collaborate in government. Indeed, in Northern Ireland, collaboration is built into the governing arrangements in the province, illustrating the challenges of building inter-party relations in power across deeply entrenched political divides. The voting system in Scotland and Wales has certainly had an impact on who governs. In Scotland, electoral competition has become more multi-party; and proportional representation has taken multi-party politics beyond the ballot box into parliament and into government. Following the 1999 and 2003 elections for the Scottish parliament, Labour / Liberal Democrat coalitions were formed. After 2007, the SNP attempted to build a coalition with the Liberal Democrats (always an unlikely event given the SNP's position on independence) and ended up forming a minority administration. In Wales, a minority Labour administration was formed in 1999, then a Labour / Liberal Democrat coalition in 2000. With an effective majority of one following the 2003 election, Labour formed a majority administration until 2005, when it lost its overall majority. Following the 2007 election, there was a prospect of Plaid joining with the Conservatives and the Liberal Democrats in a three-way coalition, but this came to nothing. Instead, Labour and Plaid formed a coalition. Given the historical tensions between Labour and Plaid, this was no easy thing. Both may be on the centre left (and ideological overlap is an important element in coalition building), but much still divides the two parties on constitutional and cultural questions.

The 2010 coalition between the Conservatives and the Liberal Democrats brought all this working together into the national public eye. In the five days following the election, much effort, and give-and-take, went into the detail of the coalition agreement between the two parties. Hung parliaments may become a more common occurrence at Westminster as they have as a result of devolution. Competition and collaboration – as across much of Europe – could become a part of British party politics, after all.[11]

capacity to govern (so important to the 'valence' model we saw in chapter 1) appeared to override older party loyalties that had been eroded by partisan de-alignment and the convergence of parties in Scotland.[12]

All of this combined to create a surge-tide effect for the SNP, pushing them ahead of Labour in the devolved 2007 poll. Such political currents ebb and flow. And following on from its devolved triumph, the SNP won a sensational by-election in the Labour heartland of Glasgow East. This was traditional working-class Britain where generations of families had got behind Labour, even as hard times led to high levels of social deprivation. Labour lost the seat to a 22 per cent swing to the SNP. The SNP could reach voters they struggled to get to before. But all tides turn – and in the 2010 general election the seat returned to Labour.

## Devolved party politics in Wales 1999–2007

In Scotland, devolved party politics has broken the hegemony of the Labour Party established in the 1980s. But has the same happened in Wales? Does the Labour Party still rule politics in the principality? Or is the picture more complex?

In elections in 1999 and 2003, the Labour Party won a majority of the votes cast and seats in the new assembly, with Plaid in second place and the Conservatives in third. The Liberal Democrats trailed in fourth place (and it is worth remembering that Wales in the early part of the twentieth century was a stronghold of liberal politics). In the 2007 devolved elections, Labour's share of the vote fell by over 7 per cent and the party lost 4 seats overall. While Plaid and the Conservatives both increased their shares of the vote and the number of seats in the assembly at this election, the position of Liberal Democrats barely changed. The key message from this poll was not so much Labour's decline as the continued fragmentation of support for the opposition parties.

The results from the 2005 general election also point to Labour's weaker position in Wales. The party's share of the vote in the principality fell by 6 per cent, with the loss of 5 seats. Plaid also lost votes and seats; and the per-

**TABLE 8.2**   Devolved election results in Wales 1999–2007: share of vote and number of seats

|  | 1999 % vote (seats) | 2003 % vote (seats) | 2007 % vote (seats) |
|---|---|---|---|
| Labour | 36.5 (28) | 38.3 (30) | 30.9 (26) |
| Plaid Cymru | 29.5 (17) | 20.5 (12) | 21.7 (15) |
| Conservatives | 16.2 (9) | 19.5 (11) | 21.9 (12) |
| Lib Dems | 13 (6) | 13.4 (6) | 13.3 (6) |
| Others | 4.9 (0) | 8.3 (1) | 12.2 (1) |

*Source*: Tetteh, 'Election Statistics 1918-2007', table 16.

formance of the Tories and the Liberal Democrats was up. But, in the Westminster elections with first-past-the-post voting, Labour was able to cling on to its status of first party of Wales, though its position was largely about the relative weakness and fragmentation of the opposition.[13] The effective number of parties by vote has, since the 1970s, been at or below 3 in elections for Westminster; by seats, the figure drops to at or below 2. In the general election results for 2001 and 2005, while there was little movement in this figure according to seats won at Westminster, in terms of votes cast the party system in Wales had become more fragmented, reaching a figure of 3.59 in 2005.[14]

## Devolved party systems and multi-level governance

It was anticipated that the creation of new devolved bodies in Scotland and Wales would change the dynamics of British government and party politics, further embedding what political science calls multi-level governance. This has seen traditional hierarchical models of public administration replaced with more complex and decentralized multi-tier systems for running public affairs. In simple terms, this means that the UK is run not just from Westminster, but also from Edinburgh, Cardiff and Belfast – and somehow, these different administrations have to find some way of working together. This unleashing of 'centrifugal forces' would reshape British party politics by creating new centres of political and administrative power.[15] Devolved party politics would march to a different tune from that set by Westminster. Voters in these regionally bounded political jurisdictions would have to be courted. Different political cleavages would come into play. The established national parties would have to adapt their political strategies and party structures to reflect these new demands – and, in doing so, shape the political preferences of voters. And proportional representation would give real opportunities to smaller parties to turn votes into seats and even to join the 'major' parties in power.

The decline in two-party politics in Britain has seen a fragmentation of the party system as voters have switched to supporting a broader range of parties, including nationalist ones in Scotland and Wales. Devolution has taken this process of fragmentation a step further by creating a new tier of politics that further consolidates the pluralism across the electoral, legislative and executive arenas. Elections to these new devolved bodies in Scotland and Wales, as we have seen, are more multi-party; the parliament in Scotland and the assembly in Wales have representatives from a broader range of parties; and the executives in both regional capitals have involved coalition governments. It has not proved business as usual for British government and politics. What were 'Labour heartlands' are no more. Predominant party systems have become more multi-party.

Devolution has also had an impact on the structure, organization and political strategies of Labour, the Conservatives and the Liberal Democrats. Traditionally, Britain's national parties were just that – shaped by the demands of national campaigns orchestrated from London by central party offices that were closely bound up with the political leadership at Westminster and the national media. Like Dick Whittington, all ambitious politicians (and journalists) were drawn to London, the apex of power of the British state. But the centrifugal forces unleashed by devolution have, to a certain extent, worked to pull national government and national parties apart. With multi-level governance across the UK has come the pressure on political parties to organize and operate at the sub-national level. The devolution of power and responsibilities for many areas of public affairs has given the elections for these sub-national bodies real meaning.

This has posed a problem of leadership. For the three national parties in particular, there are now party leaderships and parliamentary groups established in the devolved administrations (and in the case of the Lib Dems, the party leaderships had an early taste of power, as we have seen). These political leaders in Scotland and Wales co-exist with the national leaderships and parliamentary groups based around Westminster politics. This has brought tensions as national parties have tried to impose their will on devolved parties, most notably when the Labour Party moved unsuccessfully to block Rhodri Morgan becoming first minister in Wales.

Inevitably, these multiple leaderships give rise to problems when national and devolved parties can't agree the line on policy issues – made doubly difficult because of the devolution of responsibilities for many areas of domestic policy. Post-devolution, there has been a political parting of ways, giving rise to institutionalized ideological polarization within parties. The Labour Party in Wales rebranded itself 'Welsh Labour' in an effort to distance itself from the New Labour government at Westminster. Within the constraints of the devolution settlement, Welsh Labour in government in Cardiff attempted to put some clear red water between itself and the Blair government in London.[16] In Scotland too, the Labour Party in Edinburgh under Jack McConnell sought to chart a different course from that of the Labour government in the UK capital. In Wales and Scotland, Labour administrations staked out distinct policies on schooling, housing, the funding of higher education, the NHS and personal care of the elderly to the left of the national party in government in London.

These differences between national and devolved parties come to the fore at general election time when campaign strategies have to be agreed and coordinated. The almost continuous cycle of elections contributes to the blurring of national and devolved responsibilities and has knock-on effects for subsequent elections. Experience from the 2005 and 2010 general elections suggests that in Scotland and Wales there was no hard and fast division between national issues and devolved policy questions: parties campaigned on both, despite the fact that only national policies in Scotland and Wales were at stake, although, in 2010, the debate about the size of public spending cuts would have an inevitable impact on devolved policy-making. But even if it were possible to draw clear lines between elections at different levels, multi-level governance has brought real challenges of coordination for political parties operating across the UK.

All devolved parties operating across sub-national jurisdictions have, then, sought to gain a degree of autonomy from their national parties. But are voters behaving differently as a result of the new political systems put in place by devolution? There is some evidence that voters are doing their political sums on one basis for national elections and on another for devolved elections – for example, supporting the SNP in devolved elections because they will 'stand up for Scotland'. The higher share of the vote for nationalist parties in these contests compared with UK elections tends to confirm this. There is also evidence of vote-splitting. In the 1999 devolved election in Scotland, an estimated 20 per cent of the electorate split their votes between the constituency and regional ballots; and around 29 per cent did in 2003. In Wales, around 25 per cent of voters changed parties across the two ballots in 1999.[17]

## Party politics in Northern Ireland – another country?

Visit Belfast today and there few outward signs of Northern Ireland's troubled past. The road blocks are gone and what is left of the British army in the province returned to barracks. Life in Northern Ireland since the late 1990s has become more settled, even if memories remain deeply embedded in the individual and collective memories of local people. Politics, too, has returned to the province – and is one largely free from the shadow of the masked gunman or bomber. Indeed, politics has been the saviour of Northern Ireland. The gun in that old cliché has just about given way to the ballot box, and political democracy has proved a means to come to some sort of reconciliation of the divides that have torn Northern Ireland (and Ireland) apart for generations.

But party politics in Northern Ireland remains very different from politics in the rest of the United Kingdom – and probably always will be. For a start, the main parties on the British mainland, the Conservatives, Labour and the Liberal Democrats, have no significant presence in the party system in the province. From the early 1970s, politics in Northern Ireland was left to Northern Irish parties. These parties generally divide not on left/right lines, but on religion and the authority of the British state in the province. The main political cleavages are ethno-nationalist, not socio-economic. They are about identity, not class. However, there are within each community political divides based on class, and these are important to understanding some of the changes that have taken place in the party system in Northern Ireland since the late 1990s, as we shall see later.

For many years, the main party representing the unionist or loyalist Protestant communities of Northern Ireland, whatever their class, was the Ulster Unionist Party (UUP). The UUP was the conservative party in Northern Ireland politics. It supported traditional social relations and the established institutions of church and state in the province, including the Anglican Church of Ireland. The UUP also had close links with the Protestant Orange Order. The governing body of the party is the Ulster Unionist Council and today all members of the party are members of this body which elects the leadership and decides major policy positions. To a certain extent, the UUP was also the Conservative Party in Ulster: the UUP were affiliated to the National Union of Conservative and Unionist Associations and the party's MPs at Westminster generally took the Tory whip. In 2009 this relationship was re-established when the UUP and the Conservative Party agreed to form an alliance to fight general and European elections under the name Ulster Conservatives and Unionists – New Force.

The UUP ran politics in the province for the best part of fifty years. Following the partition of Ireland in 1920, the six counties of Northern Ireland were governed by a devolved parliament in Stormont, Belfast, until its suspension in 1972. To start with, elections to Stormont were by proportional representation, but after 1929 they were by simple plurality. This meant the majority community in the province, the unionist or loyalist Protestants, and its political party, the UUP, dominated government and politics. In the final election to the Belfast parliament in 1969, the UUP won 36 seats, 3 were taken by independent unionists, 2 by the Northern Ireland Labour Party, 6 by nationalists representing the largely Catholic communities, and 5 others by a mix of socialists, republicans and independents. This was a predominant party system manufactured to ensure that political power and decisions about the distribution of resources rested with one community to the exclusion of all others. This wouldn't last: the idea that majority rule equalled democracy in Northern Ireland was unsustainable.

In the late 1960s, a civil rights movement sprang up in the province that called into question the authority and privileges of Protestant unionist government. The movement called for equal rights, specifically for the minority Catholic community, not simply in politics, but in all walks of life in the province. The civil rights movement led to the formation of the party that would become the main vehicle for Catholic nationalist politics in Northern Ireland for much of the next three decades: the Social Democratic and Labour Party (SDLP). As a nationalist party, the SDLP is committed to the peaceful creation of a united Ireland governed from Dublin. The SDLP is also an expression of the ambitions of the largely Catholic communities for economic and social reform within the broad framework of traditional church morality. Like the SNP and Plaid in Scotland and Wales, the SDLP's brand of nationalism is progressive and reformist, that of a social democratic party on the centre left of the political spectrum. The party has close links with the British Labour Party and other social democratic parties across Europe. The SDLP is also about as close as British politics comes to the continental European Christian democratic strand of politics rooted in a communitarian Catholicism against the power of the secular state.

The main competition for support among Catholic nationalist communities for the SDLP has come not from other mainstream political parties but from republicans – in particular, the Irish Republican Army (IRA) and its political counterpart Sinn Fein. Some history is necessary here. The IRA was founded in 1919 to fight against British rule of Ireland. Following the Anglo-Irish war between Britain and these Irish forces the main body of the IRA became the basis for the new army of the Irish Free State – now the Republic of Ireland. Those members of the IRA who opposed the settlement with Britain that brought about the partition of Ireland between north and south fought a civil war (1921–3) alongside the nationalist political party Sinn Fein (meaning 'we ourselves'), founded in 1905 and which too rejected the treaty with Britain that divided Ireland. The civil war had a lasting impact on the politics of Ireland, forming the basis for support for the country's two main political parties, Fianna Fail and Fine Gael. Fianna Fail was led by former Sinn Fein leader Eamon de Valera who had in defeat conceded a two-state solution for Ireland, even if his party remained committed to creating a united Ireland in the longer term. Those members of Sinn Fein and the IRA who did not accept this settlement continued, on and off, a campaign of terrorism in pursuit of their republican ambitions for a united Ireland.

By the late 1960s, in the midst of the civil rights movement in Northern Ireland, factions inside Sinn Fein and the IRA (and by this time it is difficult to disentangle the two groups) broke away from the main body of the organization to form Provisional Sinn Fein and the Provisional IRA. These groups were committed to a far more aggressive policy of military action against loyalist and British rule in Northern Ireland. Violence escalated as paramilitary groups on both sides of the religious divide sought, as they saw it, to protect their own communities. The British army, deployed onto the streets of the province in 1969, increased their presence. The 'troubles' intensified and the death toll rose alarmingly. On 30 January 1972, the British army fired on a banned civil rights march in the city of Derry in the county of Londonderry. Thirteen marchers died. 'Bloody Sunday' inflamed an already divided province. The Stormont parliament that had ruled the province since partition was suspended under the Northern Ireland (Temporary Provisions) Act. Direct rule from London was established under a secretary of state. But the measure was anything but temporary. It would last, more or less, for the next thirty-five years.

Following a referendum in March 1973 on British rule in Northern Ireland, an attempt was made to bring peace to the province by a return to home rule through a power-sharing assembly elected by proportional representation bringing the two sides of the divided community together. Elections were held in June 1973 and after protracted negotiations, an executive was agreed led by the UUP's Brian Faulkner and the SDLP's Gerry Fitt. The more hard-line unionists and nationalists hated it. Faulkner's position in unionist politics was challenged. In May 1974, a strike by Protestant workers, led in part by the founder of the evangelical Free Presbyterian Church of Ulster Ian Paisley, dealt a death blow to the new assembly and to any idea of power-sharing between unionists and nationalists. The strike would also harden the division of unionism in Northern Ireland between the UUP, willing to seek a compromise between the two communities in the province, and Paisley's Democratic Unionist Party formed in 1971 to advance a more radical and uncompromising unionist politics.

The Conservative government of Margaret Thatcher attempted to revive power-sharing in the early 1980s. Elections were held in October 1982 and the new assembly met on and off for the next four years, but little came of it. Northern Ireland would be ruled directly by the British government until the endless cycle of violence and death brought the province to the brink of civil war – and to its knees.

Extraordinarily, democratic politics survived – and in the 1990s would provide the basis for what appears to be a lasting settlement for the government of Northern Ireland. But that new settlement would involve a significant shift in power within the party politics of the loyalist and nationalist communities.

## A divided polity

Between 1974 and 1997, general election results for Northern Ireland show that two parties dominated politics in the province – or, to be more precise, dominated democratic politics in their respective communities. The party system in Northern Ireland involves, in effect, competition between parties within these communities, not between parties across these community divides. Unionist parties are, by and large, seeking support from Protestant loyalists; nationalist and republican parties from Catholic voters. The only significant party to operate between communities was the 'non-sectarian' liberal Alliance Party formed in 1970. For a time in the late 1970s and 1980s, the party won a respectable share of the vote but no seats.[18] The party, as we shall see shortly, won seven seats in the 2007 devolved elections – and in 2010, its first seat at Westminster.

On the loyalist side, the UUP was during this period the leading party of the Protestant unionist community – and because of the numerical advantage of this community in Northern Ireland, this made the UUP the leading party in Ulster. The main support for the UUP, as well as its membership base, was drawn from the province's Protestant middle class who held positions of power right across Ulster society. The UUP was staunch in its loyalty to the British state, but it also showed itself willing to engage in power-sharing arrangements for Northern Ireland. In this respect, the UUP was at odds with the DUP which opposed power-sharing in the 1970s – and which remained hostile to it in the 1990s (which made 2007 such an extraordinary year for Northern Ireland politics). But the DUP was also divided from the UUP by class and church. The DUP drew its members and electoral support from the

Protestant working class who, by the early 1970s, were facing not only greater economic insecurity than ever before but also a challenge to their traditional privileged position within Ulster from the civil rights movement demanding equal rights for the Catholic working class. The party also had close links with Protestant evangelical churches in the province, including Paisley's Free Presbyterians. From 1974, support for the DUP grew, but still, in 1997, Paisley's party only won a little over 13 per cent of the vote and just two seats at Westminster.

On the nationalist side, the SDLP was the leading party in votes and seats in parliament from 1974 until 1997. The party drew support from across the Catholic community in its campaigns for social and constitutional reform. By the 1980s, the SDLP's main competition for Catholic votes came from the republican Sinn Fein – and the key political divide between them was constitutional, not socio-economic. Both were, broadly speaking, centre left parties. But they disagreed on the role of power-sharing in devolved government as the path to a united Ireland.

The question of involvement in political processes had divided republicanism in Northern Ireland in the late 1960s, leading to the breakaway Provisional Sinn Fein. While in the 1970s some republicans engaged with mainstream politics, Sinn Fein didn't. This started to change in the 1980s. In April 1981, Bobby Sands, an IRA prisoner in the Maze Prison convicted for firearms offences and on hunger strike claiming political rights for IRA prisoners, won Fermanagh and Tyrone in a by-election for parliament following the death of the sitting republican MP (the SDLP did not stand against Sands). Sands died the following month and the seat was held by Sands's election agent, Owen Carron, who, in effect, was the first Sinn Fein MP in the modern era. It signalled a shift in strategy by the party.

Sinn Fein (and the IRA) had spent the best part of a decade building a formidable political and military machine across nationalist communities in Northern Ireland, often rooted in community-based initiatives such as housing associations. But the party preferred armed force to the ballot box. Nevertheless, the victories by Sands and Carron saw Sinn Fein move increasingly into electoral politics at both a national and local level – part of a dual strategy that became known as the 'armalite and the ballot box'. The party polled well in the 1982 elections for the Northern Ireland Assembly, winning 5 seats. In 1983, the leader of the party, Gerry Adams, won West Belfast, but didn't take his seat in the House of Commons, holding it at the 1987 election. At the 1983 poll, Sinn Fein won 13.4 per cent of the vote in the province; in 1987, 11.4 per cent. Sinn Fein also did well in local government elections. In 1985, the party won 12 per cent of the vote and gained 59 seats (by 2005, 23 per cent of voters supported the party, leading to 126 seats, second only to the DUP). But support for the party dropped in the late 1980s and early 1990s – and Adams lost his seat in the 1992 general election, only to win it back in 1997.

## The realignment of Northern Irish politics

Looking at these general election results in Northern Ireland over more than twenty years, it is clear that party politics in the province started to change in the 1990s. Underpinning these changes were hugely significant agreements involving the key players in Northern Ireland that have brought a large measure of peace to the province. These agreements involved not only the British and Irish governments but also the political parties on both sides of the community divide, including Sinn Fein and the DUP. Indeed, the paradox of this peace process is that those parties that were most suspicious of it were its greatest beneficiaries.

The foundation of this settlement was the 1985 Anglo-Irish Agreement that gave the government in Dublin a formal role in Northern Ireland's affairs. Following secret talks between the British government and the IRA in the early 1990s, the 1993 Anglo-Irish Pact was signed, allowing for republican and loyalist paramilitaries to enter peace talks conditional on three-month ceasefires. Ceasefires and talks followed and in 1998 the Good Friday Agreement was signed. This set out the terms for a new devolved power-sharing assembly in the province. Sinn Fein and loyalist paramilitaries welcomed the peace moves and the agreement was overwhelmingly supported in referendums on both sides of the Irish border.

The leaders of the main parties in Northern Ireland who had been instrumental in getting their respective communities to sign up to the Good Friday Agreement, UUP leader David Trimble and the SDLP's John Hume, won the Nobel Peace Prize for their efforts. But for both parties, the agreement was to

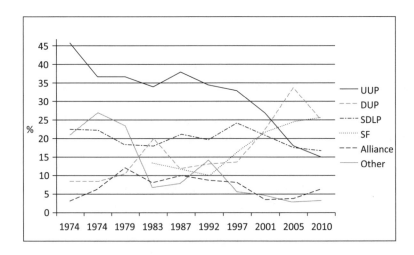

*Source: Tetteh, 'Election statistics 1918–2007'; BBC Online*

**Figure 8.2** *General election results for Northern Ireland seats, 1974–2005, share of vote*

signal a significant shift in political support in both nationalist and loyalist politics. In particular, the UUP's position in unionist politics was holed by opposition to the idea of power-sharing with Sinn Fein from Paisley's DUP. At the 2001 general election, support for the UUP fell. In 2005, the party that had dominated loyalist politics for so many decades was crushed, as was Trimble, who lost his seat in the UUP rout and resigned as leader. The DUP surged ahead, winning a third of the vote and nine seats in parliament. On the nationalist side, Sinn Fein too gained in strength in the UK-wide polls. In 1997, the party's share of the vote increased and it won two seats. In 2001, it nosed in front of the SDLP in its share of the vote, winning four seats to the SDLP's three. This lead was consolidated in 2005, when Sinn Fein won just over 24 per cent of the vote and five seats. Local election results held at the same time as the 2005 general election also showed a shift in power on both sides: the DUP won 30 per cent of the vote against the UUP's 18; and Sinn Fein won 23 per cent to the SDLP's 17.4 per cent.

## Devolution to Northern Ireland

The Good Friday Agreement paved the way for new devolved institutions in Northern Ireland. The 108-member Northern Ireland Assembly, established under the Belfast Agreement and the Northern Ireland (Elections) Act, was first elected in June 1998 using the single transferable vote to ensure the fair representation of nationalist and unionist communities. The assembly has legislative authority over devolved policy, but no powers to raise taxation. The Northern Ireland government is based on a twelve-member power-sharing cabinet that requires a cross-section of support in the assembly. A first and a deputy first minister share leadership of the executive committee, both elected by qualified majority vote to ensure support from both unionist and nationalist politicians. However, devolved government of the province was dogged by the continuing problems with the decommissioning of IRA arms. In October 2002, the assembly was suspended – for the fourth time – and direct rule from Westminster was resumed. This continued until an agreement was signed in St Andrews in 2006 that led, in 2007, to fresh elections to the Belfast assembly.

Going back to the first election to the Northern Ireland parliament on 25 June 1998, we can see in the bar charts in figure 8.3 that the UUP and the SDLP retained their lead in Northern Ireland politics. However, in the next election in 2003, this had evaporated. The DUP was now the largest unionist party and Sinn Fein was running neck and neck with the SDLP. In 2007, the DUP and Sinn Fein pulled ahead in the loyalist and nationalist communities respectively; making them the leading parties in Northern Ireland politics.

So, what has driven the realignment of the party system in Northern Ireland? In the post-Good Friday Agreement political scene, the UUP lost out.

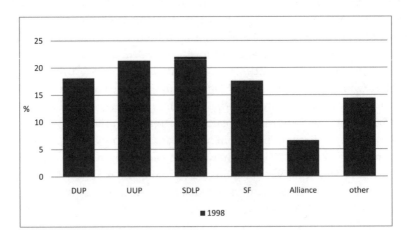

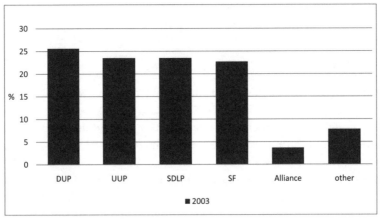

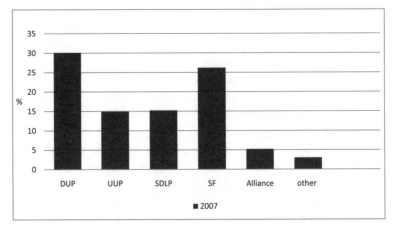

Source: BBC Online

Figure 8.3 *Northern Ireland devolved elections results, percentage of the vote, 1998, 2003 and 2007*

This was in part because its main competitor for the loyalist vote, the DUP, changed tactics, becoming less militantly loyalist and presenting itself as the party best able to defend loyalist interests in any devolved politics. In so doing, the DUP was able to broaden its appeal among Protestants beyond the working class to middle-class voters who had traditionally formed the bedrock of UUP support. In this way, the UUP was painted as a party too willing to give concessions to Sinn Fein. Indeed, unhappiness with Trimble's leadership of the UUP came not just from the DUP but also from within his own party. So, after 1998, the DUP switched from being opponents of the Good Friday Agreement to arguing that only it could defend unionist communities in the face of Sinn Fein. On the other side of Northern Ireland politics, Sinn Fein proved adept at mobilizing nationalist voters in a way that cut into the support base for the SDLP. And, like the DUP among loyalist voters, Sinn Fein presented themselves as the best party to defend Catholic nationalist interests.

## Northern Ireland's party systems – and their future

Underlying these changes in party tactics were important shifts in political cleavages in Ulster. Traditionally, as we have seen, the only political divide that mattered in the Northern Ireland party system was religion – and with religion came a powerful sense of identity, either of nationalist commitment to Ireland or of loyalist commitment to the United Kingdom. But this political cleavage only tells part of the story. As Jonathan Tonge puts it: 'Elections in Northern Ireland remain sectarian headcounts; what matters is the breakdown of votes within the blocs.'[19] There is not one *demos* but two in democratic politics in the province. And this breakdown matters enormously in terms of the future prospects for the UUP and SDLP.

The party system in Northern Ireland is better understood, then, as two party systems. Generally, on the loyalist side, the UUP and the DUP divide on class lines, as well as on their attitude towards constitutional reform, as we have seen. Among nationalist parties, there is little in the way of a class division; the SDLP and Sinn Fein part company over how to go about achieving what is a shared goal, a united Ireland. The devolved political settlement established what are known as 'consociational' constitutional arrangements that seek to embed entrenched social divisions in power-sharing forms of government. These forms of arrangements have the effect of encouraging parties to maximize their support from within their own communities rather than to appeal to others, thereby reinforcing the dual character of party politics in the province. As a result, to win votes, parties have engaged in political strategies that put defence of their community above cross-community alliance building.[20]

So, the DUP attacked the UUP in terms of defending Protestant communities against a power-sharing deal that handed power to 'terrorists' – Sinn Fein. Equally, Sinn Fein presented itself as the best party to defend Catholic nationalist interests and aspirations on the longer road to their goal of a united Ireland. By moving towards the centre ground of politics, moderating its left wing, Sinn Fein also limited any ideological divides among nationalist voters. What has happened in Northern Ireland since the 1990s is that, on the loyalist side, the socio-economic divides that traditionally separated unionist parties from one another have become far less important in comparison to the ethno-nationalist divisions – over constitutional reform. On the nationalist side too, the left/right divide is second to the ethno-nationalist. On both sides – and in both party systems – the parties that have prospered during the peace process are those that have stood up for their communities – whether this makes for good policy or not.

By the same token, both the DUP and Sinn Fein have, over the course of a decade or more, become far more pragmatic, in particular over the question of power-sharing. So, while electoral politics in Northern Ireland means that parties compete by saying they won't work together – or if they do, they will stand up for those who voted for them – in the legislative and executive spheres, these parties have become more pragmatic because they have to work with each other (and if they don't, the British government threatens to go back to direct rule from London). Having said this, while all sides enjoy the devolution of power to the province, this hasn't made the sharing of this power easy at all – in particular, in relation to police and justice powers. Indeed, the deal between the DUP and Sinn Fein to create a justice minister in 2010 in the province required Alliance Party leader David Ford to take on this post.

The price of pragmatism is high in Northern Ireland politics. In the 2009 European elections, the DUP vote was cut by opposition to power-sharing from former DUP politicians led by Jim Allister. Allister formed the Traditional Unionist Voice and won 13.7 per cent of first-preference votes under the province's single transferable vote for European elections. The DUP won 18.2 per cent at this stage – and Sinn Fein topped the poll with 26 per cent. The new alliance between the UUP and the Conservative Party won 17.1 per cent of the vote.

The position of the DUP in Northern Ireland was further shaken in 2010 when Paisley's successor as DUP leader and first minister in Northern Ireland, Peter Robinson, found himself embroiled in scandal. In the general election that followed, a resigned Robinson lost his seat to the Alliance Party, a result that otherwise saw very little change in the balance of power between parties in Northern Ireland. While the proximate causes of Robinson's problems were the financial and love affairs of his wife Iris, herself a leading politician in the province, underlying them were continuing tensions at the heart of Northern Ireland politics. While the majority of people in both communities support devolution, there is still considerable opposition inside unionist politics (not least within the DUP) to the very thought of sharing power with Sinn Fein. On the other side of the community, there remain dissident republicans in the Real IRA and the Continuity IRA who continue to believe that bombs not ballot boxes will bring about a united Ireland. The peace process in Northern Ireland has long been about the search for a common democratic narrative – and since the late 1980s, this has meant involving the 'extremes'.[21] This has not been easy for those parties long committed to democratic politics. Forced inter-party cooperation in government has been difficult. The challenge today is to ensure that parties talk to each other and consider the *polis* of Northern Ireland, not just their own communities. The spectre of sectarianism still haunts politics in Northern Ireland. The 'troubles' of the 1970s and 1980s are unlikely to return. But equally, the path forward is a difficult one.

## Further reading and research resources

The chapter by Mitchell and Seyd, 'Fragmentation in the party and political systems', in Robert Hazell's edited volume *Constitutional Futures* (Oxford: Oxford University Press, 1999), provides a useful starting point for thinking about the consequences of devolution for British party politics. The devolved administrations themselves are an excellent source of data and commentary on electoral politics. The 2007 elections in Scotland are analysed in S. Herbert, R. Burnside, M. Earle, M. Edwards, T. Foley and I. McIver (eds.), *Election 2007*, The Scottish Parliament, Scottish Parliament Information Centre, 07/21, 8 May 2007, www.scottish.parliament.uk/business/research/briefings-07/SB07-21.pdf. Detailed analysis of post-devolution elections can be found at two ESRC-funded centres, the Scottish Elections Survey, www.scottishelectionstudy.org.uk/; and the 2011 Welsh Election Study, www.aber.ac.uk/en/interpol/research/research-projects/welshelectionstudy.

The complex politics of Northern Ireland is tackled in Aughey, *The Politics of Northern Ireland*, and the consequences for the model of devolved politics in Northern Ireland on the province's party system in Tilley, Evans and Mitchell, 'Consociationalism and the evolution of political cleavages in Northern Ireland'.

# CHAPTER NINE

# Politics and Its Discontents

## Five days in May

The 2010 general election was the most exciting in living memory. Surely this was a political drama to catch voters' attentions. The poll was always going to be tight. With the Liberal Democrat surge following the first televised 'prime ministerial' debate, it only got tighter. Not only were the majority of voters ready for a change of government, there were also very many who couldn't make up their minds which party to support. Every second on the campaign trail appeared to matter. There was also the real prospect of the smaller parties getting in on this national political act. The Scottish National Party and Plaid Cymru were running from positions of power in devolved government in Edinburgh and Cardiff. The United Kingdom Independence Party and the British National Party polled well in the European elections the previous year; and expectations were high that Britain might see its first Green Party MP. In some parts of the country, this wasn't just three-party politics – multi-party politics was in full swing.

Once the polling stations closed (some with crowds of voters still waiting to cast their ballots), election fever continued. The result, a hung parliament, had been widely predicted. This made what followed no less gripping. Political horse-trading between parties on forming coalition governments might be common practice across many parts of continental Europe (and in the devolved bodies across the UK), but it appeared quite alien to Westminster politics. February 1974 was the only real point of comparison. Five days of negotiations in May 2010 produced a Conservative/ Liberal Democrat coalition – and the prospect, for political anoraks, that this could be the most interesting period of government for decades.

All this excitement, however, could not hide some uncomfortable truths about British party politics and its discontents. Turnout in general elections has been in long slow decline. In 1950, just over 84 per cent of eligible voters cast their ballots. By 1997, this was nearer 70 per cent. The UK is no different in this trend from most other mature democracies as they reach a certain point in their social, economic and cultural modernization. By contrast, countries across the world that have experienced rapid development since 1945, especially in Asia (e.g. Thailand) and South America (e.g. Peru), have seen substantial increases in the number of people voting in elections.[1]

In the longer term, the combination of the decline in partisanship examined in chapter 1, and a corresponding and related decline of traditional 'mobilizing agencies' – such as political parties, trade unions and churches – has eroded turnout in the UK. The likelihood of a person voting is related to the strength of their identification with a political party. As party identification has fallen in the population – and voting become more of a political choice – so has turnout. From time to time, a tight electoral contest produced a jump in numbers voting, for example in 1992 when turnout rose to 78 per cent. But political participation at the polling stations went from bad to worse in 2001. Turnout collapsed to just 59 per cent, edging up a notch in 2005 to 61 per cent. The fact that both contests were one-sided and the results foregone conclusions partly accounts for the low turnout in these elections. The worry is that the experience of not voting – and not thinking voting is something that a person should do – in particular for first-time voters, becomes engrained in future political habits as people get older.

The desire for change, not least of political leadership, pushed turnout up to 65 per cent in 2010. But one good election does not make a political summer. There remain lingering anxieties about the state of British democracy. Beyond the headline figures on turnout, for example, lie even more worrying differences in participation rates in elections across different social groups. Young people, poorer people and voters from black and minority ethnic communities are just not going to the polling stations in the same numbers as older, richer white voters. Moreover, the fragmentation of party politics has left British government with a problem of legitimacy: a sense that it fails to represent the 'will of the people', however imperfect this might be. Labour's victory in 2005 came dangerously close to the point where it lacked such authority. Its 66-seat majority in the House of Commons was secured with just 35 per cent of the popular vote – that is, just over a third of those who did vote, not of those who could have cast their ballot. No government had rested on such a low share since 1923. In terms of the electorate as a whole, the 2005 Labour government was supported by only 21 per cent of the country, a slice of the electorate considerably smaller than the proportion of non-voters.

In 2010, David Cameron's Conservatives 'won' with 36 per cent of the vote; only a coalition with the Liberal Democrats brought some democratic respectability – and political legitimacy. With opinion polls in the months after the election suggesting the coalition's 59 per cent of the popular vote was not all it seemed (one poll for BBC *Newsnight* had 40 per cent of Lib Dem voters stating they would not have voted for the party if they had known it would go into coalition with the Tories[2]), the pressure for electoral reform to give greater authority to the winning party or parties is likely to become unstoppable.

The fragmentation of party politics, as we have seen in this book, is reflective of the greater pluralism of modern British society; the opportunities that proportional representation offers for smaller parties in devolved and

European elections; and the more professional vote-seeking strategies of these parties. But political fragmentation also reflects the anti-political mood of the electorate and the capacity of some political parties – some at the ideological extremes – to feed off this sentiment by offering populist anti-Westminster politics. The rise of the BNP in Britain – and far right politics more generally in Europe – over the past decade is the clearest evidence of this.

### Trust and politics

One underlying concern is trust – or lack of it – in politicians and political institutions. Since 1983, the polling company Ipsos MORI has tracked levels of trust in various professions. Respondents are asked whether they trust different professions to tell the truth or not. As we can see from figure 9.1, languishing at the bottom of this trust league were 'politicians generally' with 13 per cent of people trusting them, and government ministers with 16 per cent (and not much has changed over nearly three decades). These rock-bottom scores in 2009 didn't come as any surprise. They followed the publication by the *Daily Telegraph* of what MPs claimed on expenses. The waves of press and public outrage were unrelenting, and did nothing to dispel a popular view that not only did politicians have their snouts firmly in the public trough, but also they couldn't be trusted to run the country. The BBC commissioned its own poll in the wake of these revelations – and the results were as damning, if not more so. More than 60 per cent of respondents said that MPs represent their own interests; and around half of all people thought all, most or about half of MPs were actually corrupt (this figure jumped to over 90 per cent when the responses for 'a few' were added in).[4]

Surveys of public opinion suggest that voters are just as cynical about government by political parties as they are about individual politicians: both put their interests above those of the country. When asked how much they personally trust political parties, just over 10 per cent of respondents on a ten-point scale scored them 0 ('not at all') and 84 per cent scored them between 0 and 5.[5] These data from 2006 were taken at a time of great difficulty for the incumbent Labour government – and the public's trust in politics is very much tied up with the particular circumstances of the day. Nonetheless, not just in Britain but in other parts of Europe as well, there have for some time been significant levels of disenchantment with the performance of political parties in policy-making, their links with external interests and their wider role within liberal democratic government.[6]

Does it matter whether the public trust politicians or not? After all, a bit of healthy scepticism may be no bad thing. Today, citizenship is taught in schools in an attempt to engage new generations of young people in politics. Back in the 1950s and 1960s, such civic education was taken for granted. Citizens voted in high numbers and there was considerable esteem for those working in government. In this 'civic culture', voters felt not only that their

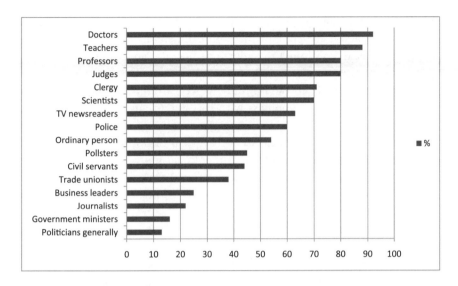

Source: Ipsos MORI, trust in professions, 2009, www.ipsos-mori.com/researchpublications/researcharchive/poll.aspx?oItemId=15&view=wide

Figure 9.1 *Who the public trust*

voices were listened to, but that politicians and civil servants knew best and could be trusted to get on with the business of politics and public administration. Over the years, a lot of this culture has worn away. Society has changed. The public have become less deferential not just to politicians, but to a wide range of professions and major institutions. Better-educated, more 'critical citizens' are less forgiving of political elites, just as they are more demanding in all walks of life, not least as expectations have risen.[7] But in more difficult times, when politicians struggle to deliver on their promises, and with a 24/7 news media shining a continuous light on government, a downward spiral of distrust and disillusionment eats away at the relationship between politicians and voters that is at the core of any shared democratic culture. In his book *Why We Hate Politics*, the political scientist Colin Hay suggests that mainstream political actors are largely to blame for this estrangement between government and voters by taking the politics out of politics ('depoliticization'): by calling into question the capacity of government to deliver public goods, shifting policy to non-governmental bodies and giving in to globalization as a *force majeure*.[8]

But while voters may not trust politicians further than they can throw them, not trusting is not the same as not voting. Indeed, those who are distrustful may in fact be more likely to vote. In a study of the 1997 general election, an election in part dominated by the lack of trust in John Major's Conservative government, Charles Pattie and Ron Johnston argued that while voters' trust in government appeared to be in decline, this didn't account for the decline in voting in 1997. Interestingly, despite widespread concerns across society about the state of the political system in the mid 1990s, the 'relatively cynical' continued to endorse democratic government in Britain, even if they thought it didn't deliver what they wanted.[9] In the annual *Audit of Political Engagement* from the Hansard Society, around a third of people in 2009 expressed a broad happiness with the system governing the country. The figure has declined a little since the first audit in 2004; and the slice of voters who think the system needs a great deal of improvement has crept up to nearly a quarter. So, while an anti-political sentiment has grown, the extent to which voters reject the system of government in Britain remains limited. The general public still believes that voting is something a good citizen should do it, even if they may not actually do it when election time comes. The problem is that this sense of civic duty is falling, especially among younger voters.[10]

There are, then, some worrying indicators of the health of British democracy. But is party politics part of the problem or part of the solution? One view is that the era of the political party as the main focus of political participation is coming to a close. Future political activism and civic participation will be sustained by not just new political organizations but also new models of democracy rejecting the elitist assumptions of the representative forms that have dominated politics since the nineteenth century.

## Getting people mobilized

Membership of, and involvement in, political organizations is an important indicator of the health of democratic politics. By joining such organizations, citizens take part in some way in politics; and the very existence of political organizations helps to bring that activism into life by providing the opportunities and resources for people to get involved. In this way, traditional institutions such as political parties, churches and trade unions, as well as a wide range of other pressure groups, serve as mobilizing agencies. That is, they act to get people mobilized; and without them, it is assumed, the level of political activism would be lower.

Underlying many of the concerns with political parties today is their capacity to do this mobilizing, and their position as the principal agencies of political participation in contemporary society. As we saw in chapters 1 and 2, as the class-based political sociology was eroded and, in certain respects, reconfigured in post-war Britain, the traditional agencies of political mobilization came under threat. The public stopped joining parties in such great numbers. This decline in membership is broadly the same across developed countries, although the comparative picture is mixed. For example, across Western Europe, some countries – such as Germany and Belgium – saw party membership grow between the 1960s and 1980s, or remain stable (e.g. Sweden). More recent changes in party membership since the early 1980s also show important variation across countries. Membership has fallen substantially in some countries (notably France and Italy), but less so in other countries, such as Austria, where nearly one in five people were still party members in the late 1990s, far higher than the more typical 5–10 per cent of the electorate joining parties. The UK is very much at the low end of this range – and there is evidence that membership is at or below 2 per cent of the population.[11] In all events, today in Britain, party membership for all three main parties can be counted in a few hundreds of thousands, not millions. With the launch of something new – the Social Democratic Party in the 1980s, 'New Labour' in the 1990s, 'Cameron's Conservatives' in the 2000s – the falling trends in party membership reversed, usually temporarily, before heading back down again.

The leadership of political parties, to some extent, turned their backs on card-carrying members, preferring instead to communicate with the voters at large via the mass broadcast media. For electoral professional parties, political foot soldiers were not critical to winning the election battle in the era of catch-all politics. This perspective can be overdone. Contemporary electoral campaigning has become more localized, acknowledging the complex political geography of the UK. For all parties, big or small, where they work they have more chance of winning, as we have seen in this book. To do this, members remain an important campaigning resource. The major drivers of the decline in party membership are the host of social trends that have more generally weakened the linkages and the loyalties between voters and political parties. The electorate has become less partisan in its voting; so too have citizens become less likely to join political parties and to carry out activities such as canvassing on the streets or by telephone at election time.

One argument is that the shifting political sociology of late 20th- and early 21st-century society prompted a change in political activism away from parties to newer forms of mobilizing agencies. In particular, social change underpinned the growth of what have variously been called non-governmental organizations (NGOs), pressure groups, cause groups, single-issue groups, new social movements (or social movement organizations) and public interest groups. These new kids on the political block that have sprung up in such apparent numbers since the 1960s, it has been argued, are not only more attractive to the less socially anchored citizen, but also better able than political parties to take the lead in a more issue-based political environment. It is also suggested, more radically, that this political shift offers a new model of democracy in a world of professionalized, elitist and undemocratic party politics. This is leading to the 'death' of the political party as the principal agency of political mobilization capable of getting citizens involved in politics.[12]

## New patterns of political agency

The emergence of new forms political agency since the 1960s certainly challenges traditional approaches to the study of politics. As Pippa Norris argues, what we understand by political participation, and how we might frame this understanding theoretically, needs updating 'to take account of how opportunities for civic engagement have evolved and diversified over the years'.[13] In the post-war years, political parties and traditional interest groups were the mainstays of twentieth-century pluralist liberal democracies. In the politics of the twenty-first century, not only is there an explosion of political agencies trying to get their points of view across, but also they are expanding the range of activities that we think of as political action.

So what kind of political groups have been on the rise? Norris distinguishes between three sets of agencies. The first are interest groups. These range from professional and trade associations (including, of course, trade unions) to groups set up to campaign on a particular issue or cause, such as the environment, peace and human rights. All these groups are in different ways pressure groups, in that they seek to influence policy-makers in government on behalf of their cause or interest group. These groups have traditionally been based on a membership (making up the professional or trade association) – and have a formal structure and organization. 'Cause' groups, such as Amnesty and Greenpeace, set up in the 1960s and 1970s, are also well organized and formally structured and based on a membership model of political activism.

The second set of agencies is new social movements (NSMs). These, by contrast with traditional interest groups, are political bodies that are less structured and formal in organization. Typical examples are the movements that sprang up to campaign for women's rights, the environment and human rights, and against nuclear weapons. Membership of these NSMs is less formal and more open; and the focus of political activity extends beyond changing policy-makers' minds to creating alternative lifestyles and communal ways of living. The distinction between NSMs and pressure groups can, as Norris concedes, be 'fluid and imprecise'. Many of the bodies making up, for example, green and human rights movements are remarkably similar to the interest groups that, in theory, they are displacing – and may be better thought of as social movement organizations.

The final group of agencies identified by Norris are transnational advocacy networks. Again, the distinction between these networks and NSMs may be fine, but the less formal and more fluid characteristics of NSMs are taken a step further. Transnational advocacy networks are multinational 'loose coalitions' of groups today using the latest communication technologies to challenge established institutions and policies, often using direct political action. The most obvious example is the anti-globalization movement.

The shift in political agency away from parties and traditional professional and trade association interest groups is partly about structure and organization: a move from formal bureaucratic bodies to something more informal and less structured. But it is also about the kind of political action these groups, movements and networks engage in – their political 'repertoires'.

Taking full advantage today of the opportunities for social networking presented by the internet, NSMs and transnational advocacy networks are thought to engage in a much broader range of political activities, including street protests, consumer boycotts, occupations and other examples of direct action, beyond the more formalized world of pluralist liberal democratic policy-making. Significantly, these shifts in politics involve a move away from traditional nation-state-centred politics: not only is the new political action directed at international agencies such as multinational businesses or the G8 or G20 groups, but the organization of the activity is global in character and organization.

But what hard evidence is there that these apparently new forms of political agency and political action have been on the rise in recent decades? And does this evidence support the argument that traditional mobilizing agencies such as parties are giving way to a new type of politics and a new model of democracy?

## Noise and numbers

On the surface, the growth in political pressure groups seems self-evident. The thoughts and activities of such groups are widely reported in the media and elsewhere. As we saw in chapter 7, the coalition of groups lining to protest on climate change, globalization and world poverty is both large in number and broad in membership, ranging from traditional non-governmental organizations such as Oxfam to radical socialists and greens, Christian groups and anarchists. They make a lot of noise, take up a lot of space, and grab lots of attention and media headlines. But hard evidence on the number of groups is difficult to come by. This is partly because pressure groups come and go: political life spans are often short. Some groups exist only as long as the interest or cause they're promoting does. Political activism associated with the world of pressure groups is linked to, and often a response to, specific events, such as the war in Iraq or Afghanistan. As a result, surveys of political activism may not register individual protest action that is so bound up with a particular situation that may yet arise.

Another way of getting a handle on the scale of political activism is by looking at the membership of pressure groups. This has increased significantly over a period of two decades. By the early 1990s, membership of environmentalist groups was put at 5 million. But again, a note of caution is needed. Much of this growth came through a small number of household names in green politics, in particular Friends of the Earth and Greenpeace – and in human rights protest politics, Amnesty International.[14]

Evidence from wider studies of citizenship and political engagement also point to a thriving political world beyond parties. Drawing on survey evidence from eight developed countries from the early 1970s through to the mid 1990s, Norris argues that protest activities such as signing petitions, going on demonstrations, or taking part in a consumer boycott, an unofficial strike or an occupation of a building have become more common. There has also been a rise in such protest politics in a broader range of countries;[15] and that protest politics has shifted from being something that 'young radicals' did to something that a significant part of the population do (something like a third in some surveys). In this way, protest politics has become 'normalized', perhaps, in part, as yesterday's younger generations of protestors grow up and keep protesting. But this evidence also shows that protesting is in all likelihood linked to education: the better-educated are more likely to donate money, take to the streets or write to their MP (and vote, of course), just as they have done in previous generations of protest politics.

In the UK, around a third of people, according to research, are members of groups as diverse as sports clubs, trade unions, residents' associations, professional bodies, churches and conservation and disability groups. On this list of groups Britons join, only a relatively small number can be classed as political. The list is dominated by the 29 per cent of people (around 13 million) signed up to motoring organizations – largely, it has to said, just in case they break down. Another 8 per cent or 3 million are members of a sports club; 6 per cent or 2 million belong to a gym (whether they go or not is another question . . . ). But when it comes to membership of environmental or animal rights groups, or women's groups, or groups campaigning on human rights or consumer rights or disability issues, the percentage of citizens joining these groups falls to the 1 per cent category. Once these small slices are put together, however, something like 250,000 to 500,000 people are members of these more overtly political organizations.[16] This is a reasonable chunk of British society involved in some way in a political organization outside party politics. As a point of comparison, the current combined membership of the Conservative, Labour and Liberal Democratic parties stands at a little under 500,000.

There is, to be sure, a question mark over what this involvement entails and who is actually participating. A majority of members of groups don't do very much beyond making a donation; just over 40 per cent had never been to a group meeting; and over half never participate in decision-making or speak at meetings.[17] The research also shows that becoming a member of a group, just as with political participation generally, is something that better-educated and well-off people do more of than less educated poorer groups.

Further evidence on political participation in the UK is found in Hansard's annual survey of political engagement. This survey confirms the low (and falling) rates of engagement with political parties. In 2009, just 3 per cent of the adult population reported having donated money and paid a membership fee to a political party. By contrast, those reporting having donated to and joined a charity or campaigning organization – while down on previous rates – still make up over a third of the population. Overall, using the eight indicators of political activism we can see in figure 9.2, around 11 per cent of adults can be classed as political activists, having done at least three of these activi-

| Political activity | % of British population in 2009 |
|---|---|
| Signed a petition | 36 |
| Boycotted certain products for political, ethical or environmental reasons | 18 |
| Presented my views to a local councillor or MP | 17 |
| Urged someone to get in touch with a local councillor or MP | 12 |
| Been to a political meeting | 4 |
| Taken part in a demonstration, picket or march | 3 |
| Donated money or paid a membership fee to a political party | 3 |
| Taken part in a political campaign | 3 |
| None of these | 51 |

*Source:* Audit of Political Engagement 6, *figure 12, p. 27.*

Figure 9.2 *Getting involved. If you have done three or more of these activities over the past two or three years, you are counted as politically active*

ties over the previous two years. This may not be setting the bar very high when it comes to assessing the size of the pool of activism. It is worth noting that just over half of adults had not done any of these eight activities. Again, concerns persist that white middle-class men or women are much more likely to participate in politics than other groups in society. The survey also found, as we saw earlier, that, while a great many people thought that political participation was a really important part of being a good citizen, this didn't turn into practice. A third of the population, for example, think that joining a political party is an important component of being a good citizen.[18]

Despite, then, the problems the established political parties are having in attracting voters and members, political engagement more broadly understood is in reasonable health. What can appear like apathy at the polls is balanced by participation in a wide range of groups and organizations that are engaging in political activity. There is, of course, a danger that at the margins we stretch to the limits of credulity what counts as political; and there are obvious concerns about which social groups are participating and how much individuals are getting involved. These are important questions when we consider the significance of the apparent shift in political activity away from political parties for our understanding of them and their position in contemporary democracy. Is the growth of a more informal pressure-group politics beyond elections and the Westminster village forcing us to re-think democratic mobilization?

## From party politics to protest group politics?

The growth in membership of pressure groups does point to a vibrant world of politics beyond the mainstream. However, there are problems with how significant these figures are. To start with, as we have seen, the growth in members is disproportionally with large mega-groups such as Greenpeace and Amnesty. There is also a concern with the retention of members and the depth of political participation. In large social movement organizations, an annual turnover of 30–40 per cent of members is commonplace.[19] This high turnover suggests that most members don't do very much. Like political parties, pressure groups need members to provide financial and human resources, as well as giving the organization political credibility as an activist group. More active members are needed to carry out the tasks that ensure that the organization continues to be high-profile; but the slice of active members is small by comparison with the total membership. The commitment demanded of most members is actually very low: it is 'cheap participation' because the costs of membership are low and 'activists' can make a political statement by joining without the much higher cost, in terms of time and money, that more traditional forms of political activism demand. Members, in other words, aren't really members; they are more like subscribers to a magazine, mail-order catalogue or internet service. Having said this, while groups such as Amnesty are able to recruit large numbers of inactive members, they are experiencing greater problems in recruiting and sustaining active members, whom they still need in order to be a credible and effective pressure group.[20]

The high turnover of members leads some analysts to describe such social movement organizations as 'protest businesses'. Whatever the very real commitment of activists to a particular cause, the driving force behind these protest groups is the marketing systems necessary to attract new fee-paying members to fund the group's political activities – systems, it has to be said, that have proved extraordinarily successful at delivering members on a year-by-year basis, whatever the problems of retention. As a result, these organizations have become professionalized in much the same way as political parties have. The majority of members do little more than donate money; there is little on-going commitment; and their 'membership' gives them few, if any, rights within the organization. The 'new politics' is not so very different from the old politics; and clear distinctions between traditional mobilizing agencies and new social movements are dubious.

Political parties have more recently adopted some of the techniques used by pressure groups to attract members by lowering the costs to potential joiners, for example, by offering cut-price 'supporters' membership' that demands little of the new recruit. But political parties, for good reasons, struggle in this marketplace for activists. On the face of it, it would make sense for political parties to become much more like pressure groups; and, to a certain extent, they have by running single-issue campaigns. These, though, can back-fire when not enough voters are interested (the Conservatives 'saving the pound') or the issue moves off the agenda (Respect and the war in Iraq). It is worth remembering that pressure groups have thrived in a more issue-based political environment because they do less – and not as much is expected from them. Pressure groups don't have to run local councils, stand candidates in devolved or European elections, organize parliamentary parties to run the business of government and scrutinize legislation across a broad range of domestic and international issues. It is expected that political parties do all of these things. As a consequence, parties find it difficult to compete with the likes of Amnesty and Greenpeace and a host of smaller campaigning pressure groups.

The study of politics has quite rightly shifted its focus to include a wider range of mobilizing agencies often doing new – or at least non-mainstream – things. This is a welcome balance to the argument that citizens are turning their back on politics and political action (and the narrow focus on voting patterns can present a distorting picture in this respect). Contemporary debate on the future of political parties should consider, as Pippa Norris puts it, the 'multiple alternative avenues for political expression'.[21] Having said this, while our attention is often drawn to the radical groups engaging in headline-grabbing direct action, the real powerhouses of politics beyond the party scene are altogether more traditional in their structure and ethos. Indeed, a number of historical studies have pointed out that not only is the new social movement politics not actually very new, but also the radical, alternative groups of one generation soon become the established and institutionalized organizations of another.[22]

The fact that radical activist groups 'grow up' (as the activists themselves might do) may be no bad thing. Indeed, the bureaucratization of organizations as they get bigger can turn them into far more influential groups on public opinion and public policy. Amnesty and Greenpeace are no less politically significant for being highly professional organizations with large memberships that are in the main inactive. Moreover, the fact that pressure groups continue to attract members, even if they don't do very much or stay members for very long, may also add to, not subtract from the pluralist democratic culture of contemporary society. These groups are able to engage with citizens in part because they focus on a limited range of issues and require little in the way of active participation. When pressure groups like Amnesty do stray beyond their established remit – for example when they ran a pro-abortion campaign – they run the danger of alienating some of their members and supporters (in Catholic schools, colleges and communities, in this case). There is also a concern that the marketing machines of large pressure groups focus on those groups in society who already are more likely to engage in politics, thereby helping to perpetuate the inequalities that exist in political participation.

## What needs to change

For more than a century, the established narrative of British liberal democracy has relied on political parties to connect voters to government, citizens to the state. In the modern world of universal suffrage, and in a society of divided interests and opinions, politics was an activity carried out by dedicated organizations: political parties. The great strength of these organizations, it was argued, was their capacity to aggregate the plurality of interests and opinions into something that made democratic government possible. Political parties were *the* agents of political participation. The public joined them. Voters with a host of opinions were offered choices at the ballot box across a range of domestic and international issues. Parties serious about power were forced to look beyond their narrow partisan perspective. The political marketplace created a national debate among all kinds of different people. Political parties helped to inform that debate and to mobilize support for particular approaches to government. They also acted a bulwark against the unelected administrative state and powerful lobby groups in civil society.

There is, as we have seen in this book, considerable debate about how much *active* participation takes place in political parties and other mobilizing agencies. To the theorists of elitist democracy, notably Robert Michels, the answer was not very much. Long membership lists were no indication of organizational democracy. Indeed, the lack of active participation was not really a problem from the elitist perspective. Politics required particular skills and expertise, not least those of leadership. It was something best left to career professionals, not amateur activists. Parties were recruiting grounds for each generation of politicians. From student union or trade union to cabinet table, parties were the making of the political life.

Today, this narrative of British democracy is under question perhaps as never before. Voters distrust political parties, see them as out-of-touch and think them incapable of making a difference in government. There is a real sense that political parties have lost the capacity to engage with the electorate and to act as the principal agent of political participation. At the same time, voters have turned away from the established parties towards non-mainstream parties and pressure groups very often on the political extremes. A spectre of political fragmentation and ideological polarization is haunting British democracy. But what can parties do to re-engage with voters and restore trust and authority to politics?

Part of the problem, as we have seen in this book, is that over the past half a century political parties have changed because the world has changed. As organizations seeking power through democratic election, parties have responded to a less partisan society by becoming far less partisan themselves – and the process is mutually reinforcing. To appeal to voters more willing to make political choices at the ballot box, not just follow well-established social patterns of voting, political parties have become more professional campaigning organizations, and have distanced themselves from the social groups that once provided the bedrock of their members and voters. The link between party and civil society has weakened. As times get tougher, this has fed a sense that politicians and their parties have lost touch, especially with 'their people'. Party leaderships having suffered painful defeats will often seek to get back in touch with these voters, usually prolonging the agony of having to make tougher decisions later.

But parties, big and small, have also been slow to change. One important issue is representation. Voters often complain that politicians 'aren't like us'. To some extent, they never were. In more partisan times, however, parties did look and sound more like the social groups that joined them and voted for them. As we have all become a little less attached to particular political parties, it may not be surprising that parties have come to appear and speak in ways that attract broader slices of the electorate. Having said this, old habits die hard. The Labour and Conservative parties, in particular, have been slow in – and in many respects resistant to – making the kinds of changes necessary to broaden the range of candidates standing in elections, in particular to include more women and those from black and minority ethnic communities. Part of the problem, as we have seen, is that reforms to influence candidate selection tend to increase the power of central party offices over local party bodies, bodies that the parties are also trying to revive. The professionalization of politics has also driven the growth in numbers of politicians being recruited from the inside.

What could help to restore some faith in politics is a less partisan approach to picking politicians. Parties will always be the main route into politics for the aspiring government minister. But the selection of candidates could move beyond the committee rooms of local parties. 'Open primaries', for example, might catch on. These allow all voters, not just party members, to have the final choice over the candidate to fight an election. The Conservatives tried it in Totnes, Devon, in 2009 and it worked. The hustings were open to the public – and the aspiring MPs had to make their pitch to a broader cross-section of voters, not just the usual party suspects.

Engaging the public in politics will be a tough challenge. The modern citizen not only is less partisan, but also has more opportunities to get involved in politics (whatever concerns there might be about the depth of this participation). Joining or even just supporting a party has become less attractive. And with today's communication technologies, electoral professional parties can do more with less. One option is to increase the incentives for individuals to join, for example by giving members greater power over party affairs, and offering more cut-price membership deals – for young people, for example. Another approach is to use the techniques of 'deliberative democracy' to provide the opportunities and resources (including social networking) for members and the public to voice their opinions in what are sophisticated and sometimes virtual focus groups (Labour tried it in the 2000s with the 'People's Panel' and the 'Big Conversation'). There are dangers here for the leaderships of political parties. They need members to be active in getting the party's message across to voters, but not so active that they prevent difficult decisions, unpopular with committed supporters, being made.

The funding of parties also needs reform. As things stand, we have the worst of both worlds: parties struggle to pay the bills, and the dependency on trade unions and rich individuals and corporations fuels cynicism in politics. Clear steps can be taken. The 2007 report from the former civil servant Hayden Phillips recommended caps on campaign spending during and between elections (and spending at the constituency level is key here) and on the size of donations to political parties. The report also proposed more state funding linked to the support parties win in elections. Tax incentives could also be introduced to encourage more people to donate money to parties. But reform has not been easy. Getting politicians to agree on what needs to change has proved difficult, in particular over the caps on the size of donations. And while voters don't like the current funding model, they don't want more of their taxes paying for party politics. More public funding also brings the danger of creating 'cartel parties' in the UK, further removed from voters.[23]

There is also the corrosive impact of cynicism on politics, which may be even harder to shake. To a great many voters, not only are politicians all alike (which in many respects, they are), but what divides them and their parties pales into insignificance compared to what unites them. What has emerged, it is argued, is a self-serving political class with its own interests and ways of doing things. This only serves to alienate and antagonize voters who can't spot the difference between any of them. What British politics needs is a good dose of ideology. But does it?

One reason why parties have become less ideological is because the world has become less ideological. The major ideological conflict of the first half of the twentieth century, between East and West, state communism and liberal capitalism, is over. In the UK, the post-Thatcherite consensus combines support for the free market and the state.[24] The Conservatives under David Cameron, only in part because of their coalition with the Liberal Democrats, will, just as New Labour did under Tony Blair, move on from the position they inherit, not try to turn the clock back. The political arguments today revolve around the details of the mixed economy: the balance between the invisible hand of the market and the visible hand of the state.

Parties have also become less ideological because voters have become less partisan. Ideological convergence has been driven by the electoral necessities of catch-all politics, especially under a voting system that penalizes parties that head to the extremes. In a more personalized and presidential form of government and politics, when parties are competing for votes on the basis of how good their leaders are, their priorities in government and how well they can deliver policies, differences between parties can appear vanishingly small. This can have an impact on turnout in elections with voters not really thinking there is much of a choice; and feed the sense that all politicians are the same. But whether voters really want a see-sawing of ideologically driven policy is another matter. Voters may want real choices at the ballot box, but they also want their politicians to stop arguing with each other. That's quite a juggling act for parties to pull off.

Moreover, there is no strong evidence that the majority of voters, even when given the opportunity of expressing their preferences more fully in elections using proportional representation, are necessarily going in any more radical directions. To be sure, British politics has become more fragmented and multi-party – and in the 2009 European elections, UKIP came second in the poll and the BNP won two seats. But the main beneficiary of partisan de-alignment has been the centrist Liberal Democrats and the two moderate social democratic minority nationalist parties in Scotland and Wales, the SNP and Plaid (and for these two parties, the great divide from the mainstream is the constitutional state, not the state of the economy). Beyond the consensus, the Green Party has over time become much more focused on winning elections and engaging in public policy-making. UKIP is very much a one-policy party; and the BNP, despite its attempt to adopt a more voter-friendly approach, remains a fringe player that clearly benefited from an unpopular Labour government. These small parties, and the host of independents winning seats in local government across the country, do, to a certain extent, 'fill the gap in political representation'[25] left by parties operating in the broad post-Thatcherite consensus. But care needs to be taken not to exaggerate the size and significance of this politics beyond the mainstream.

## Power to the people?

If political parties need to change, do voters have to be more realistic about what to expect – and what we might expect from voters themselves? Is there a limit to 'people power'? This question goes to the heart of the debate between those who support the traditional model of party democracy and those who search for a more direct and participatory model. The evidence on citizen participation is far from conclusive. Indeed, the hypothesis that citizens want to participate more (or that they don't) is almost impossible to prove or disprove empirically, given there might be conditions in which people might want to get more involved if they were given the chance and resources to do it. This has always been the nub of 'developmental' models of democracy (whether liberal or radical) that believe that supporting more citizen participation can lead to more active citizenship in political governance.[26] In the end, the debate between party-based representative models and more participatory direct models of democracy is a normative one bound up with all sorts of value judgements about what constitutes the political good. The danger for supporters of more participation is that the normative value of democracy gets in the way of what citizens in practice will actually do – and not just what they say that they might do.[27] There may be

## Box 9.1 Power to the people?

The state of British democracy was reviewed by the Power Commission chaired by the barrister and campaigner Helena Kennedy. The Commission's 2006 report argued that the public (especially young people and black and minority ethnic groups) had become 'disengaged' from 'formal democratic politics'. Voters were 'alienated', not apathetic. Political parties were part of the problem. Their top-down organization discouraged citizens from getting involved. The voting system was also out-dated and should be far more proportional. And parties should be given state funding to prevent the corruption of politics. The Commission also pointed to a more radical model of democracy. More power should be given directly to the people. Citizens should have more opportunity to participate in the policy-making and decision-making processes of the state. This participation would be supported by 'democracy hubs' providing information and advice. Deliberative democracy, in which an informed citizen body participates in government, would provide a radical alternative to elitist party democracy at Westminster. This echoed the 'back to Greece' arguments for more direct forms of democracy put forward by Andrew Adonis and Geoff Mulgan in the mid 1990s for the think tank Demos – and which had made their way into a host of consultative measures by the Labour government aimed at getting the public more involved in the policy-making process (e.g. the People's Panels).

Critics of the Power Commission lined up to defend party politics against what some saw as the report's populist sentiments. The political scientist and Conservative peer Philip Norton accused the Commission of playing fast and loose with what it meant by 'the people': 'Does the term refer to everybody in the country, to the majority of the people, to those who shout the loudest or to those who can be bothered to participate?' Tim Bale, Paul Taggart and Paul Webb contested the view that the upsurge in 'informal' politics (e.g. joining pressure groups or signing petitions) was very significant, given that most were one-off activities demanding little time or commitment. Indeed, rather than being excluded, the public on the whole chose not to get involved: 'What many of us run scared from is anything ongoing, anything time-sapping, anything conflictual and (and to name two of the twenty-first century's cardinal sins) anything "difficult" and "boring".' The danger of giving the people more direct power is that those whose voices are already heard in politics and policy-making – not just the educated middle classes who like nothing more than writing angry letters of complaint but also powerful interest groups – will be further entrenched. Party democracy ensures that a wide range of interests and perspectives are represented in government and acts as a shield against lobby groups from all sides.

*Sources: Hansard*, HL, 60615–10, col. 363, 15 June 2006; T. Bale, P. Taggart and P. Webb, 'You can't always get what you want: populism and the Power inquiry', *Political Quarterly*, 77, 2 (2006), pp. 195–203

opportunities to introduce certain elements of direct democracy into how political parties operate – for example, using open shortlists and making MPs subject to possible recall – although supporters of party democracy argue that representative and direct forms are like oil and water and cannot be mixed.[28]

If politicians and political parties need to be more honest and open about what they do, then voters also need to be more realistic and less naïve about what politics can and cannot do. Gerry Stoker, in his *Why Politics Matters*, puts it in a way that is worth quoting at length:

> Politics is prone to crises because it faces one of the toughest challenges available to human societies. It is about how, given our inherent interdependence, we can learn to manage conflicts and construct pillars of cooperation. There is no end-game in politics, but rather a cycling of issues and solutions that produces one temporary fix after the other, with an occasional and powerful expression of some more permanent institutionally reinforced boundary markers. Politics has a natural rhythm that tends to create a certain level of dissatisfaction and disenchantment. It imposes collective decisions on us all, its processes of communication and exchange are time-consuming and irksome and implementation and decision outcomes involve resource distributions and practical actions and interventions that cannot always be either comprehended or valued by those on the receiving end of them. Politics . . . is almost designed to disappoint. Yet it does an important job for us by enabling our voice to be heard among many and then compromises to be made and deals struck so that in vital areas conflicts can be contained and cooperation achieved.[29]

In the end, we need political parties – and strong ones too. Indeed, as long as society remains a complex mix of interests and viewpoints that have to be pulled together, we will need some means not only to channel political participation but also to connect citizens with government in a realistic, legitimate, accountable and effective manner. Political parties may need reform, but if they didn't exist, we'd have to invent them. This isn't an argument for complacency. As we have seen in this book, as British society has changed, so have political parties – sometimes all too slowly. Contemporary Britain is a less deferential, far more diverse, individualistic and egalitarian place than it was fifty or so years ago. Modern political parties were built on the bedrock of simple social divisions that have long since fractured. Understandably, political parties have come to reflect this changing society as they cast their electoral nets more widely. In these more fragmented and contingent times, it is also perhaps not surprising that political parties struggle, not least with public expectations, especially when facing the pressure groups that have thrived in a more issue-based world. Indeed, the pressure of expectations is huge given the constraints imposed on the autonomy of all policy-makers by globalization, long-term social trends and the membership of supra-national bodies such as the European Union. None the less, it is the very complexity of modern society, and the necessity of finding compromises and doing deals that we can all accept, that means we need political parties more than ever before.

## Further reading and research resources

On the general political mood and the extent to which citizens have become disengaged from politics and political parties, see Norris's *Democratic Phoenix*; Pattie, Seyd and Whiteley's *Citizenship in Britain*; Dalton's *Citizen Politics*;

Stoker's *Why Politics Matters*; and Hay's *Why We Hate Politics*. For the best guide to democratic thinking, see David Held's *Models of Democracy*. The annual survey of political engagement by the Hansard Society can be found at www.hansardsociety.org.uk/blogs/parliament_and_government/pages/audit-of-political-engagement.aspx. The 2006 report by the Power Commission (*Power to the People: The Report of Power: An Independent Inquiry into Britain's Democracy*, http://makeitanissue.org.uk/devlog/2007/01/the_power_commission_was_estab.php) needs to be read with Bale, Taggart and Webb's response, 'You can't always get what you want'.

# Notes

## Introduction

[1] Paul Whiteley, 'Where have all the members gone? The dynamics of party membership in Britain', *Parliamentary Affairs*, 62, 2 (2009), pp. 242–57.

## 1 The British party system

[1] The Electoral Commission, register of political parties, http://registers. electoralcommission.org.uk/regulatory-issues/regpoliticalparties.cfm.

[2] Paul Webb, *The Modern British Party System* (London: Sage, 2000).

[3] Giovanni Sartori, *Parties and Party Systems: A Framework for Analysis* ([1976] Colchester: ECPR Press, 2005).

[4] The ENP was first produced by two Finnish political scientists, Markku Laakso and Rein Taagepera: ' "Effective" number of parties: a measure with application to West Europe', *Comparative Political Studies*, 12, 1 (1979), pp. 3–27.

[5] See Russell J. Dalton, 'The quantity and the quality of party systems: party system polarization, its measurement, and its consequences', *Comparative Political Studies*, 41, 7 (2008), pp. 899–920.

[6] See Adrian Blau, 'The effective number of parties at four scales: votes, seats, legislative power and cabinet power', *Party Politics*, 14, 2 (2008), pp. 167–78.

[7] N. Huntington and T. Bale, 'New Labour: new Christian Democracy?', *Political Quarterly*, 73, 1 (2002), pp. 44–50.

[8] Russell J. Dalton, *Citizen Politics: Public Opinion and Political Parties in Advanced Industrial Democracies* (Washington, DC: CQ Publishers, 2008, 5th edition).

[9] See R. Taagepera and B. Grofman, 'Rethinking Duverger's law: predicting the effective number of parties in plurality and PR systems – parties minus issues equals one', *European Journal of Political Research*, 13, 4 (2006), pp. 341–52; Heather Stoll, 'Social cleavages and the number of parties', *Comparative Political Studies*, 41, 11 (2008), pp. 1439–65.

[10] S. E. Finer, *The Changing British Party System, 1945–1979* (Washington, DC: American Institute for Public Policy Research, 1980).

[11] David Denver, *Elections and Voters in Britain* (London: Palgrave Macmillan, 2007, 2nd edition), p. 159.

[12] Figures from Paul Webb, 'The continuing advance of the minor parties', *Parliamentary Affairs*, 58, 4 (2005), pp. 757–75.

[13] Webb, *The Modern British Party System*.

[14] Figures from Edmund Tetteh, 'Election statistics 1918–2007' (House of Commons Research Paper, RP 08/12, 2008).

[15] C. Copus, A. Clark, H. Reynaert and K. Steyvers, 'Minor party and independent politics beyond the mainstream: fluctuating fortunes but a permanent presence', *Parliamentary Affairs*, 62, 1 (2009), pp. 4–18.

[16] Blau, 'The effective number of parties at four scales'.

[17] Denver, *Elections and Voters in Britain*, table 4.1, p. 68.

[18] Denver, *Elections and Voters in Britain*, table 4.3, p. 72.

[19] For a sensible take on this, see Denver, *Elections and Voters in Britain*.

[20] See G. Evans (ed.), *The End of Class Politics? Class Voting in Comparative Context* (Oxford: Oxford University Press, 1999); J. Thamassen (ed.), *The European Voter: A Comparative Study of Modern Democracies* (Oxford: Oxford University Press, 2005).

[21] Denver, *Elections and Voters in Britain*.

[22] See P. Nieuwbeerta and N. Dirk de Graaf, 'Traditional class voting in twenty postwar societies', in Evans (ed.), *The End of Class Politics?*

[23] H. D. Clarke, D. Sanders, M. Stewart and P. Whiteley, *Political Choice in Britain* (Oxford: Oxford University Press, 2004).

[24] Denver, *Elections and Voters in Britain*, table 4.5, p. 87.

[25] Ronald Inglehart, *The Silent Revolution: Changing Values and Political Styles among Western Publics* (Princeton: Princeton University Press, 1977).

[26] Webb, *The Modern British Party System*, p. 55.

[27] Patrick Dunleavy, 'Facing up to multi-party politics', *Parliamentary Affairs*, 58, 3 (2005), pp. 503–32, p. 504.

## 2  Political parties

[1] Maurice Duverger, *Political Parties: Their Organization and Activity in the Modern State* ([1951, in French] London: Methuen, 1964).

[2] Richard Katz and Peter Mair, 'Changing models of party organization and party democracy: the emergence of the cartel party', *Party Politics*, 1, 1 (1995), pp. 5–28.

[3] Duverger, *Political Parties*, figure 6, pp. 68–9.

[4] Duverger, *Political Parties*, p. 71.

[5] R. Michels, *Political Parties: A Sociological Study of the Oligarchical Tendencies of Modern Democracy* (New York: Free Press, 1962).

[6] Figures in this section are from J. Marshall, *Membership of UK Political Parties*, SN/ SG/5125, House of Commons Library, 2009.

[7] See Pippa Norris, *A Virtuous Circle: Political Communications in Postindustrial Societies* (Cambridge: Cambridge University Press, 2000), p. 137; D. Farrell and P. Webb, 'Political parties as campaign organizations', in R. J. Dalton and M. Wattenberg (eds.), *Parties without Partisans* (Oxford: Oxford University Press, 2002).

[8] D. Denver, G. Hands and I. MacAllister, 'The electoral impact of constituency campaigning in Britain, 1992–2001', *Political Studies*, 52 (2004), pp. 289–306; see also J. Fisher and D. Denver, 'Evaluating the electoral effects of traditional and modern modes of constituency campaigning in Britain 1992–2005', *Parliamentary Affairs*, 62, 2 (2009), pp. 196–210.

[9] Norris, *A Virtuous Circle*, p. 148.

[10] Chrysa Lamprinakou, 'The party evolution model: an integrated approach to party organisation and political communication', *Politics*, 28, 2 (2008), pp. 103–11.

[11] Angelo Panebianco, *Political Parties: Organisation and Power* (Cambridge: Cambridge University Press, 1988).

[12] Katz and Mair, 'Changing models of party organization and party democracy'.

[13] Figures from Tetteh, 'Election statistics 1918–2007'; Richard Woods, 'Rise of the executive MP', *The Sunday Times* (16 May 2010).

[14] Whiteley, 'Where have all the members gone?'

[15] Sarah Childs, *Women and British Party Politics* (London: Routledge, 2008).

[16] Justin Fisher, 'Economic performance or electoral necessity? Evaluating the system of voluntary income to political parties', *British Journal of Politics & International Relations*, 2, 2 (2000), pp. 179–204.

[17] Fisher, 'Economic performance or electoral necessity?'; see also Fisher, 'Hayden Phillips and Jack Straw: the continuation of British exceptionalism in party finance?' *Parliamentary Affairs*, 62, 2 (2009), pp. 298–317.

[18] Ingrid van Biezen, 'Political parties as public utilities', *Party Politics*, 10, 6, (2004), pp. 701–22.

[19] Katz and Mair, 'Changing models of party organization and party democracy'.

[20] R. K. Carty, 'Parties as franchise systems: the stratarchical organizational imperative', *Party Politics*, 10, 1 (2004), pp. 5–24.

[21] See P. Seyd and P. Whiteley, 'British party members: an overview', *Party Politics*, 10, 4 (2004), pp. 355–66.

[22] Whiteley, 'Where have all the members gone?'

## 3   The Conservative Party post-Thatcherism

[1] Anthony Seldon and Stuart Ball (eds.), *Conservative Century: The Conservative Party since 1900* (Oxford: Oxford University Press, 1994).

[2] Denver, *Elections and Voters in Britain*, p. 92.

[3] Ian Gilmour, *Dancing with Dogma: Britain under Thatcherism* (London: Simon & Schuster, 1992).

[4] William Keegan, *Mrs Thatcher's Economic Experiment* (Harmondsworth: Penguin, 1984).

[5] W. Waldegrave, review of P. Norton and A. Aughey, *Conservatives and Conservatism*, *The Times*, 24 September 1981; see also M. Oakeshott, 'On being Conservative', in *Rationalism in Politics and Other Essays* ([1962] Indianapolis: Liberty Press, 1991).

[6] See Roger Scruton, *The Meaning of Conservatism* (Basingstoke: Palgrave Macmillan, 2001, 3rd edition).

[7] See Stuart Hall, 'The great moving right show', in S. Hall and M. Jacques, *The Politics of Thatcherism* (London: Lawrence and Wishart, 1983).

[8] See Tim Bale, 'The logic of no alternative? Political scientists, historians and the politics of Labour's past', *British Journal of Politics & International Relations*, 1, 2 (1999), pp. 192–204, p. 196.

[9] Andrew Gamble, *The Free Economy and the Strong State: The Politics of Thatcherism* (Basingstoke: Macmillan, 1994).

[10] Simon Jenkins, *Thatcher and Sons: A Revolution in Three Acts* (London: Allen Lane, 2006), and 'Thatcher's legacy', *Political Studies Review*, 5, 2 (2007), pp. 161–71.

[11] Mark Garnett, 'Banality in politics: Margaret Thatcher and the biographers', *Political Studies Review*, 5, 2 (2007), pp. 172–82, p. 172.

[12] See Philip Norton (ed.), *The Conservative Party* (London: Prentice Hall, 1996).

[13] P. Whiteley, P. Seyd and J. Richardson, *True Blues: The Politics of Conservative Party Membership* (Oxford: Oxford University Press, 1994).

[14] Whiteley, Seyd and Richardson, *True Blues*.

[15] C. Rallings, M. Thrasher and R. Johnston, 'The slow death of a governing party: the erosion of Conservative local electoral support in England 1979–97', *British Journal of Politics & International Relations*, 4, 2 (2002), pp. 271–98.

[16] Roger Scruton, *The Conservative Idea of Community* (London: Conservative 2000 Foundation, 1996); John Gray, *Beyond the New Right: Markets, Government and the Common Environment* (London: Routledge, 1993).

[17] John Gray and David Willetts, *Is Conservatism Dead?* (London: Profile Books, 1994/7).

[18] E.g. A. Duncan and D. Hobson, *Saturn's Children* (London: Politico's, 1999).

[19] Philip Cowley and Jane Green, 'New leaders, same problems: the Conservatives', in A. Geddes and J. Tonge (eds.), *Britain Decides: The UK General Election 2005* (Basingstoke: Palgrave Macmillan, 2005); T. Heppell, *Choosing the Tory Leader: Conservative Party Leadership Elections from Heath to Cameron* (London: Tauris Academic Studies, 2007).

[20] Tim Bale, *The Conservative Party: From Thatcher to Cameron* (Cambridge: Polity, 2010).

[21] Cowley and Green, 'New leaders, same problems'.

[22] Theresa May, speech to Conservative Party conference, Bournemouth, 7 October 2002, www.guardian.co.uk/politics/2002/oct/07/conservatives2002.conservatives1.

[23] A. Anthony, 'The second coming of Iain Duncan Smith', *The Observer*, 29 June 2008, www.guardian.co.uk/society/2008/jun/29/youngpeople.socialexclusion.

[24] See I. Duncan Smith, G. Streeter and D. Willetts (eds.), *There is Such a Thing as Society* (London: Politico's, 2002); David Willetts, 'Compassionate Conservatism and the war on poverty', speech to Centre for Social Justice, 6 January 2005, www.davidwilletts.co.uk/2005/01/06/compassionate-conservative.

[25] Michael Ashcroft, *Smell the Coffee: A Wakeup Call for the Conservative Party* (London: Politico's Media, 2005).

[26] Peter Oborne, 'Forward', in S. Lee and M. Beech (eds.), *The Conservatives under David Cameron: Built to Last?* (Basingstoke: Palgrave Macmillan, 2009).

[27] David Denver, 'The results: how Britain voted', in Geddes and Tonge (eds.), *Britain Decides*.

[28] Denver, 'The results'.

[29] P. Norton, 'David Cameron and Tory success: architect or by-stander', in Lee and Beech (eds.), *The Conservatives under David Cameron*.

[30] Kieron O'Hara, *After Blair: David Cameron and the Conservative Tradition* (Cambridge: Icon Books, 2007).

[31] Oborne, 'Forward'.

[32] Bale, *The Conservative Party*.

[33] Robert McIlveen, 'Ladies of the Right: an interim analysis of the A-list', *Journal of Elections, Public Opinion & Parties*, 19, 2 (2009), pp. 147–57.

[34] Francis Elliot and Sam Coates, 'Women take a back seat in Cameron's Tory Party', *The Times*, 28 April 2009.

[35] Francis Elliot, 'Greenhorns with no green credentials: Tory wannabes push party to the right', *The Times*, 30 April 2009.

[36] Fraser Nelson, 'To keep your seat, stick to your principles', *The Times*, 14 May 2010.

[37] Bale, *The Conservative Party*.

## 4 'New Labour' and the Labour Party

[1] A. Heath, R. Jowell and J. Curtice, *Labour's Last Chance? The 1992 Election and Beyond* (Aldershot: Dartmouth, 1994).

[2] R. Heffernan and M. Marqusee, *Defeat from the Jaws of Victory: Inside Kinnock's Labour Party* (London: Verso, 1992).

[3] G. Radice and S. Pollard, *Any Southern Comfort?* (London: Fabian Society, 1994).

[4] See I. Crewe, 'The Labour Party and the electorate', in D. Kavanagh (ed.), *The Politics of the Labour Party* (London: George Allen and Unwin, 1982).

[5] H. M. Drucker, *Doctrine and Ethos in the Labour Party* (London: George Allen and Unwin, 1979).

[6] Lewis Minkin, *The Contentious Alliance* (Edinburgh: Edinburgh University Press, 1991).

[7] Shaw, *The Labour Party since 1945*, p. 219.

[8] J. Rentoul, *Tony Blair* (London: Little, Brown, 1995).

[9] Sassoon, *One Hundred Years of Socialism*.

[10] S. Meredith, 'New Labour: "The road less travelled"?' *Politics*, 23, 3 (2003), pp. 163–71.

[11] Bale, 'The logic of no alternative?'

[12] C. Pattie, 'New Labour and the electorate', in S. Ludlam and M. J. Smith (eds.), *New Labour in Government* (Basingstoke: Palgrave, 2001).

[13] D. Butler and D. Kavanagh, *The British General Election 1997* (Basingstoke: Macmillan, 1997).

[14] C. Pattie, 'Re-electing New Labour', in S. Ludlam and M. J. Smith (eds.), *Governing as New Labour: Policy and Politics under Blair* (Basingstoke: Palgrave, 2004).

[15] P. Dunleavy, 'The political parties', in P. Dunleavy, A. Gamble, I. Holliday and G. Peele, *Developments in British Politics 4* (Basingstoke: Macmillan, 1993), p. 135.

[16] K. Alderman and N. Carter, 'The Labour Party and the trade unions: loosening the ties', *Parliamentary Affairs*, 47, 3 (1994), pp. 321–37.

[17] P. Seyd and P. Whiteley, *Labour's Grass Roots* (Oxford: Clarendon Press, 1992).

[18] See P. Seyd and P. Whiteley, 'New Labour and the party: members and organization', in Ludlam and Smith (eds.), *New Labour in Government*; Meg Russell, *Building New Labour* (Basingstoke: Palgrave Macmillan, 2005).

[19] Webb, *The Modern British Party System*, pp. 244–5; P. Webb and J. Fisher, 'Professionalism and the Millbank tendency: the political sociology of New Labour's employees', *Politics*, 23, 1 (2003), pp. 10–20.

[20] Jill Sherman and Philip Webster, 'Union tired of "feeding the hand that bites us" may pull Labour funds', *The Times*, 17 June 2009.

[21] See Seyd and Whiteley, 'New Labour and the party: members and organization', in Ludlam and Smith (eds.), *New Labour in Government*; P. Seyd and P. Whiteley, *New Labour's Grassroots : The Transformation of the Labour Party Membership* (Basingstoke: Palgrave, 2002); see also P. Seyd, 'New parties / new politics', *Party Politics*, 5, 3 (1999), pp. 383–406.

22  These details are from Childs, *Women and British Party Politics*, pp. 25–33.

23  Childs, *Women and British Party Politics*.

24  P. Cowley, *The Rebels: How Blair Mislaid His Majority* (London: Politico's, 2005).

25  Patrick Diamond (ed.), *New Labour's Old Roots: Revisionist Thinkers in Labour's History 1931–1997* (Exeter: Imprint Academic, 2004).

26  A. Giddens, *The Third Way: The Renewal of Social Democracy* (Cambridge: Polity, 1998).

27  See Colin Hay, *The Political Economy of New Labour* (Manchester: Manchester University Press, 1999).

28  D. Coates, *Prolonged Labour: The Slow Birth of New Labour in Britain* (Basingstoke: Palgrave Macmillan, 2005).

29  M. J. Smith, 'Understanding the "politics of catch-up": the modernization of the Labour Party', *Political Studies*, 42, 4 (1994), pp. 708–15.

30  Mark Bevir, *New Labour: A Critique* (London: Routledge, 2005).

## 5    The Liberal Democrats: from protest to power

1  Colin Copus, 'Liberal Democrat councillors: community politics, local campaigning and the role of the political party', *Political Quarterly*, 78, 1 (2007), pp. 128–38.

2  Vernon Bogdanor, 'The Liberal Democrat dilemma in historical perspective', *Political Quarterly*, 78, 1 (2007), pp. 11–20.

3  Butler and Butler, *British Political Facts since 1979*, p. 125.

4  Matthew Taylor, 'The birth and rebirth of the Liberal Democrats', *Political Quarterly*, 78, 1 (2007), pp. 21–31, p. 31.

5  Duncan Brack, 'Liberal Democrat leadership: the cases of Ashdown and Kennedy', *Political Quarterly*, 78, 1 (2007), pp. 78–88.

6  E. Fieldhouse, D. Cutts and A. Russell, 'The Liberal Democrat performance in the 2005 general election', *Journal of Elections, Public Opinion and Parties*, 16, 1 (2006), pp. 77–92.

7  See S. Driver and L. Martell, *New Labour* (Cambridge: Polity, 2006).

8  P. Cowley and M. Stuart, *A Long Way from Equidistance: LibDem Voting in Parliament, 1997–2007*, revolts.co.uk briefing paper (14 January 2008), www.revolts.co.uk/A%20long%20way%20from%20equidistance.pdf.

9  David Cutts, '"Where we work we win": a case study of local Liberal Democrat campaigning', *Journal of Elections, Public Opinion and Parties*, 16, 3 (2006), pp. 221–42.

10  See D. Cutts and N. Shryane, 'Did local activism really matter? Liberal Democrat campaigning and the 2001 general election', *British Journal of Politics & International Relations*, 8, 3 (2006), pp. 427–44.

11  Cutts, 'Where we work we win', p. 239.

12  A. Russell and E. Fieldhouse, *Neither Left nor Right? The Liberal Democrats and the Electorate* (Manchester: Manchester University Press, 2005).

13  This section draws on John Curtis, 'New Labour, new protest? How the Liberal Democrats profited from Blair's mistakes', *Political Quarterly*, 78, 1, pp. 117–27.

14  P. Whiteley, P. Seyd and A. Billinghurst, *Third Force Politics: Liberal Democrats at the Grassroots* (Oxford: Oxford University Press, 2006).

15  These figures are based on the number of ballot papers sent out to individual party members in the elections for leader and president between 1988 and 2008.

[16] A. Russell, E. Fieldhouse and D. Cutts, 'De facto veto? The parliamentary Liberal Democrats', *Political Quarterly*, 78, 1 (2007), pp. 89–98.

[17] Whiteley, Seyd and Billinghurst, *Third Force Politics*.

[18] Siobhan Kennedy, 'Clegg revamps Lib Dems' party structure to seize control from the committee men', *The Times*, 16 July 2008, p. 15.

[19] D. Denver, A. Clark and L. Bennie, 'Voter reactions to a preferential ballot: the 2007 Scottish local elections', *Journal of Elections, Public Opinion and Parties*, 19, 3 (2009), pp. 265–82.

[20] See, in particular, David Laws, 'Reclaiming liberalism: a liberal agenda for the Liberal Democrats', in P. Marshall and D. Laws (eds.), *The Orange Book: Reclaiming Liberalism* (London: Profile Books, 2004); J. Astle, D. Laws, P. Marshall and A. Murray, *Britain after Blair: A Liberal Agenda* (London: Profile Books, 2006); see also Richard Grayson, 'Social democracy or social liberalism? Ideological sources of Liberal Democrat policy', *Political Quarterly*, 78, 1 (2007), pp. 32–9; Ed Randall, 'Yellow versus orange – never a fair fight: an assessment of two contributions to liberal politics separated by three-quarters of a century', *Political Quarterly*, 78, 1 (2007), pp. 40–9.

## 6  Putting the boots away? The far right in British politics

[1] Roger Eatwell,'The extreme right and British exceptionalism: the primacy of politics', in P. Hainsworth (ed.), *The Politics of the Extreme Right: From the Margins to the Mainstream* (London: Pinter, 2000), pp. 172–92.

[2] Matthew Goodwin, 'The extreme right in Britain: still an "ugly duckling" but for how long?' *Political Quarterly*, 78, 2 (2007), pp. 241–50, p. 241; Nigel Copsey, *Contemporary British Fascism: The British National Party and the Quest for Respectability* (Basingstoke: Palgrave, 2004).

[3] Sandra Laville and Matthew Taylor, 'A racist, violent neo-nazi to the end: BNP founder Tyndall dies', *The Guardian*, 20 July 2005, http://politics.guardian.co.uk/otherparties/story/0,9061,1532048,00.html.

[4] Nigel Fielding, *The National Front* (London: Routledge & Kegan Paul, 1981), pp. 38–9.

[5] Goodwin, 'The extreme right in Britain'.

[6] Jessica Yonwin, *Electoral Performance of Far-Right Parties in the UK*, SN/SG/1982, Social and General Statistics Section, House of Commons Library, June 2004, table 1.

[7] Goodwin, 'The extreme right in Britain', p. 243.

[8] Matthew Goodwin, 'Activism in contemporary extreme right parties: the case of the British National Party (BNP)', *Journal of Elections, Public Opinion and Parties*, 20, 2 (2010), pp. 31–54.

[9] Matthew Goodwin, 'Research, revisionists and the radical right', *Politics*, 28, 1 (2008), pp. 33–40, p. 33.

[10] Mark Neocleous and Nick Startin, '"Protest" and fail to survive: Le Pen and the great moving right show', *Politics*, 23, 3 (2003), pp. 145–55.

[11] Paul Taggart, 'New populist parties in Western Europe', *Western European Politics*, 18, 1 (1995), pp. 34–51.

[12] Cas Mudde, *The Populist Radical Right in Europe* (Cambridge: Cambridge University Press, 2007). See also *Political Studies Review* 7, 3 (2009), review symposium on Mudde's research.

13  Martin Fletcher, 'The British National Party gains strength', *The Times*, 19 April 2007, www.timesonline.co.uk/tol/news/politics/article1672185.ece.

14  Goodwin, 'The extreme right in Britain'.

15  Fletcher, 'The British National Party gains strength'.

16  Fletcher, 'The British National Party gains strength'.

17  Tetteh, 'Election statistics 1918–2007'.

18  'Minister says BNP tempting voters', BBC Online, http://news.bbc.co.uk/1/hi/uk_politics/4913164.stm.

19  Peter John, Helen Margetts, David Rowland and Stuart Weir, *The BNP: The Roots of its Appeal, Democratic Audit* (Human Rights Centre, University of Essex, 2006), www.democraticaudit.com/breaking-news/far-right.php.

20  See Pippa Norris, *Radical Right: Voters and Parties in the Electoral Market* (Cambridge: Cambridge University Press, 2005).

21  Stan Taylor, *The National Front in English Politics* (Basingstoke: Macmillan, 1982).

22  Andrew Geddes, 'Immigration and European integration at the election', in A. Geddes and J. Tonge, *Britain Decides: The UK General Election 2005* (Basingstoke: Palgrave Macmillan, 2005), p. 292.

23  L. Chappell, J. Clifton, G. Gottfried and K. Lawton, *Exploring the Roots of BNP Support* (London: Institute for Public Policy Research, 2010).

24  Matthew Goodwin and Robert Ford, 'The BNP's breakthrough', *New Statesman*, 16 April 2009; see also Goodwin, 'In search of the winning formula: Nick Griffin and the "modernization" of the British National Party', and Ford, 'Who might vote for the BNP?: survey evidence on the electoral potential of the extreme right in Britain', in R. Eatwell and M. J. Goodwin (eds.), *The New Extremism in 21st Century Britain* (London: Routledge, 2010).

25  Robert Booth, Simon Rogers and Paul Lewis, 'What the BNP list says about its members', *The Guardian*, 20 October 2009; Marshall, *Membership of UK Political Parties*.

26  Goodwin, 'Activism in contemporary extreme right parties'; Goodwin, 'In search of the winning formula', in Eatwell and Goodwin (eds.), *The New Extremism in 21st Century Britain*.

27  Marshall, *Membership of UK Political Parties*.

28  Ford, 'Who might vote for the BNP?'

29  Goodwin, 'Activism in contemporary extreme right parties'.

30  See Amir Abedi and Thomas Carl Lundberg, 'Doomed to failture? UKIP and the organizational challenges facing right-wing populist anti-political establishment parties', *Parliamentary Affairs*, 62, 1 (2009), pp. 72–87.

31  See Fiona Hamilton, 'Fringe parties look to exploit furore about expenses', *The Times*, 13 May 2009, p. 8.

## 7   Reds and Greens

1  A. Thorpe, *The British Communist Party and Moscow, 1920–1943* (Manchester: Manchester University Press, 2000).

2  Michael Crick, *The March of Militant* (London: Faber and Faber, 1986).

3  Tetteh, 'Election statistics 1918–2007', table 11.

4  Tetteh, 'Election statistics 1918–2007'.

5  Tetteh, 'Election statistics 1918–2007'.

6  Webb, 'The continuing advance of the minor parties'.

[7] Pippa Norris, *Democratic Phoenix: Reinventing Political Activism* (Cambridge: Cambridge University Press, 2002).

[8] Ronald Ingehart, *The Silent Revolution: Changing Values and Political Styles among Western Publics* (Princeton: Princeton University Press, 1977).

[9] Quoted in Michael Barratt Brown, *Models in Political Economy* (Harmondsworth: Penguin, 1984), p. 113.

[10] Chris Rootes, 'Britain: Greens in a cold climate', in D. Richardson and C. Rootes (eds.), *The Green Challenge: The Development of Green Parties in Europe* (London: Routledge, 1995).

[11] Tetteh, 'Election statistics 1918–2007'.

[12] Rootes, 'Britain: Greens in a cold climate', in Richardson and Rootes (eds.), *The Green Challenge*.

[13] A. Jordan and W. Maloney, *The Protest Business? Mobilizing Campaign Groups* (Manchester: Manchester University Press, 1997), p. 12; see also Jordan and Maloney, *Democracy and Interest Groups: Enhancing Participation?* (Basingstoke: Palgrave, 2007).

[14] Sarah Birch, 'Real progress: prospects for Green Party support in Britain', *Parliamentary Affairs*, 62, 1 (2009), pp. 53–71.

[15] Rootes, 'Britain: Greens in a cold climate', in Richardson and Rootes (eds.), *The Green Challenge*, p. 86.

[16] Webb, 'The continuing advance of the minor parties'.

[17] Birch, 'Real progress', p. 56.

[18] Birch, 'Real progress', pp. 64–5.

[19] 'Big smiles and faded hopes in a tale of two elections', *The Times*, 8 May 2010, pp. 14–15.

[20] Birch, 'Real progress'.

[21] Webb, 'The continuing advance of the minor parties', see table 2.

## 8   Party politics after devolution

[1] Webb, 'The continuing advance of the minor parties'.

[2] Richard Rose, *Understanding the United Kingdom* (London: Longman, 1982).

[3] Linda Colley, *Britons: Forging the Nation 1707–1837* (New Haven and London: Yale University Press, 1992).

[4] See Vernon Bogdanor, 'Devolution: decentralisation or disintegration?' *Political Quarterly*, 70, 2 (1999), pp. 185–94.

[5] Butler and Butler, *British Political Facts since 1979*, p. 110.

[6] Denver, *Elections and Voters in Britain*, p. 159.

[7] James Mitchell, 'Scotland: expectations, policy types and devolution', in A. Trench (ed.), *Has Devolution Made a Difference?* (Exeter: Imprint Academic, 2004); Mitchell, 'The election in Scotland', in Geddes and Tonge (eds.), *Britain Decides*.

[8] Webb, 'The continuing advance of the minor parties', table 1, p. 759.

[9] John Curtis, 'Turnout and electoral behaviour', in S. Herbert, R. Burnside, M. Earle, M. Edwards, T. Foley and I. McIver (eds.), *Election 2007*, The Scottish Parliament, Scottish Parliament Information Centre, 8 May 2007, 07/21, p. 41, www.scottish.parliament.uk/business/research/briefings-07/SB07-21.pdf.

[10] Marshall, *Membership of UK Political Parties*, table 3, p. 19.

[11] Further reading: Finer, The Changing British Party System, 1945–1979; A. Lijphart, Patterns of Democracy: Government Forms and Performance in Thirty-Six Countries (New Haven: Yale University Press, 1999); Paun et al., 'Hung parliaments and the challenges for Westminster and Whitehall': how to make minority and multi-party governance work, *Partiamentary Affairs*, 81, 2, pp. 213–27 (2010). The Liberal Democrat David Laws gives his account of the negotiations leading to the coalition government in *22 Days in May* (London: Biteback, 2010); and the Conservative Rob Wilson gives his in *5 Days to Power* (London: Biteback, 2010). The Institute for Government is a good source for analysis of the power-sharing arrangements in Westminster and Whitehall: www.instituteforgovernment.org.uk.

[12] See D. Denver, R. Johns, J. Mitchell and C. Pattie, 'The Holyrood elections 2007: explaining the results', paper presented to EPOP conference, Bristol, 2007, www.scottishelectionstudy.org.uk/paperspubs.htm.

[13] Jonathan Bradbury, 'Wales: the second post-devolution general election', in Geddes and Tonge (eds.), *Britain Decides*.

[14] Webb, 'The continuing advance of the minor parties', table 2, p. 761.

[15] J. Mitchell and B. Seyd, 'Fragmentation in the party and political systems', in R. Hazell (ed.), *Constitutional Futures* (Oxford: Oxford University Press, 1999).

[16] John Osmond, 'The emergence of Welsh civic consciousness', in Trench (ed.), *Has Devolution Made a Difference?*

[17] Denver, *Elections and Voters in Britain*, p. 177.

[18] The 'other' parties winning seats in the 1970s include the Vanguard Unionist Progressive Party (three seats in 1974) and the United Ulster Unionist Party (one seat in 1979).

[19] Jonathan Tonge, 'Northern Ireland: meltdown of the moderates or the redistribution of moderation?' in Geddes and Tonge (eds.), *Britain Decides*, p. 135.

[20] J. Tilley, G. Evans and C. Mitchell, 'Consociationalism and the evolution of political cleavages in Northern Ireland, 1989–2004', *British Journal of Political Science*, 38 (2008), pp. 699–717; A. Little, *Democracy and Northern Ireland* (Basingstoke: Palgrave, 2004).

[21] See Arthur Aughey, *The Politics of Northern Ireland: Beyond the Belfast Agreement* (London: Routledge, 2005); Aughey, 'Northern Ireland narrative of British democracy', *Policy Studies* (forthcoming).

## 9   Politics and its discontents

[1] Norris, *Democratic Phoenix*.

[2] 'Four in 10 Lib Dem voters reject coalition – poll', *Newsnight*, BBC Online, http:// news.bbc.co.uk/1/hi/programmes/newsnight/8854870.stm.

[3] www.ipsos-mori.com/researchpublications/researcharchive/poll. aspx?oItemId=15&view=wide.

[4] Mark Easton, 'Parliament in peril', 2 June 2009, BBC Online www.bbc.co.uk/ blogs/thereporters/markeaston/2009/06/parliament_in_peril.html.

[5] European Social Survey, *Final Activity Report* (Centre for Comparative Social Surveys, City University London, 2010).

[6] Paul Webb, 'Political parties in Western Europe: linkage, legitimacy and reform', *Representation*, 37, 3 (2000), pp. 203–14. See also Dalton, *Citizen Politics*, ch. 12.

[7]  See P. Norris, 'The growth of critical citizens', in Norris (ed.), *Critical Citizens: Global Support for Democratic Governance* (Oxford: Oxford University Press, 1999); R. Dalton, *Democratic Challenges, Democratic Choices* (Oxford: Oxford University Press, 2004).

[8]  Colin Hay, *Why We Hate Politics* (Cambridge: Polity, 2007).

[9]  C. Pattie and R. Johnston, 'Losing the voters' trust: evaluations of the political system and voting at the 1997 British general election', *British Journal of Politics & International Relations*, 3, 2 (2001), pp. 191–222.

[10]  *Audit of Political Engagement 6: The 2009 Report* (London: Hansard Society, 2009), www.hansardsociety.org.uk/blogs/publications/archive/2009/04/01/audit-of-political-engagement-6.aspx; S. Butt and J. Curtice, 'Duty in decline? Trend in attitudes to voting', in *British Social Attitudes 2009–2010: The 26th Report* (London: Sage, 2010).

[11]  *Audit of Political Engagement 6*; Marshall, *Membership of UK Political Parties*.

[12]  G. Parry, G. Moyser and N. Day, *Political Participation and Democracy in Britain* (Cambridge: Cambridge University Press, 1992); P. Webb, 'Are British political parties in decline?' *Party Politics*, 1, 3 (1995), pp. 292–322.

[13]  Norris, *Democratic Phoenix*, p. 188; see also Hay, *Why We Hate Politics*.

[14]  Jordan and Maloney, *The Protest Business*, pp. 12–13, p. 175 and table 1.1; see also Jordan and Maloney, *Democracy and Interest Groups*. See also charts 3 and 4 in Marshall, *Membership of Political Parties*, p. 16.

[15]  Norris, *Democratic Phoenix*, see tables 10.4 and 10.5; see also Hay, *Why We Hate Politics*.

[16]  C. Pattie, P. Seyd and P. Whiteley, *Citizenship in Britain: Values, Participation and Democracy* (Cambridge: Cambridge University Press, 2004), pp. 96–8, table 3.13.

[17]  Pattie, Seyd and Whiteley, *Citizenship in Britain*, p. 99, table 3.14.

[18]  *Audit of Political Engagement 6*.

[19]  Jordan and Maloney, *The Protest Business?* p. 166.

[20]  'Research into the development of Amnesty International UK youth and student groups' (final report, Social Research Centre, Roehampton University, for Amnesty International UK, June 2008).

[21]  Norris, *Democratic Phoenix*, p. 212.

[22]  See D. S. Meyer and S. Tarrow (eds.), *The Social Movement Society: Contentious Politics for a New Century* (Lanham: Rowman and Littlefield, 1998); C. Tilly, *Social Movements 1768–2004* (Boulder: Paradigm, 2004).

[23]  Peter Riddell, 'Public raises its hackles at parties, policies and funding', *The Times*, 12 December 2007.

[24]  Driver and Martell, *New Labour*.

[25]  Copus, Clark, Reynaert and Steyvers, 'Minor party and independent politics beyond the mainstream'.

[26]  See David Held, *Models of Democracy* (Cambridge: Polity, 2006, 3rd edition); Bale, Taggart and Webb, 'You can't always get what you want'.

[27]  Gerry Stoker, *Why Politics Matters* (Basingstoke: Palgrave Macmillan, 2006).

[28]  Peter Kellner, 'Down with people power', *Prospect*, 160 (July 2009).

[29]  Stoker, *Why Politics Matters*, p. 203.

# Bibliography

Abedi, A. and Lundberg, T. C. (2009) 'Doomed to failture? UKIP and the organizational challenges facing right-wing populist anti-political establishment parties', *Parliamentary Affairs*, 62, 1, pp. 72–87.

Adonis, A. and Mulgan, G. (1994) 'Back to Greece: the scope for direct democracy', *Demos Quarterly*, 3, pp. 1–28.

Alderman, K. and Carter, N. (1994) 'The Labour Party and the trade unions: loosening the ties', *Parliamentary Affairs*, 47, 3, pp. 321–37.

Anderson, P. and Mann, N. (1997) *Safety First: The Making of New Labour* (London: Granta Books).

Ashcroft, M. (2005) *Smell the Coffee: A Wakeup Call for the Conservative Party* (London: Politico's Media).

Astle, J., Laws, D., Marshall, P. and Murray, A. (2006) *Britain after Blair: A Liberal Agenda* (London: Profile Books).

*Audit of Political Engagement 6: The 2009 Report* (2009) (London: Hansard Society).

Aughey, A. (2005) *The Politics of Northern Ireland: Beyond the Belfast Agreement* (London: Routledge).

Bale, T. (1999) 'The logic of no alternative? Political scientists, historians and the politics of Labour's past', *British Journal of Politics & International Relations*, 1, 2, pp. 192–204.

Bale, T. (2010) *The Conservative Party: From Thatcher to Cameron* (Cambridge: Polity).

Bale, T., Taggart, P. and Webb, P. (2006) 'You can't always get what you want: populism and the power inquiry', *Political Quarterly*, 77, 2 (2006), pp. 195–203.

Ball, S. (1998) *The Conservative Party since 1945* (Manchester: Manchester University Press).

Beech, M. and Lee, S. (2008) *Ten Years of New Labour* (Basingstoke: Palgrave Macmillan).

Bevir, M. (2005) *New Labour: A Critique* (London: Routledge).

Birch, S. (2009) 'Real progress: prospects for Green Party support in Britain', *Parliamentary Affairs*, 62, 1, pp. 53–71.

Blake, R. (2010) [1970] *The Conservative Party from Peel to Major* (London: Faber & Faber).

Blau, A. (2008) 'The effective number of parties at four scales: votes, seats, legislative power and cabinet power', *Party Politics*, 14, 2, pp. 167–78.

Bogdanor, V. (1999) 'Devolution: decentralisation or disintegration?' *Political Quarterly*, 70, 2, pp. 185–94.

Bogdanor, V. (2007) 'The Liberal Democrat dilemma in historical perspective', *Political Quarterly*, 78, 1, pp. 11–20.

Brack, D. (2007) 'Liberal Democrat leadership: the cases of Ashdown and Kennedy', *Political Quarterly*, 78, 1, pp. 78–88.

Burchell, J. (2002) *The Evolution of Green Politics: Development and Change within European Green Parties* (London: Earthscan).

Butler, D. and Butler, G. (1994) *British Political Facts 1900–1994* (Basingstoke: Macmillan, 7th edition).

Butler, D. and Butler, G. (2006) *British Political Facts since 1979* (Basingstoke: Palgrave Macmillan).

Butler, D. and Kavanagh, D. (1997) *The British General Election 1997* (Basingstoke: Macmillan).

Butler, D. and Stokes, D. (1974) *Political Change in Britain: The Evolution of Electoral Choice* (London: Macmillan, 2nd edition).

Butt, S. and Curtice, J. (2010) 'Duty in decline? Trend in attitudes to voting', in A. Park et al. (eds.), *British Social Attitudes 2009–2010: The 26th Report* (London: Sage).

Chappell, L., Clifton, J., Gottfried, G. and Lawton, K. (2010) *Exploring the Roots of BNP Support* (London: Institute for Public Policy Research).

Childs, S. (2008) *Women and British Party Politics* (London: Routledge).

Clarke, H. D., Sanders, D., Stewart, M. and Whiteley, P. (2004) *Political Choice in Britain* (Oxford: Oxford University Press).

Coates, D. (2005) *Prolonged Labour: The Slow Birth of New Labour in Britain* (Basingstoke: Palgrave Macmillan).

Colley, L. (1992) *Britons: Forging the Nation 1707–1837* (New Haven and London: Yale University Press).

Colomer, J. (2005) 'It's parties that choose electoral systems (or Duverger's Laws upside down)', *Political Studies*, 53, 1, pp. 1–21.

Committee on Standards in Public Life (1998) *The Funding of Political Parties in the United Kingdom*, Cm. 4057-I (London: HMSO).

Cook, C. (1998) *A Short History of the Liberal Party 1900–1997* (London: Macmillan).

Copsey, N. (2004) *Contemporary British Fascism: The British National Party and the Quest for Respectability* (Basingstoke: Palgrave).

Copus, C. (2007) 'Liberal Democrat councillors: community politics, local campaigning and the role of the political party', *Political Quarterly*, 78, 1, pp. 128–38.

Copus, C., Clark, A., Reynaert, H. and Steyvers, K. (2009) 'Minor party and independent politics beyond the mainstream: fluctuating fortunes but a permanent presence', *Parliamentary Affairs*, 62, 1, pp. 4–18.

Cowley, P. (2005) *The Rebels: How Blair Mislaid His Majority* (London: Politico's).

Cowley, P. and Kavanagh, D. (2010) *The British General Election of 2010* (Basingstoke: Palgrave Macmillan).

Cowley, P. and Norton, P. (1999) 'Rebels and rebellions: Conservative MPs in the 1992 parliament', *British Journal of Politics & International Relations*, 1, pp. 84–105.

Cowley, P. and Norton, P. (2002) 'What a ridiculous thing to say! (which is why we didn't say it): a response to Timothy Heppell', *British Journal of Politics & International Relations*, 4, 2, pp. 325–9.

Crewe, I. and King, A. (1995) *SDP: The Birth, Life and Death of the Social Democratic Party* (Oxford: Oxford University Press).

Crick, M. (1986) *The March of Militant* (London: Faber and Faber).

Curtis, J. (2007) 'New Labour, new protest? How the Liberal Democrats profited from Blair's mistakes', *Political Quarterly*, 78, 1, pp. 117–27.

Curtis, J. (2007) 'Turnout and electoral behaviour', in S. Herbert, R. Burnside, M. Earle, M. Edwards, T. Foley and I. McIver (eds.), *Election 2007*, The Scottish Parliament, Scottish Parliament Information Centre, 07/21.

Cutts, D. (2006) '"Where we work we win": a case study of local Liberal Democrat campaigning', *Journal of Elections, Public Opinion and Parties*, 16, 3, pp. 221–42.

Cutts, D. and Shryane, N. (2006) 'Did local activism really matter? Liberal Democrat campaigning and the 2001 general election', *British Journal of Politics & International Relations*, 8, 3, pp. 427–44.

Daalder, H. and Mair, P. (1983) *Western European Party Systems: Continuity and Change* (London: Sage).

Dalton, R. J. (2004) *Democratic Challenges, Democratic Choices* (Oxford: Oxford University Press).

Dalton, R. J. (2005) *Citizen Politics: Public Opinion and Political Parties in Advanced Industrial Democracies* (Washington, DC: CQ Publishers, 2008, 5th edition).

Dalton, R. J. (2008) 'The quantity and the quality of party systems: party system polarization, its measurement, and its consequences, *Comparative Political Studies*, 41, 7 (2008), pp. 899–920.

Dalton, R. J. and Wattenberg, M. (eds.) (2002) *Parties without Partisans* (Oxford: Oxford University Press).

Dangerfield, G. (2008) *The Strange Death of Liberal England* (London: Serif).

Denham, A. and O'Hara, K. (2008) *Democratising Conservative Leadership Selection: From Grey Suits to Grass Roots* (Manchester: Manchester Univerity Press).

Denver, D. (2007) *Elections and Voters in Britain* (London: Palgrave Macmillan, 2nd edition).

Denver, D., Clark, A. and Bennie, L. (2009) 'Voter reactions to a preferential ballot: the 2007 Scottish local elections', *Journal of Elections, Public Opinion and Parties*, 19, 3, pp. 265–82.

Denver, D., Hands, G. and MacAllister, I. (2004) 'The electoral impact of constituency campaigning in Britain, 1992–2001', *Political Studies*, 52, pp. 289–306.

Diamond, P. (ed.) (2004) *New Labour's Old Roots: Revisionist Thinkers in Labour's History 1931–1997* (Exeter: Imprint Academic).

Driver, S. and Martell, L. (2006) *New Labour* (Cambridge: Polity).

Drucker, H. M. (1979) *Doctrine and Ethos in the Labour Party* (London: George Allen and Unwin).

Duncan, A. and Hobson, D. (1999) *Saturn's Children* (London: Politico's).

Duncan Smith, I., Streeter, G. and Willetts, D. (eds.) (2002) *There is Such a Thing as Society* (London: Politico's).

Dunleavy, P. (1993) 'The political parties', in P. Dunleavy, A. Gamble, I. Holliday and G. Peele (eds.), *Developments in British Politics 4* (Basingstoke: Macmillan).

Dunleavy, P. (2005) 'Facing up to multi-party politics', *Parliamentary Affairs*, 58, 3, pp. 503–32.

Duverger, M. (1964) [1951] *Political Parties: Their Organization and Activity in the Modern State* (London: Methuen).

Eatwell, R. and Goodwin, M. J. (eds.) (2010) *The New Extremism in 21st Century Britain* (London: Routledge).

Electoral Commission (2004) *The Funding of Political Parties* (London: Electoral Commission).

Evans, G. (ed.) (1999) *The End of Class Politics? Class Voting in Comparative Context* (Oxford: Oxford University Press).

Fieldhouse, E., Cutts, D. and Russell, A. (2006) 'The Liberal Democrat performance in the 2005 general election', *Journal of Elections, Public Opinion and Parties*, 16, 1, pp. 77–92.

Fielding, N. (1981) *The National Front* (London: Routledge & Kegan Paul).

Fielding, S. (2002) *The Labour Party: Continuity and Change in the Making of New Labour* (Basingstoke: Palgrave Macmillan).

Finer, S. E. (1980) *The Changing British Party System, 1945–1979* (Washington, DC: American Institute for Public Policy Research).

Fisher, J. (1999) *British Political Parties* (Basingstoke: Palgrave Macmillan).

Fisher, J. (2000) 'Economic performance or electoral necessity? Evaluating the system of voluntary income to political parties', *British Journal of Politics & International Relations*, 2, 2, pp. 179–204.

Fisher, J. (2009) 'Hayden Phillips and Jack Straw: the continuation of British exceptionalism in party finance?' *Parliamentary Affairs*, 62, 2, pp. 298–317.

Fisher, J. and Denver, D. (2009) 'Evaluating the electoral effects of traditional and modern modes of constituency campaigning in Britain 1992–2005', *Parliamentary Affairs*, 62, 2, pp. 196–210.

Gallagher, M. and Mitchell, P. (eds.) (2008) *The Politics of Electoral Systems* (Oxford: Oxford University Press).

Gamble, A. (1994) *The Free Economy and the Strong State: The Politics of Thatcherism* (Basingstoke: Macmillan).

Garnett, M. (2007) 'Banality in politics: Margaret Thatcher and the biographers', *Political Studies Review*, 5, 2, pp. 172–82.

Geddes, A. and Tonge, J. (eds.) (2005) *Britain Decides: The UK General Election 2005* (Basingstoke: Palgrave Macmillan).

Gibson, R., Nixon, P. and Ward, S. (2003) *Political Parties and the Internet: Net Gain?* (London: Routledge).

Giddens, A. (1998) *The Third Way: The Renewal of Social Democracy* (Cambridge: Polity).

Gilmour, I. (1992) *Dancing with Dogma: Britain under Thatcherism* (London: Simon & Schuster).

Goodwin, M. (2007) 'The extreme right in Britain: still an "ugly duckling" but for how long?' *Political Quarterly*, 78, 2, pp. 241–50.

Goodwin, M. (2008) 'Research, revisionists and the radical right', *Politics*, 28, 1, pp. 33–40.

Goodwin, M. (2010) 'Activism in contemporary extreme right parties: the case of the British National Party (BNP)', *Journal of Elections, Public Opinion and Parties*, 20, 2, pp. 31–54.

Gray, J. (1993) *Beyond the New Right: Markets, Government and the Common Environment* (London: Routledge).

Gray, J. and Willetts, D. (1997) *Is Conservatism Dead?* (London: Profile Books).

Grayson, R. (2007) 'Social democracy or social liberalism? Ideological sources of Liberal Democrat policy', *Political Quarterly*, 78, pp. 32–9.

Hainsworth, P. (ed.) (2000) *The Politics of the Extreme Right: From the Margins to the Mainstream* (London: Pinter, 2000).

Hall, S. (1983) 'The great moving right show', in S. Hall and M. Jacques (eds.), *The Politics of Thatcherism* (London: Lawrence and Wishart).

Hay, C. (1999) *The Political Economy of New Labour* (Manchester: Manchester University Press).

Hay, C. (2007) *Why We Hate Politics* (Cambridge: Polity).

Heath, A., Jowell, R. and Curtice, J. (1994) *Labour's Last Chance? The 1992 Election and Beyond* (Aldershot: Dartmouth).

Heffernan, R. and Marqusee, M. (1992) *Defeat from the Jaws of Victory: Inside Kinnock's Labour Party* (London: Verso).

Held, D. (2006) *Models of Democracy* (Cambridge: Polity, 3rd edition).

Heppell, T. (2002) 'The ideological composition of the parliamentary Conservative Party 1992–97', *British Journal of Politics & International Relations*, 4, 2, pp. 299–324.

Heppell, T. (2007) *Choosing the Tory Leader: Conservative Party Leadership Elections from Heath to Cameron* (London: Tauris Academic Studies).

Heppell, T. and Hill, M. (2005) 'Ideological typologies of contemporary British conservatism', *Political Studies Review*, 3, 3, pp. 335–55.

Herbert, S., Burnside, R., Earle, M., Edwards, M., Foley, T. and McIver, I. (eds.) (2007), *Election 2007*, The Scottish Parliament, Scottish Parliament Information Centre, 07/21.

Huntington, N. and Bale, T. (2002) 'New Labour: new Christian Democracy?' *Political Quarterly*, 73, 1, pp. 44–50.

Ingle, S. (2008) *The British Party System: An Introduction* (London: Routledge).

Inglehart, R. (1977) *The Silent Revolution: Changing Values and Political Styles among Western Publics* (Princeton: Princeton University Press).

Jarrett, D. (1965) *Britain 1688–1815* (Harlow: Longman).

Jenkins, S. (2006) *Thatcher and Sons: A Revolution in Three Acts* (London: Allen Lane).

Jenkins, S. (2007) 'Thatcher's legacy', *Political Studies Review*, 5, 2, pp. 161–71.

John, P., Margetts, H., Rowland, D. and Weir, S. (2006) *The BNP: The Roots of its Appeal* (Democratic Audit, Human Rights Centre, University of Essex).

Jones, T. (1996) *Remaking the Labour Party: From Gaitskell to Blair* (London: Routledge).

Jordan, A. and Maloney, W. (1997) *The Protest Business? Mobilizing Campaign Groups* (Manchester: Manchester University Press).

Jordan, A. and Maloney, W. (2007) *Democracy and Interest Groups: Enhancing Participation?* (Basingstoke: Palgrave).

Katz, R. and Mair, P. (1995) 'Changing models of party organization and party democracy: the emergence of the cartel party', *Party Politics*, 1, 1 (1995), pp. 5–28.

Kavanagh, D. (ed.) (1982) *The Politics of the Labour Party* (London: George Allen and Unwin).

Keegan, W. (1984) *Mrs Thatcher's Economic Experiment* (Harmondsworth: Penguin).

Kellner, P. (2009) 'Down with people power', *Prospect*, 160, July, pp. 40–3.

Kenny, M. (2009) 'Taking the temperature of the political elite 2: the professionals move in?' *Parliamentary Affairs*, 62, 2, pp. 335–49.

Laakso, M. and Taagepera, R. (1979) '"Effective" number of parties: a measure with application to West Europe', *Comparative Political Studies,* 12, 1, pp. 3–27.

Lamprinakou, C. (2008) 'The party evolution model: an integrated approach to party organisation and political communication', *Politics*, 28, 2, pp. 103–11.

Laws, D. (2010) *22 Days in May* (London: Biteback).

Lee, S. and Beech, M. (eds.) (2009) *The Conservatives under David Cameron: Built to Last?* (Basingstoke: Palgrave Macmillan).

Lee, S. and Beech, M. (eds.) (2011) *The Cameron–Clegg Government: Coalition Politics in the Age of Austerity* (Basingstoke: Palgrave).

Lijphart, A. (1984) *Democracies: Patterns of Majoritarian and Consensus Government in Twenty-one Countries* (New Haven: Yale University Press).

Lijphart, A. (1999) *Patterns of Democracy: Government Forms and Performance in Thirty-Six Countries* (New Haven: Yale University Press).

Little, A. (2004) *Democracy and Northern Ireland* (Basingstoke: Palgrave).

Lovenduski, J. (2005) *Feminizing Politics* (Cambridge: Polity).

Ludlam, S. and Smith, M. J. (eds.) (1996) *Contemporary British Conservatism* (London: Macmillan).

Ludlam, S. and Smith, M. J. (eds.) (2001) *New Labour in Government* (Basingstoke: Palgrave).

Ludlam, S. and Smith, M. J. (eds.) (2004) *Governing as New Labour: Policy and Politics under Blair* (Basingstoke: Palgrave).

Lynch, P. and Garner, R. (2005) 'The changing party system', *Parliamentary Affairs*, 58, 3, pp. 533–54.

McHugh, D. (2006) 'Wanting to be heard but not wanting to act? Addressing political disengagement', *Parliamentary Affairs*, 59, 3, pp. 546–52.

McIlveen, R. (2009) 'Ladies of the right: an interim analysis of the A-list', *Journal of Elections, Public Opinion and Parties*, 19, 2, pp. 147–57.

McKenzie, R.T. (1964) [1955] *British Political Parties* (London: Heinemann).

Mair, P. (ed.) (1990) *The West European Party System* (Oxford: Oxford University Press).

Maor, M. (1997) *Political Parties: Comparative Approaches and the British Experience* (London: Routledge).

Marshall, J. (2009) *Membership of UK Political Parties*, SN/SG/5125, House of Commons Library.

Marshall, P. and Laws, D. (eds.) (2004) *The Orange Book: Reclaiming Liberalism* (London: Profile Books).

Meredith, S. (2003) 'New Labour: "The road less travelled"?' *Politics*, 23, 3, pp. 163–71.

Meyer, D. S. and Tarrow, S. (eds.) (1998) *The Social Movement Society: Contentious Politics for a New Century* (Lanham: Rowman and Littlefield)

Minkin, L. (1991) *The Contentious Alliance* (Edinburgh: Edinburgh University Press).

Mitchell, J. (2004) 'Scotland: expectations, policy types and devolution', in A. Trench (ed.), *Has Devolution Made a Difference?* (Exeter: Imprint Academic).

Mitchell, J. and Seyd, B. (1999) 'Fragmentation in the party and political systems', in R. Hazell (ed.), *Constitutional Futures* (Oxford: Oxford University Press).

Michels, R. (1962) *Political Parties: A Sociological Study of the Oligarchical Tendencies of Modern Democracy* (New York: Free Press).

Mudde, C. (2007) *The Populist Radical Right in Europe* (Cambridge: Cambridge University Press).

Neocleous, M. and Startin, N. (2003) '"Protest" and fail to survive: Le Pen and the great moving right show', *Politics*, 23, 3, pp. 145–55.

Nieuwbeerta, P. and Dirk de Graaf, N. (1999) 'Traditional class voting in twenty postwar societies', in G. Evans (ed.), *The End of Class Politics? Class Voting in Comparative Context* (Oxford: Oxford University Press).

Norris, P. (1999) 'The growth of critical citizens?' in Norris (ed.), *Critical Citizens: Global Support for Democratic Governance* (Oxford: Oxford University Press).

Norris, P. (2000) *A Virtuous Circle: Political Communications in Postindustrial Societies* (Cambridge: Cambridge University Press).

Norris, P. (2002) *Democratic Phoenix: Reinventing Political Activism* (Cambridge: Cambridge University Press).

Norris, P. (2005) *Radical Right: Voters and Parties in the Electoral Market* (Cambridge: Cambridge University Press).

Norton, P. (ed.) (1996) *The Conservative Party* (London: Prentice Hall).

O'Hara, K. (2007) *After Blair: David Cameron and the Conservative Tradition* (Cambridge: Icon Books).

Oakeshott, M. (1991) [1962] 'On being Conservative', in *Rationalism in Politics and Other Essays* (Indianapolis: Liberty Press).

Panebianco, A. (1988) *Political Parties: Organisation and Power* (Cambridge: Cambridge University Press).

Parry, G., Moyser, G. and Day. N. (1992) *Political Participation and Democracy in Britain* (Cambridge: Cambridge University Press).

Pattie, C. and Johnston, R. (2001) 'Losing the voters' trust: evaluations of the political system and voting at the 1997 British general election', *British Journal of Politics & International Relations*, 3, 2, pp. 191–222.

Pattie, C., Seyd, P. and Whiteley, P. (2004) *Citizenship in Britain: Values, Participation and Democracy* (Cambridge: Cambridge University Press).

Paun, A., Hazell, R., Turnbull, A., Beith, A., Evans, P. and Crick, M. (2010) 'Hung parliaments and the challenges for Westminster, and Whitehall: how to make minority and multiparty governance work', *Political Quarterly* 81, 2, pp. 213–27.

Pelling, H. (1993) *A Short History of the Labour Party* (London: Macmillan).

Pugh, M. (2002) *The Making of Modern British Politics, 1867–1945* (Oxford: Wiley-Blackwell, 3rd edition).

Quinn, T. (2004) 'Electing the leader: the British Labour Party's electoral college', *British Journal of Politics & International Relations*, 6, 2, pp. 333–52.

Quinn, T. (2010) 'New Labour and the trade unions in Britain', *Journal of Elections, Public Opinion and Parties*, 20, 3, pp. 357–80.

Rallings, C., Thrasher, M. and Johnston, R. (2002) 'The slow death of a governing party: the erosion of Conservative local electoral support in England 1979–97', *British Journal of Politics & International Relations*, 4, 2, pp. 271–98.

Ramsden, J. (1998) *An Appetite for Power: A History of the Conservative Party since 1830* (London: HarperCollins).

Randall, E. (2007) 'Yellow versus orange – never a fair fight: an assessment of two contributions to liberal politics separated by three-quarters of a century', *Political Quarterly*, 78, 1, pp. 40–9.

Rentoul, J. (1995) *Tony Blair* (London: Little, Brown).

Richardson, D. and Rootes, C. (eds.) (1995) *The Green Challenge: The Development of Green Parties in Europe* (London: Routledge).

Rose, R. (1982) *Understanding the United Kingdom* (London: Longman).

Russell, A. (2004) 'Parties and party systems: realignment or readjustment?' *Parliamentary Affairs*, 57, 2, pp. 396–407.

Russell, A. and Fieldhouse, E. (2005) *Neither Left nor Right? The Liberal Democrats and the Electorate* (Manchester: Manchester University Press).

Russell, A., Fieldhouse, E. and Cutts, D. (2007) '*De facto* veto? The parliamentary Liberal Democrats', *Political Quarterly*, 78, 1, pp. 89–98.

Russell, M. (2005) *Building New Labour* (Basingstoke: Palgrave Macmillan).

Sartori, G. (2005) [1976] *Parties and Party Systems: A Framework for Analysis* (Colchester: ECPR Press).

Sassoon, D. (1996) *One Hundred Years of Socialism: The Western European Left in the Twentieth Century* (London: I. B. Tauris).

Scruton, R. (1996) *The Conservative Idea of Community* (London: Conservative 2000 Foundation).

Scruton, R. (2001) *The Meaning of Conservatism* (Basingstoke: Palgrave Macmillan, 3rd edition).

Seldon, A. and Ball, S. (eds.) (1994) *Conservative Century: The Conservative Party since 1900* (Oxford: Oxford University Press).

Seyd, P. (1999) 'New parties / new politics', *Party Politics*, 5, 3, pp. 383–406.

Seyd, P. and Whiteley, P. (1992) *Labour's Grass Roots* (Oxford: Clarendon Press).

Seyd, P. and Whiteley, P. (2002) *New Labour's Grassroots : The Transformation of the Labour Party Membership* (Basingstoke: Palgrave).

Seyd, P. and Whiteley, P. (2004) 'British party members: an overview', *Party Politics*, 10, 4, pp. 355–66.

Shaw, E. (1996) *The Labour Party since 1945* (Oxford: Blackwell).

Smith, M. J. (1994) 'Understanding the "politics of catch-up": the modernization of the Labour Party', *Political Studies*, 42, 4, pp. 708–15.

Stoker, G. (2006) *Why Politics Matters* (Basingstoke: Palgrave Macmillan).

Stoll, H. (2008) 'Social cleavages and the number of parties', *Comparative Political Studies*, 41, 11, pp. 1439–65.

Taagepera, R. and Grofman, B. (2006) 'Rethinking Duverger's law: predicting the effective number of parties in plurality and PR systems – parties minus issues equals one', *European Journal of Political Research*, 13, 4, pp. 341–52.

Taggart, P. (1995) 'New populist parties in Western Europe', *Western European Politics*, 18, 1, pp. 34–51.

Taylor, M. (2007) 'The birth and rebirth of the Liberal Democrats', *Political Quarterly*, 78, 1, pp. 21–31.

Taylor, S. (1982) *The National Front in English Politics* (Basingstoke: Macmillan).

Tetteh, E. (2008) 'Election statistics 1918–2007' (House of Commons Research Paper, RP 08/12).

Thamassen, J. (ed.) (2005) *The European Voter: A Comparative Study of Modern Democracies* (Oxford: Oxford University Press).

Thorpe, A. (2000) *The British Communist Party and Moscow, 1920–1943* (Manchester: Manchester University Press).

Tilley, J., Evans, G. and Mitchell, C. (2008) 'Consociationalism and the evolution of political cleavages in Northern Ireland, 1989–2004', *British Journal of Political Science*, 38, pp. 699–717.

Tilly, C. (2004) *Social Movements 1768–2004* (Boulder: Paradigm).

Tonge, J. (2006) *Northern Island* (Cambridge: Polity)

Trench, A. (ed.) (2004) *Has Devolution Made a Difference?* (Exeter: Imprint Academic).

van Biezen, I. (2004) 'Political parties as public utilities', *Party Politics*, 10, 6, pp. 701–22.

Vincent, J. (1966) *The Formation of the Liberal Party 1857–1868* (London: Constable).

Ward, S., Gibson, R. and Lusoli, W. (2003) 'Online participation and mobilisation in Britain: hype, hope and reality', *Parliamentary Affairs*, 56, 4, pp. 652–68.

Ware, A. (1996) *Political Parties and Party Systems* (Oxford: Oxford University Press).

Webb, P. (1995) 'Are British political parties in decline?' *Party Politics*, 1, 3, pp. 292–322.

Webb, P. (2000) 'Political parties in Western Europe: linkage, legitimacy and reform', *Representation*, 37, 3, pp. 203–14.

Webb, P. (2000) *The Modern British Party System* (London: Sage).

Webb, P. (2002) 'Parties and party systems: more continuity than change', *Parliamentary Affairs*, 55, 2, pp. 363–76.

Webb, P. (2003) 'Parties and party systems: prospects for realignment', *Parliamentary Affairs*, 56, 2, pp. 283–96.

Webb, P. (2005) 'The continuing advance of the minor parties', *Parliamentary Affairs*, 58, 4, pp. 757–75.

Webb, P. and Fisher, J. (2003) 'Professionalism and the Millbank tendency: the political sociology of New Labour's employees', *Politics*, 23, 1, pp. 10–20.

Whiteley, P. (2009) 'Where have all the members gone? The dynamics of party membership in Britain', *Parliamentary Affairs*, 62, 2, pp. 242–57.

Whiteley, P., Seyd, P. and Billinghurst, A. (2006) *Third Force Politics: Liberal Democrats at the Grassroots* (Oxford: Oxford University Press).

Whiteley, P., Seyd, P. and Richardson, J. (1994) *True Blues: The Politics of Conservative Party Membership* (Oxford: Oxford University Press).

Willetts, D. (1992) *Modern Conservatism* (Harmondsworth: Penguin).

Wilson, R. (2010) *5 Days to Power* (London: Biteback).

Yonwin, J. (2004) *Electoral Performance of Far-Right Parties in the UK*, SN/SG/1982, Social and General Statistics Section, House of Commons Library.

# Index